AFFECTIVE LEARNING
IN INDUSTRIAL ARTS

AFFECTIVE LEARNING IN INDUSTRIAL ARTS

Editor:
Gerald L. Jennings

Authors:
Gerald L. Jennings
Lewis D. Kieft
Paul D. Kuwik
Harold E. PaDelford
H. James Rokusek
Louis Thayer

Eastern Michigan University
Ypsilanti, Michigan 48197

33rd Yearbook, 1984

*American Council on Industrial Arts
Teacher Education*

Lithographed in U.S.A.

Yearbooks of the American Council
on Industrial Arts Teacher Education
are produced and distributed by the
McKnight Publishing Company,
Bloomington, Illinois 61701

Orders and requests for information about cost and availability of yearbooks should be addressed to the company.

Requests to quote portions of yearbooks
should be addressed to the Secretary,
American Council on Industrial Arts Teacher Education,
in care of the publisher, for forwarding
to the current Secretary.

**This publication
is available in microform.**

University Microfilms International

300 North Zeeb Road
Dept. P.R.
Ann Arbor, MI 48106

ISBN: 02-672690-4

Foreword

The thirty-two yearbooks of the American Council on Industrial Arts Education (ACIATE) are outstanding and important in our profession. A number of these yearbooks have been centered on the student and the total development of the Industrial Arts student. Several yearbooks have been concerned with the role industrial arts plays in our technological culture in assisting individuals to respond to the needs of our society.

Editor Gerald L. Jennings, with his authors, has developed a notable yearbook regarding Affective Learning. Professor Jennings and his colleagues from Eastern Michigan University clearly respond to the need for Affective Learning and the challenge now found in our educational programs throughout the United States. Social issues, political pressures and technological advancement in this post-industrial era demand an increasing sensitivity in the role of our teachers in society. Tremendous implications are found in the technological changes and the role of each teacher in meeting these challenges.

How do we fully develop the complete student and transmit the enormous cultural change and evolution while at the same time meeting our responsibility to interpret and describe change? The chapter authors show perception and insight concerning these issues. They are to be commended for this yearbook, and the inspiration it will provide.

The American Council on Industrial Arts Teacher Education salutes the McKnight Publishing Company for its support and contribution to the publishing of this and other yearbooks. The McKnight Publishing Company has provided great influence and leadership in our discipline for the past thirty-three years. Our Council is truly indebted to them.

30 March, 1984

Rollin Williams, III
President, American Council on
Industrial Arts Teacher Education

Yearbook Planning Committee*

— *Term Expiring in 1984:*

Lee H. Smalley
   University of Wisconsin-Stout, Menomonie, Wisconsin

— *Terms Expiring in 1985:*

Stanley E. Brooks
   State University College at Buffalo, Buffalo, New York

G. Eugene Martin
   Southwest Texas State University, San Marcos, Texas

— *Terms Expiring in 1986:*

Daniel L. Householder
   Texas A&M University, College Station, Texas

R. Thomas Wright
   Ball State University, Muncie, Indiana

— *Terms Expiring in 1987:*

Ervin A. Dennis
   University of Northern Iowa, Cedar Falls, Iowa

Paul W. DeVore
   West Virginia University, Morgantown, West Virginia

— *Terms Expiring in 1988*

Donald P. Lauda
   Eastern Illinois University, Charleston, Illinois

Donald F. Smith
   Ball State University, Muncie, Indiana

Chairperson

M. James Bensen
   University of Wisconsin-Stout, Menomonie, Wisconsin

---

*The immediate past president of ACIATE serves as the yearbook planning committee chairperson.

Officers of the Council

W. Rollin Williams, President
   East Tennessee State University, Johnson City, Tennessee

R. Thomas Wright, Vice-President
   Ball State University, Muncie, Indiana

Everett N. Israel, Secretary
   Illinois State University, Normal, Illinois

John M. Ritz, Treasurer
   Old Dominion University, Norfolk, Virginia

M. James Bensen, Past President
   University of Wisconsin-Stout, Menomonie, Wisconsin

Yearbook Proposals

Each year, at the AIAA international conference, the ACIATE Yearbook Committee reviews the progress of yearbooks in preparation and evaluates proposals for additional yearbooks. Any member is welcome to submit a yearbook proposal. It should be written in sufficient detail for the committee to be able to understand the proposed substance and format, and sent to the committee chairman by February 1 of the year in which the conference is held. Below are the criteria employed by the committee in making yearbook selections.

ACIATE Yearbook Committee

Guidelines for ACIATE Yearbook Topic Selection

With reference to a specific topic:
1. It should make a direct contribution to the understanding and the improvement of industrial arts teacher education.
2. It should avoid duplication of the publication activities of other professional groups.
3. It should confine its content to professional education subject matter of a kind that does not infringe upon the area of textbook publication which treats a specific body of subject matter in a structured, formal way.
4. It should not be exploited as an opportunity to promote and publicize one man's or one institution's philosophy unless the volume includes other similar efforts that have enjoyed some degree of popularity and acceptance in the profession.
5. While it may encourage and extend what is generally accepted as good in existing theory and practice, it should also actively and constantly seek to upgrade and modernize professional action in the area of industrial arts teacher education.
6. It can raise controversial questions in an effort to get a national hearing and as a prelude to achieving something approaching a national consensus.
7. It may consider as available for discussion and criticism any ideas of individuals or organizations that have gained some degree of acceptance as a result of dissemination either through formal publication, through oral presentation, or both.
8. It can consider a variety of seemingly conflicting trends and statements emanating from a variety of sources and motives, analyze them, consolidate and thus seek out and delineate key problems to enable the profession to make a more concerted effort at finding a solution.

Approved, Yearbook Planning Committee
March 15, 1967, Philadelphia, PA.

Previously Published Yearbooks

*1. *Inventory Analysis of Industrial Arts Teacher Education Facilities, Personnel and Programs,* 1952.
*2. *Who's Who in Industrial Arts Teacher Education,* 1953.
*3. *Some Components of Current Leadership; Techniques of Selection and Guidance of Graduate Students; An Analysis of Textbook Emphases;* 1954, three studies.
*4. *Superior Practices in Industrial Arts Teacher Education,* 1955.
*5. *Problems and Issues in Industrial Arts Teacher Education,* 1956.
*6. *A Sourcebook of Reading in Education for Use in Industrial Arts and Industrial Arts Teacher Education,* 1957.
*7. *The Accreditation of Industrial Arts Teacher Education,* 1958.
*8. *Planning Industrial Arts Facilities,* 1959, Ralph K. Nair, ed.
*9. *Research in Industrial Arts Education,* 1960. Raymond Van Tassel, ed.
*10. *Graduate Study in Industrial Arts,* 1961. R. P. Norman and R. C. Bohn, eds.
*11. *Essentials of Preservice Preparation,* 1962. Donald G. Lux, ed.
*12. *Action and Thought in Industrial Arts Education,* 1963. E. A. T. Svendsen, ed.
*13. *Classroom Research in Industrial Arts,* 1964. Charles B. Porter, ed.
14. *Approaches and Procedures in Industrial Arts.* 1965. G. S. Wall, ed.
15. *Status of Research in Industrial Arts,* 1966. John D. Rowlett. ed.
16. *Evaluation Guidelines for Contemporary Industrial Arts Programs,* 1967. Lloyd P. Nelson and William T. Sargent, eds.
17. *A Historical Perspective of Industry,* 1968. Joseph F. Luetkemeyer, Jr., ed.
18. *Industrial Technology Education,* 1969. C. Thomas Dean and N.A. Hauer, eds. *Who's Who in Industrial Arts Teacher Education,* 1969. John M. Pollock and Charles A. Bunten, eds.
19. *Industrial Arts for Disadvantaged Youth,* 1970. Ralph O. Gallington, ed.
20. *Components of Teacher Education,* 1971. W. E. Ray and J. Streichler, eds.
21. *Industrial Arts for the Early Adolescent,* 1972. Daniel L. Householder, ed.
*22. *Industrial Arts in Senior High Schools,* 1973, Rutherford E. Lockette, ed.
23. *Industrial Arts for the Elementary School,* 1974. Robert G. Thrower and Robert D. Weber, eds.
24. *A Guide to the Planning of Industrial Arts Facilities,* 1975. D. E. Moon, ed.
25. *Future Alternatives for Industrial Arts,* 1976. Lee H. Smalley, ed.
26. *Competency-Based Industrial Arts Teacher Education,* 1977. Jack C. Brueckman and Stanley E. Brooks, eds.
27. *Industrial Arts in the Open Access Curriculum,* 1978. L. D. Anderson, ed.
28. *Industrial Arts Education: Retrospect, Prospect,* 1979. G. Eugene Martin, ed.
29. *Technology and Society: Interfaces with Industrial Arts,* 1980. Herbert A. Anderson and M. James Bensen, eds.
30. *An Interpretive History of Industrial Arts,* 1981. Richard Barella and Thomas Wright, eds.
31. *The Contributions of Industrial Arts to Selected Areas of Education,* 1982. Donald Maley and Kendall N. Starkeather, eds.
32. *The Dynamics of Creative Leadership for Industrial Arts Education,* 1983. Robert E. Wenig and John I. Mathews, eds.

---

*Out-of-print yearbooks can be obtained in microform and in Xerox copies. For information on price and delivery, write to Xerox University Microfilms, 300 North Zeeb Road, Ann Arbor, Michigan, 48106.

CONTENTS

Chapter

11

Preface

Many persons outside of industrial arts education—and even many inside—view the major focus of the discipline as being on the material world, upon things and tool processes. What in fact it deals with is human development; the development of the "whole" person.

Experiences in technology that are provided through industrial arts education are the things used to influence the behavior of children, youth and adults who study in our classrooms and laboratories. What is often overlooked is the potential that exists in those experiences for the involvement of the whole person in the learning process. While cognitive and psychomotor development are quite naturally included in daily instructional activities, the area of behavior which gives meaning to learning and provides for total involvement of the learner—the affective domain—is often given much too little attention. Significant opportunities to offer experiences for the development of the whole learner are, therefore, lost.

This yearbook attempts to provide direction for a more adequate understanding of affective learning in industrial arts education. Through a review of the bases for affective learning, its characteristics and applications in industrial arts education, it is hoped that students, teachers and administrators might more fully realize the potential that exists in the discipline to attend to the whole learner, to promote more effective instruction and more meaningful learning.

The chapters in this yearbook build one upon the other and include discussion of the psychological basis for affective development, learning experiences for affective development, the evaluation of affective learning, and the role of teacher education in promoting affective learning in industrial arts. Resources useful for further study and research on the affective domain are also highlighted.

Much appreciation is expressed for the work of the faculty at Eastern Michigan University who prepared chapters for this yearbook. Their diligence and commitment to a joint effort has made this a very significant professional and rewarding personal experience. Through it we have all grown and become more complete persons.

Jerry Jennings
Editor

Chapter 1

Affective Education: An Overview of Issues

Gerald L. Jennings, Ph.D.
Professor
Department of Business and Industrial Education
Eastern Michigan University
Ypsilanti, Michigan

A CHALLENGE TO EDUCATION

The challenge to educational programs may be greater during the decade of the 80's than at any time in the past half century. Social, political, technological and economic changes during the last twenty years have created tremendous uncertainty over what the schools should teach and how the process of educating should be carried out. Public expectations of the schools are vacillating from demands to achieve minimum performance in the basic 3-R's to more wholly inclusive requirements for preparing youths to become fully contributing and well rounded citizens. A recent study indicates that public confidence in the schools is now at the lowest point it has been during the past twenty years (Weiler, 1982, pp. 9-14) — a fact that shows itself in stronger criticism of the schools and greater reluctance to accept increases in school taxes.

Conditions faced by schools today are for the most part a product of changes that have taken place in our communities, government, commerce and technology since World War II. The social revolution of the 1950's and 60's created much greater sensitivity for the opportunities afforded different social and cultural groups in this country, and is now seen as providing more equal access and educational oppor-

14

tunity for all persons regardless of race, sex, ethnic identity or economic status. Federal government involvement in the schools has increased dramatically during the past thirty years, especially as social changes with widespread national overtones have taken place. One of the outcomes of the social and political changes is the public impression that there now exists an "American school system." (Tyler, 1983, p. 462) The number of educational activities which occur at the national level, and the mass media coverage of such events as school desegregation, federal support for numerous compensatory programs and enforcement of government mandated guidelines have helped to reinforce this image.

Social issues involving schools today are very much related to the upward shift in average age of the general population. Increasing numbers of communities are made up of older citizens with a greater interest in preparing for retirement years than in dealing with local school needs, for they now have very little vested interest in the schools. Families with children are now a much smaller percentage of the total population than in recent decades, and display much less strength at the polls than was the case fifteen years ago — a time when schools were near their peak in enrollment.

Social movements have increasingly become the basis for political issues involving the schools. The social reform period of the 1960's promoted greater freedom both in and outside the school curriculum. To many it was identified as the "progressive education" period dominated by social and political liberals. Educational experimentation took many forms as educators sought ways to deal with exploding school populations and greater social sensitivity. Those political liberals and educational progressives are now criticized for permitting the schools to become too free and too costly. It may be that today the political and social conservatives are regaining control of many community schools, as we hear the call for a return to fundamental value systems and greater restrictions on the curricular options provided for children.

Economic conditions during the latter 1970's and early 80's further complicated the position of schools. When competition for public funds for all social institutions increased, schools were often assigned a lower priority as recipients of those funds. One outcome of the recent major economic recession that has gripped our nation has been significant reductions in school budgets. This action is often translated as retrenchment—the cutting of "frills" and curriculum development services, and back-to-basics movements. Accurate figures do not exist on how many have been affected, but it is certain that significant numbers of programs in industrial arts have fallen victim to reductions in funding to education, especially in recession plagued regions of the nation.

National policy on education appears to shift dramatically as we move from one administration to the next—each offering its own solution on the role of education and proper levels of support required to maintain a particular role. Botkin, Dimancescu and Strata express the view that incongruities in national policy regarding the role of education can be explained in part by the fact that "society has failed to grasp the full significance of the transition that is now under way. We are moving from a capital-intensive, physical-resource-based economy of the first half of this century to a knowledge-intensive, human-resource-based economy of the last half." (Botkin, 1983, p. 5) Appropriate role definition and adequate support of education both depend upon a greater awareness by society of the technological changes that have taken place.

Technological advancements in recent decades have created what is now considered the post-industrial era in the history of mankind. The full implications of this era for education are not fully understood by either experts who deal with social change or the general populace. Emergence of a new information society from the former industrial society is presenting new and little understood problems for education. The communications revolution of the 1960's brought educational television and a greater awareness of alternative delivery systems. But the computer revolution which began in the 1970's may bring us an entirely new approach to the process of education that could be operating by the year 2000. It will at least provide for mass information handling and processing, but may go so far as to require the development of new kinds of communication skills which create different kinds of relationships between and among individuals and social groups.

Technology change has had a number of different impacts upon education. On the one hand, it has generated new information for use in instruction, especially for the sciences, the social sciences and applied subject areas—including industrial arts. It has provided new and improved environments for learning, as seen in new school construction which utilizes the latest in climate, light, sound and physical space control for improved instructional delivery and human comfort. Technology change provides new ways for information handling in education as evidenced by the development of a wider selection of audio-visual systems, including teaching machines, television and computers. With these components of "educational technology" there has been increased interest in the use of new instructional systems—ways in which the teaching-learning process is conducted, different from that which was utilized for many years in the past.

In addition to these impacts, technology change has presented a number of issues which educators are challenged to consider. One set of those issues relates to the social and economic problems that result from technology change. New generations of children must recognize the implications of technology change for the lives of people throughout the world. The meaning of a global economy has never been clearer than during these times of serious economic stress. The other set of issues is concerned with how schools can help persons develop into complete human beings under conditions of change that tend to create a great deal of personal and social conflict.

Schools have a responsibility to transmit the culture to each new generation. That includes the development of basic communication and social skills which permit the person to function in daily life. Beyond those expectations, schools play a major role in guiding and promoting the development of the whole person—one who can realize his or her full potential for becoming a worthy and contributing member of society.

Technology change has had both positive and negative effects on this process. It has provided the tools to solve complex problems and has freed men and women from menial and demeaning labor, so that time can be used in more humanly constructive ways—including learning about life and living. In addition, each new generation has had access to more knowledge and has been able to discover more about the world than previous generations. Technology change has also made it more practical to educate the masses—a primary objective and obligation of our democratic society. But, it has also generated an incomprehensible amount of knowledge which is confusing and frightening to those who cannot deal with it. For many individuals the assimilation of new information created from technological activity has become an overwhelming task. Alienation and isolation in the work place, as well as the community, have often been the by-products of technological advancements.

The kind of education provided for the masses in coming years may be a central issue in determining the future of this society. It is obvious that there will be a need for increasing amounts of education to the point of making it a life-long process for virtually everyone. Education will need to provide access to the skills and knowledge required for adjustments in daily activities as well as in one's life work. As the information society takes on new forms, people must be provided new tools to carry out those tasks. The primary question to be considered at this time is: Will educators recognize the need to develop the whole person—one who requires not only the knowledge and manipulative skills, but also the attitudes and values, interests and emotions appropriate for life in an increasingly complex and rapidly changing world?

The need for understanding of self and the way in which attitudes and values are shaped will be greater in the future than at any time in the history of mankind. As technology and technological advancements force new social, cultural and economic relationships, educators

ments force new social, cultural and economic relationships, educators must consider even more seriously the area of affective learning. Educators and those others in the state and federal governments who influence the direction of education must realize that the focus of schools cannot be limited to development of cognitive and manipulative skills. They must accept the role of schools in helping persons of all ages form and reform that much less defined, but no less important area of behavior described as "affect."

DEVELOPING THE WHOLE PERSON

Schools in a democratic society must show concern for the total development of the individual. This is a rather widely accepted position among responsible educators today. The only possible way to achieve total development is by designing instructional programs and operating schools to provide experiences that will evoke thinking, feeling and acting responses; which means helping learners develop certain cognitive, affective and psychomotor behaviors. The role of formal education in this process was relatively narrow in earlier times. As the character and roles of all institutions have changed, and continue to change, the specific contributions of schools in this effort to develop the whole person have increased. A thoughtful consideration of human development suggests that this is a fitting role-change for education, for there is no other institution that has a greater opportunity to influence development of the whole person than the school.

It would be difficult if not impossible to speak of any single domain or component of human development without referring to another. To promote development of thinking processes without considering the individual's feelings or emotions concerning the use of those processes and the substance of thought, invites the kind of human tragedy seen when people become enslaved by political demagogues. A good mind supported by a free spirit can provide a powerful force against tyranny. Attempts to develop functional motor skills would be totally frustrated without a conscious awareness of the routine or procedure to be followed and a motivating drive to perform. The mind, the body and the will operating in harmony result in the best possible performance. Interaction is an extremely important factor in the functioning of the domains of behavior.

There are other factors which should be recognized when speaking of human development. First, the human organism is a tremendously complex form that may never be fully understood. In spite of at least one hundred years of scientific study in human development, very little is as yet really known about it. Second, the make up and interactive character of cognitive, affective and psychomotor processes are extremely difficult to describe. If we persist in looking at one area of behavior without considering the others, our investigations will not provide wholly valid results. Certain behaviors can be analyzed and scientific techniques devised to study human responses to selected phenomena, but the conclusions derived from experimentation cannot necessarily be projected to apply in all other situations. The new conditions may significantly alter the behavior of the organism. Third, the human organism is a dynamic form capable of changing at any point in its life cycle. The true limits in development of mind or body—its full potentialities—are not known and may never be determined. We simply don't know what we are fully capable of achieving.

A discussion of affective learning must consider all of these factors. The obvious limitation of this yearbook on affective learning in industrial arts education, therefore, is that it can deal with only one part of the whole. It can provide only partial insights concerning the character of human development, and may in fact reflect the bias of emphasizing only certain qualities of affective development. A full interpretation of affective learning can only be offered in the context of a discussion of cognitive and psychomotor learning, and with reference to the whole person concept of development.

Major Domains of Behavior

Definitions of the three major domains of behavior are generally agreed upon by education psychologists and learning theorists. It is in the application of individual philosophies to learning theory that differences in meaning or interpretation become pronounced. Historically, those differences follow along the lines of behaviorist and humanist theories. Definitions provided here will tend to be rather general, in an effort to avoid the confusion of specifics when dealing with those different philosophical and psychological theories.

Cognitive development has been given the greatest attention throughout the history of formal education. Shaping of the intellect has always been a primary goal of educators. It is relatively easy to define things to "know" and ideas to "conceptualize." In fact, progress in most educational institutions today is measured in terms of how much a student knows and is able to indicate through examination (cognitive measures) what he or she has learned. Virtually all school progress is defined in terms of grades (a measure of cognitive performance) and subject areas (formalized bodies of knowledge). The great concern expressed by the public today for low student performance is with reference to cognitive behaviors. Many are saying that students leaving high schools do not "know how to read" or "cannot solve simple arithmetic problems." Quite certainly, knowing how to read and to compute is essential in life today, and educators must strive continually to refine those processes which assist students in developing cognitive skills. However, cognitive development is only one aspect of total human development and cannot be emphasized at the expense of others.

In addition to concerns expressed for what is learned, questions need to be raised about the quality or form of cognitive experience. Is the learner dealing with only the simplest of ideas and the processing of basic information, or is he/she involved with problem solving using these ideas to generate new conclusions by evaluating known factors? Cognitive development should involve, at some point, the more demanding and useful functions at the higher levels of thought processes, and not be limited to the simplest and barely useful forms of memorization.

How the learner treats new knowledge he/she acquires has significant implications for the relationship of cognition to affect. Is there any effort to deal with questions of meaning in the new knowledge for the learner? Is there any attempt to deal with questions of the value of new knowledge or with value issues created by new knowledge? And, does the learner have any feelings for the knowledge—good, bad or indifferent? These questions all involve aspects of affect and suggest the important relationship of cognitive to affective learning.

Psychomotor development has been to this point the least studied and interpreted of the major domains of behavior. Neuromuscular functions are very important for performance in the arts, including industrial arts, and physical education. According to PaDelford (1983), "Better developed motor skills in general, specific movement patterns, eye movement patterns, voice language patterns, and visualization patterns are reported . . . to measurably increase reading ability, positive behavior, ability to concentrate, and self-confidence." Much of the research performed on these functions has been related to early childhood development. (pp. 24-25) Important relationships for cognitive, affective and psychomotor development can be found in studies reviewed by PaDelford.

There is no single or wholly agreed-upon definition for the psychomotor domain. Much of the literature on it involves child development, the military, physical education and sports, with the focus on motor abilities and motor skills. According to PaDelford:

> The lack of coordination among disciplines and the paucity of research in disciplines . . . may be due, in part, to the lack of a comprehensive, acceptable taxonomy such as the Bloom (1956) tax-

onomy of the cognitive domain and the Krathwohl, *et al* (1964)
taxonomy of the affective domain. With a few notable exceptions,
little effort has been made to develop a functional model of the
psychomotor domain which is applicable to all disciplines. This may
have been caused by the difficulty of separating the psychomotor
domain concepts from the practices of developing skills." (p. 25)

Affective development involves the formation and expression of
feelings and emotions. This may include either positive or negative
feelings as well as emotionally toned attitudes, interests, appreciations, values, morals, character, and even personal and social adjustment. It is an extremely important aspect of what a child learns in
the process of forming a personality. (Ringness, 1975, p. xi) Affective
learning begins at birth with the first expressions of need for food
and love, and continues throughout life, shaping and reshaping the
individual's personality. Hart (1978) speaks of it as all of those things
that make us "give a damn." It involves the sense of who we are and
what we are about. Because affect involves all of these rather subjective characteristics, it is much more difficult to describe than the
characteristics of the cognitive domain. However, in spite of any differences in definition or emphasis given to its characteristic qualities,
it is acknowledged by virtually all informed psychologists and educators that greater attention must be given to it in the schools.

A very large amount of literature on the affective domain involves
discussion of values, value definition and values clarification. It is evident that this particular characteristic is considered to be one of the
more descriptive of affect. Value formation represents, in the minds
of many, one of the more important qualities to be considered in the
shaping of personality. Or at least, the process of developing values
encompasses most other components of affect. Terms such as feelings and emotions are much too vague and subject to misrepresenta-
tion, while values tend to have an identifiable or observable quality
about them.

Krathwohl, Bloom and Masia (1964) focus on value development
as the primary characteristic or goal of affective development. Their
well known *Taxonomy of Educational Objectives, Handbook II* presents
a values approach in delineating the affective domain. In it they have
developed a rather comprehensive classification or hierarchical
description of affective objectives intended as a guide for evaluating
affective behavior. In the process they offer an interpretation of the
affective domain as a continuum of successive levels of behavior which
can result in the internalization of affect. The process described in
the taxonomy illustrates how a given phenomenon or value passes from
a level of basic awareness to a position of some power to guide or
control the behavior of a person.

Differences in definitions of affect and emphasis on affective learning appear to follow along the lines of psychological and philosophical demarcation between behaviorists and humanists. That line may not be as real as some choose to make it. However, the point of difference is illustrated by Ringness (1975) in his comparison of behaviorists and humanists with reference to their orientation to affective learning. Behaviorists consider the environment as very important in learning. Each of us is a product of our genes and the learning we gain from our experiences. Our attitudes and values, goals, and motives, ideas and behaviors can be traced to genetic, biological and learned phenomena. Ringness states that:

> In a sense, each of us is predetermined. We react to our inner and outer environment. The choices we make are the result of that peculiar combination of knowledge, attitudes, and motives which we have accumulated and of the present environmental situation. One might even conclude that we therefore have no real choice of behavior at all. (p. 15)

Humanists might say, however, that our lives are not so stringently controlled. We can be spontaneous and self-directing, and can change if not satisfied with the way we are. According to Ringness, humanists would say that:

> People are viewed as self-determining and capable of acting rather than simply reacting. They can control their environment rather than letting it control them. Each interacts with others, hence is influenced; but at the same time each influences others. Each person is morally responsible for what he becomes. (p. 15)

A final and acceptable definition of affect beyond its generally inclusive group of variables such as attitudes, values, interests, motivation, appreciations, adjustment, etc., may rest with the person defining it. Our individual philosophical positions will probably indicate what emphasis we would give in that definition.

Relationships of the Domains of Behavior

As suggested earlier, significant relationships exist in learning between and among the three major domains of behavior. Those relationships are recognized most clearly as they involve the cognitive and affective domains. Many studies will be found concerning the development of attitudes in relation to the learning of a given subject area. The relationship of cognitive and affective processes is discussed in a general context by Jean Piaget in *Intelligence and Affectivity: Their Relationships During Child Development* (1981). He summarizes his views on this relationship by saying:

> Affective states that have no cognitive elements are never seen, nor are behaviors found that are wholly cognitive . . . affective (plays) the role of an energy source on which functioning but not the structure of intelligence would depend. It would be like gasoline, which activates the motor of an automobile but does not modify its structure. (p. 5)

The relationship of cognition and affect is seen by Lewis and Rosenblum (1978) as circular in nature and influenced by the individual's efforts to adapt to the environment. They view it as:

> . . . affects giving rise to cognition that give rise to new affects and in turn to new cognitions. This flow—or circular rather than lineal model—incorporates our belief in interaction both within and between individuals as well as the holistic approach to behavior; that is, all these behaviors occur within a single organism as a consequence of that organism's adaptation to a continuously changing environment. (p. 9)

Piaget (1981) also explains the function of affectivity in influencing behavior while conducting tasks involving cognitive processes.

> For a student to solve an algebra problem or a mathematician to discover a theorem, there must be intrinsic interest, extrinsic interest, or a need at the beginning. While working, states of pleasure, disappointment, eagerness, as well as feelings of fatigue, effort, boredom, etc., come into play. At the end of the work, feelings of success or failure may occur; and finally, the student may experience aesthetic feelings stemming from the coherence of his solution. (p. 3)

The relationship of affective factors to psychomotor functions is similar in nature to that of affect and cognition. The motives, drives and sense of fulfillment or accomplishment experienced in motor activity are essential both in the performance and completion of the task. Interaction is continuous and a necessary ingredient.

A RATIONALE FOR AFFECTIVE EDUCATION

Support for affective education has been offered by many highly regarded educators, virtually all of whom see it as so vital to the learning process that without it education would be virtually meaningless. Combs (1982) believes that it is unlikely that learning would influence behavior without affect. And schools that ignore or reject affective aspects of behavior run the risk of being ineffective (p. 495). Aspy and Roebuck (1982) refer to the importance of affective education for improving the learning environment:

In school settings where affective concerns are attended, the student works in a climate of trust, respect, and expectancy of the highest possible individual achievement. Learning is, therefore, maximized and high standards are perceived as eustress rather than distress. (p. 489)

Hart (1978) comments on the criticisms being leveled at education for its failure to provide a good education in the basics (3 R's):

What must not be overlooked is the fact that human affective characteristics and functioning are as basic as, or more basic than, any of (the basics) in accomplishing the superordinate goals of a culture for its people. Tools, techniques, and funds of knowledge without desires, values and emotions that motivate choice-making and lead to action make learning little more than a senseless exercise or simulation game with no reality model or extension. (p. 2)

At least four fundamental reasons can be offered in the defense of affective education. First, it is simply common sense to provide opportunities in schools for affective learning. One of the strongest criticisms of schools today is with reference to declining academic performance of students. There may be a number of reasons for this problem, including poor planning of instruction within individual disciplines; the use of outdated materials or methodologies; or, the unrealistic demands on teachers and staff to deal with excessively large numbers of students of widely varied ability without adequate support services. It may also be due to the climate or condition created in the school by any number of these factors. In all, it can add up to a great deal of distress and discontent among teachers and students. Virtually anybody in a work setting is going to perform below normal expectations if negative conditions exist. A reasonable degree of contentment can result in greater performance. Affective education attempts to influence the school climate by emphasizing human rather than material needs.

A second reason for dealing with affective education is illustrated by the experiences of major industries in the United States with the competition of foreign import products. American industry has learned the hard way, through the loss of major markets in recent years, that when management and labor work together to achieve a commonly accepted goal under conditions that reduce levels of antagonism, the chances for success and improved output increase. Affective education tends to be learner-centered. Students have an opportunity to participate in decision-making concerning learning activities in classrooms where affective learning is stressed.

Educational researchers have frequently discussed the importance of interpersonal skills to improved performance of teachers and administrators. This is also true with students. Affective education focuses upon improving the interpersonal skills of all persons involved in a situation. In schools that value affective learning, administrators, teachers and students consciously work to develop and improve their own interpersonal skills. Well planned programs and fully equipped schools will never be able to overcome deficiencies in education where the interpersonal relationships of personnel are unsatisfactory.

Finally, because affective education makes an effort to establish favorable conditions for learning and places emphasis upon the learner's needs, it can get at two of the most persistent and educationally disruptive forces in the schools—absenteeism and vandalism. These are problems considered by the public as well as teachers to be major indicators of the decline of education. Affective education cannot in and of itself provide all that is needed to realize these advantages, but it can add a great deal to efforts directed at their establishment. (Aspy and Roebuck, 1982, pp. 488-493)

Carkhuff (1982) has presented reasons similar to these in a discussion of affective education in the age of productivity. His interpretation of the evolution of mankind indicates that the present "electronic revolution" has created a whole new set of circumstances influencing man's productive capabilities. Existing production systems assume unlimited human and material resources. Nations cannot continue to support these outdated systems, and a new formula or equation for improving productivity is needed. Through a review of 137 studies of living, learning and working outcomes, Carkhuff determined that the solution rests in improving human output through more appropriate affective education. He believes that greater productivity in schools can result from greater attention being given to human resources. Carkhuff states:

> The actualization of human productivity is found in the human processing that enables humans to analyze, operationalize, and technologize the means to minimizing or even eliminating resource inputs and maximizing or even actualizing results outputs.
>
> The greatest assistance in accomplishing these productivity purposes lies in the affective-interpersonal development of all parties involved—students as well as teachers, parents as well as administrators, industry as well as local, state, and federal government. The greatest and most inexpensive resources are effective humans, skilled in communicating with each other to share data bases concerning inputs, processes, and outputs. (p. 486)

The realization that learning itself is directly influenced by affective experiences provides one of the strongest arguments for schools to recognize affective education. Combs (1982) points to four affective factors that are known to influence the learning process cirtically. With appropriate attention to these factors, learning can be enhanced:

1. Self-concept: Students need to believe in themselves if they are to learn appropriate behaviors. Without the support provided in a good self-concept the student cannot realize even partially his or her potential.

2. Challenge or Threat: The challenge a student senses from dealing with a problem that he/she is interested in and feels able to cope with successfully is quite different from the sense of threat experienced when confronted with problems they may not feel able to handle. A reduction in threat inducing situations and an increase in challenging experiences can promote learning.

3. Values: There is a need for the learners to identify goals and behaviors they choose to reach and develop. Values are the generalized beliefs that serve as basic guidelines for this selection process. Schools can deal with some values quite readily without conflicting with what may be considered "personal" value systems. Valuing knowledge, skills, critical thinking, lifelong education and good citizenship for example would be an appropriate goal for schools to consider.

4. Belonging and Being Cared for: The sense of acceptance and being a part of something is essential to growth and development. Schools can readily provide opportunities for students through group and peer activities to develop feelings of belonging and being accepted. (p. 496)

There are, of course, critics of affective education. Much of the criticism emphasizes the vagueness and continuously changing quality of affect as interpreted by persons of differing philosophical or psychological orientations. It will also be found that criticism results from some earlier abuses in educational practices where the development of feelings and emotions was closely associated with sensory or "touchy-feely" encounters and not based upon sound and comprehensive principles of psychology. Diane Divorky (1978) makes the point that the field of affective education "is amorphous, the goals and objectives immeasurable, and rhetoric often incomprehensible." (p. 47) The behaviorist might criticize it primarily on the point that you cannot observe attitudes, values or appreciations as their development relies too much on time and situational factors to provide an adequate basis for measurement. However, the humanist might argue that such efforts at precise measurement of behavior are attempts to place individuals of greatly varying make-up in artificially defined groupings. The arguments and issues raised by these positions clearly emphasize "the need for meticulous care and monitorial progress in the development of affective components." (Beeler, 1978, p. 8)

The revolution in new technologies that is virtually reshaping every social, political, and economic institution today provides a basis for even one more argument in support of affective education. The issue is that there is a very great deal of affective activity involved in coping with problems presented by the technological revolution. The influence of technological change is all pervasive. Making decisions concerning the appropriateness of developing some technological system, such as a space satellite, extends in its influence far beyond questions of what and how to do so. It draws in major issues of why and for what purposes, as well as at what expense to other things. Stanley (1978) makes the point in summarizing a discussion on the influence of technological advances on the conscience, that "technological norms and values can erode other norms and values." (p. 8) This is not to suggest that technology is automatically bad, but rather to indicate the need for careful attention to how to deal with changes in norms and values influenced by technological activity.

AFFECTIVE EDUCATION AND VALUES IN A TECHNOLOGICAL AGE

Throughout the history of mankind new technological developments have provided both advantages and disadvantages, goods and evils. Early uses of technology were directed at the earth's hostile environment. Since that time man has virtually tamed the environment and eliminated disease, poverty and hunger for a major percentage of the earth's people. He is now on the threshhold of great biological advances in the area of genetics. At the same time, man faces overpopulation and the prospect of massive food shortages, environmental pollution and the destruction of natural resources, uncontrolled production of weapons for war and the growing potential for annihilation of the human race. He has controlled nature but cannot seem to control his inventive tendencies toward self-destruction. Lauda (1971) stated in his epilogue to *Advancing Technology* that:

> Whether we view technology negatively, positively, or consider it unworthy of study, we find ourselves making value decisions about it . . . Technology has positive and negative characteristics. Both must be judged consistently and accurately, for over-optimism can be as threatening to the future as pessimism. However, the greatest pitfall for man is sheer ambivalence. (pp. 534-35)

The point in this statement seems quite clear: studies of technology must consider the motivation for any new innovation, its impact on mankind, and its meaning to all people on the earth.

Raising questions about technological activity forces us to deal with value issues. A high-technology, knowledge-based free society is going to be faced with questions concerning traditional values simply because the process of planning for use and then using new technological invention causes values to change. Traditional values often fail to function adequately when technology leads to changes in social conditions. They are not necessarily destroyed, but are, through a process of accommodation, altered or reformulated to fit demands of the new conditions. (Mesthene 1970, pp. 45-48)

An illustration of this process is seen in the response of labor unions to the increased use of robots in manufacturing processes. Robots can provide tremendous advantages for improving production rate and quality control, which must be achieved to make products competitive in a free market system. Another outcome with the use of robots, however, is that workers are displaced from traditional jobs. Labor unions which are designed to protect jobs now find themselves unable to enforce those basic values in the interest of workers. Accommodations must be made in the union's position to acknowledge the requirements for higher production and to assure some form of employment for the workers.

Technology can promote conflict as the gap between principle and practice is increased. This gap is described as the difference between what we are able to do and what we are willing to do. We may be able to produce enough food in the United States to feed all of the world's hungry, but we are not able to make that food available to those masses without upsetting the entire system for maintaining a balance of trade among nations—a principle that must be applied with consistency for the general welfare of nations.

The point was made earlier in this discussion that technological developments in a free society create conflict. In nations run by totalitarian governments there is no conflict, as questions cannot be asked concerning the appropriateness of government actions. Children and youth in a free society must be provided an opportunity to study all issues raised by new technological developments, to consider alternatives and to present their views as well as listen to the views of others concerning problems created by the new developments. The educational system should provide the setting and means for this process of inquiry.

Technologists today find themselves dealing with issues of values and the impact of technology on society as they never have in the past. The potential for abuses in the application of technology has become too evident for even the most dedicated technologist to ignore. Those who create new technologies, including scientists, engineers and technologists, must look beyond the simple physical gratifications provided by new technologies and deal with the larger needs of mankind—mental as well as moral. They must face the priority obligation of implementing universal values that will survive over the long haul. Those decisions cannot be left to philosophers, religious leaders or politicians, for earlier approaches using only the input of those groups are now obsolete. Workable values which take into account the larger and more significant needs of mankind over time must be shaped by the input of those who develop technologies as well as those who use them. (Watkins, 1977, p. 1965)

As industrial arts education moves toward education to describe the technological world and man's technological activity, the responsibility for dealing with learning in the affective domain, and especially value formulation relating to technological developments, will increase. Children, youth and adults will need to understand, not only what is taking place in the physical world as a result of technological development, but what their own feelings, emotions and values are with reference to those phenomena. To study technological process or applications without considering those deeper issues will simply perpetuate conditions of the past wherein man has been able only to react to the surge of technological events and never really direct them. New generations will simply never be able to make their own future if the old approach continues to be used. (Toffler, 1970)

INDUSTRIAL ARTS AND AFFECTIVE EDUCATION

Industrial arts education reflects the same confusion in acknowledging affective learning as found in other disciplines. At the same time, cognitive and psychomotor learning is well represented in the content, goals and activities for programs in industrial arts. The same condition holds true for virtually all other disciplines. Birnie (1978), in a discussion of this problem in science education, offers several reasons for the lack of attention to affective education.

1. Because entering the world of personal values is seen as indoctrination or brainwashing.
2. Because our methods and materials have been ineffective in reaching affective goals.
3. Because we do not have evaluation techniques and instruments to tell us whether or not we have been successful in achieving affective outcomes.

4. Because we believe that behavior is the only thing that really matters in education; that affect is an unfit subject for scientific study.
5. Because we have assumed that there is a direct relationship between knowing and behavior (that, for example, the child who can list endangered species will, therefore, be concerned with their survival). (p. 29)

These same reasons may also hold true for industrial arts education. It would seem, at least, that the overriding reason for neglecting affective learning is that it would create many more problems and generate numerous unanswerable questions for the teacher. It is simply easier to deal with the more obvious and clearly describable phenomena pertaining to cognitive and psychomotor development.

Another way to view the problem would be to suggest that the philosophical and psychological orientations most appropriate for implementing affective education may not be sufficiently evident among industrial arts teachers to assure its being given adequate attention in their classrooms. This may be because (1) the underlying philosophy of the discipline does not support affective education, (2) the kind of instructional content, methods and materials appropriate for affective learning have not been sufficiently developed, or (3) industrial arts teacher education programs do not give adequate emphasis to affective education. It is likely that all three of these conditions have played a part in creating the neglect of affective learning in industrial arts that exists today. However, it should be entirely possible to correct these conditions if the profession chooses to do so and gives attention to those things which would provide support for a new orientation to affective learning. Some reflection on philosophical and psychological orientations among certain professionals in industrial arts education might offer an indication of the prospects for such a pattern of change.

There is nothing in the underlying philosophy for industrial arts education that would restrict the inclusion of affective learning experiences in industrial arts programs. If anything, it has been an inherent part of the discipline from the early beginning. The difficulty is more likely defined in terms of the kind of emphasis provided and the extent to which efforts have been made to give affective learning description.

One of the early proponents of a philosophy encompassing affective learning experiences in industrial arts was Frederick Gordon Bonser. His child-centered approach to education emphasized the socialization of children. From his studies of Bonser's work, McPherson (1978) states:

According to Bonser, the specific purpose of objectives to be accomplished in industrial arts were: (1) a health purpose; (2) an

economic purpose; (3) an art or aesthetic purpose; (4) a social purpose and (5) a recreational purpose. These purposes were to be
accomplished by utilizing the psychological or natural impulses of
children toward expression or action. Bonser identified six psychological impulses naturally expressive in children. They were: (1) the
impulse to manipulative activity; (2) the impulse to investigate; (3) the
impulse to art activities; (4) the impulse to play; (5) the impulse to
communicate, and (6) the social impulse.

    The role of industrial arts was to contribute to the develop-
ment of these natural impulses into effective habits or attitudes by
providing educational direction. The educational experiences should
therefore be based on the child's psychological and mental growth.
(p. 233)

McPherson, in his discussion on the role of industrial arts in the
establishment of humanism in American education, has allied Bonser
with the group of educators responsible for giving description to the
Progressive Education Movement, including Francis W. Parker, John
Dewey, William H. Kilpatrick and James C. Russell. In that affective
education finds its greatest support among humanistic theories, it can
be stated that Bonser, as an influential leader in industrial arts education, was defining a significant role for industrial arts in affective
education.

Further support for the role of industrial arts in affective education is offered by Gordon Wilber (1954) in his discussion of industrial
arts in general education. He speaks of the need to deal with the total
organism in education and says:

    Emotions become important not in their peculiar manifestations
but as they are indicative of disequilibrium within the individual.
A further implication of the wholeness of learning situations makes
it appear that an individual not only learns the lesson which a
teacher is presenting but may be developing certain very definite
attitudes—likes and dislikes—and emotional reactions in addition.
The matter of concomitant learning, therefore, becomes of unusual
importance.

    In like manner, modern psychology seems to show that learning
takes place much more quickly and easily when it is the result of
experience carried on in relationship to pupil goals and purposes.
(p. 12)

Wilber indicates that industrial arts can "meet the needs of individuals in the basic aspects of living" (a principal aim of general education). (p. 15) He states that:

    There are two groups of needs which can be especially well met by
the industrial arts program. These are the need for a feeling of

belonging to and being accepted by a group, and the need for a feeling of success. (p. 26)

He continues to emphasize the significance of this process to the learner by saying: "The possibility of promoting this feeling of success for all children is of such importance that industrial arts might be justified on this basis alone." (p. 27)

Waetjen (1953) believes there is a key role for industrial arts in shaping learner attitudes and values through peer group experiences. He sees an increasing need in modern technological society for the learner to develop a group identity—one where the individual finds an opportunity to make a significant contribution to the welfare of the group and where an individual's security can be realized. Industrial arts can make a major contribution to the development of social relationships through varied group activities in industrial arts laboratories, according to Waetjen. "Industrial arts in our schools, in addition to representing the industrial life of our society, has the task of helping our youth to learn to live in a highly inter-dependent world." (p. 9)

Another aspect of affective development considered by Waetjen as pertinent to the role of industrial arts is the formation of an appropriate self-concept, which is closely associated with the development of social relationships. Waetjen (1954) indicates that "self-concept could be defined as being the perceptions a person has of his abilities, personal traits, and physique; his attitudes and values; his feelings about himself, particularly in relation to other people." (p. 3) It is while a student formulates perceptions of the world around him that he also acquires and differentiates perceptions of himself to form an integrated concept of self.

Waetjen (1957) emphasizes the great importance of self-concept to learning in a chapter of the Sixth ACIATE Yearbook. He draws from phenomenological psychology and the writings of Arthur Combs, Donald Snygg, Earl Kelley, and Carl Rogers to establish a rationale for the place of self-concept. Its influence is seen in the following:

> The self-concept, which develops through time and serves as an interpretive force, gives meaning to events in terms of the individual's present organization and needs as perceived at the moment of action. Also, self-concept governs perceptions through its selective action. In effect, self-concept screens perceptions, permitting those which are compatible and offering resistance to perceptions more incompatible with the conception of self. (p. 80)

The key point Waetjen makes in the chapter is:

> ... that human beings have the tendency and urge to develop, mature and expand themselves while moving in the direction of self-actualization. Humans are "becoming" creatures. (p. 90)

Industrial arts has a great deal to contribute in this process. Implications for industrial arts and industrial arts teacher education which Waetjen develops from his review of psychological theories in this chapter have a good deal to say about the way in which we can approach affective learning. The implications are summarized as a set of hypotheses to be considered for more thorough research.

1. Industrial arts teachers play a contributing role in the self-evolvement of the student, in the same way as other teachers, parents or any important persons in the student's life.

2. Industrial arts teachers and industrial arts teacher education promotes the uniqueness of the individual student.

3. A first step industrial arts teacher education can take in planning a curriculum to prepare teachers is to describe in behavioral terms the kind of teacher that should be produced. Experiences can then be provided for students to obtain appropriate behavioral changes.

4. Industrial arts teacher educators cannot expect their students to experience instruction in the same way. They will each experience it in an individual way.

5. Industrial arts teachers can expect students to be influenced by the roles and behaviors manifested by the teachers. Values and attitudes are learned through identification with teachers.

6. Teachers are able to accept errors or mistakes made by students without reflecting blame or ineptness. Notions of "good" and "bad" are not so emotionally loaded when this attitude is maintained.

7. Industrial arts teachers are able to accept the attitude that all people have the capacity and desire to learn; and every effort is made to understand when the student is in the process of achieving developmental tasks.

8. Industrial arts teachers provide activities which not only portray the industrial characteristics of society, but also yield rich interpersonal contacts.

9. Group processes are utilized in industrial arts classrooms and laboratories in an effort to remove the teacher from the role of a "fountain of information," to engender positive feelings in students, and increase the rate and permanence of learning.

10. Industrial arts classrooms provide an environment that stimulates the creative instincts in the learner. Creativity may be displayed through a product.

(Waetjen, 1957, 80-94)

> However, a person can just as well demonstrate creativity. . . .
> through his unique ability to solve problems, through being able to
> maintain a high quality of human relationships, or being able to
> see new relationships and meanings in existing knowledge. Crea-
> tivity may then be thought of not as an end product, but as the inter-
> action between the individual with his unique purposes and goals,
> and the conditions, materials, people and processes in the indi-
> vidual's life. (Waetjen, 1957, p. 90)

The last of these hypotheses points to the strong relationship of
cognitive processes and affective development. Creative tendencies
in the learner can be facilitated through problem solving, which
involves cognitive functions, when affective factors such as personal
and interpersonal relationships are taken into consideration. It should
also be seen in these hypotheses that through the large variety of activities and experiences which can be offered in a well designed industrial arts program, the student can acquire a positive self-concept
while becoming a self-actualized person.

Much of the discussion regarding industrial arts curricula in
recent years has focused upon content derivation and structure. Professional journals, books and conferences for industrial arts personnel
have involved countless references to new directions for the discipline
—virtually all emphasizing technology as a basis for curriculum and
technological activity as the source for deriving new content structures. The pattern of those discussions during the 1970's has been
effectively documented by James Zeigler and others in the 28th
ACIATE Yearbook. (Martin, 1979, pp. 169-187) Indications also are
that the 1980's will be marked by a concerted national effort to review
the role of industrial arts education in a technologically oriented
society, as the American Industrial Arts Association sets course on
a comprehensive and detailed study of the question. (Starkweather,
1983) Whether that study will deal exclusively with content derivation and structure is not as yet known.

A central issue with regards to these efforts seems to be one of
the emphasis placed upon analyzing the structure of knowledge for
industrial arts without consideration for the learner and the psychological bases for learning experiences in this area of education. In
other words, will the greater effort be given to defining and describing
components appropriate for cognitive development with little regard
for affective experiences? This has been the pattern since the mid-
1960's; will it continue to be the pattern through the 1980's?

A notable exception to this somewhat singular interest of the
discipline will be found in the efforts of Donald Maley at the University
of Maryland. During his years at that institution he has repeatedly

emphasized the need to develop the "whole boy and girl." There is little doubt that his illustrations of curriculum approaches, such as that found in the Maryland Plan (Smith, 1970) emphasize affective as well as cognitive and psychomotor development. That fact can be noted in his reference to the Plan for the junior high grades.

> The Maryland Plan for a junior high school program in Industrial Arts should *not* be called "A plan for the organization of Industrial Arts content." This statement would be only a partial description since content organization is not the entire program. The program also involves specific teaching methodology. It is the blending of the selected teaching methodology with the content that produces the Maryland Plan. (p. 24)

It is also stated in the Maryland Plan that a number of guidelines were used in directing its development. Emphasis is given as much to human needs as to the more traditional sources used in the design of instructional content and activities in industrial arts education— tool, material, process, and job analysis.

> The human needs analysis was a prime factor in this development. The result is a program with content and methodology based on a concern for the individual and for what happens to him. In Industrial Arts a common alternative to human needs analysis has been the thing or job analysis approach to content and methodology. (p. 7)

In his own interpretation of the history and development of the Maryland Plan, Maley (1979) states:

> The content and experiential elements of the program grew out of a thorough examination of the contemporary society and the needs of people living in it. The content, activities, and instructional strategies were integrated into a working plan with a strong concern for individual differences in abilities, interests, motivations, goals, and ambitions of the students to be served. The program has a place in it at each grade level for students of all levels of ability. (p. 144)

Maley uses developmental tasks as a key reference point and guide for understanding human needs. Developmental tasks (Havighurst, 1972; Tryon and Lilienthal, 1950) have been used to describe the human condition at the several stages of life in terms of a wide variety of needs. There is a strong psychological orientation in the quality of needs described in developmental tasks. In using the choice of human needs analysis as the focal point for instructional planning, Maley probably comes closer to acknowledging education or development for the "whole" person, including significant affective factors, than any other contemporary writer in industrial arts education. The Maryland Plan was conceived in the 1950's and has been implemented in public schools continuously since that time.

More recently Maley (1980) elaborated on his theories for industrial arts to serve the whole learner in the publication *Industrial Arts Puts the Whole Boy and Girl in the School in 1980.* In this booklet, he offers ten propositions as a basis for discussion of his curriculum proposal. It is quite apparent that cognitive, affective and psychomotor features were considered in the development of those propositions.

1. The nature of learning involves a range of inter-related factors and elements which interface with and depend upon a variety of human processes.
2. The Industrial Arts activity is based on the idea that the learner is involved in an experience that is multisensory. As such, it has the potential for the learner to use the senses of smell, taste, touch, sight and hearing.
3. The Industrial Arts activity has a rich potential for a strong intellectual involvement in such functions as creating, analyzing, assimilating, and perceiving.
4. The Industrial Arts activity has the potential for a deep personal involvement as such experiences deal with the factors of interests, likes, aspirations, curiosities, motivations, dreams, emotions, values, cares, satisfactions, and fears of the learner.
5. The Industrial Arts activity has the great potential for the learner's involvement in the motor functions which relate to fine muscle control, large muscle control, and the coordination of the physical and mental capabilities of the individual.
6. There are strong connections between the motor activities and the intellectual factors of creating, analyzing, assimilating, and perceiving. These same potentials for connections exist between the personal and the motor.
7. The Industrial Arts activity provides a rich arena for the student to engage in learning experiences directed toward the achievement of developmental tasks at the several levels or growth periods.
8. The wholeness of the educational and growth processes for the learner is based on the concept that the intellectual, personal, motor, and developmental task factors are dependent on each other.
9. The dimensions of wholeness in an educational sense for the individual is achieved when the learning process maximizes the

human potential for involvement in that process. That is to say, if one can learn about the properties of wood through the senses of smell and touch, and there is no opportunity to use those senses in the learning experience, then the concept of wholeness is not fulfilled.

10. The flexibility of the program and comprehensiveness of its structure plus the additional ingredient of a creative, imaginative, effective teacher are essentials to the process of educating the whole child. (pp. 1-3)

There exist, therefore, precedents for the serious consideration of affective learning in industrial arts education. Whether educators in the discipline recognize or acknowledge those precedents is not known. However, the preponderance of literature with a heavy emphasis on cognitive and psychomotor learning activities suggests either a reluctance to accept a focus on the affective, or a significant level of confusion concerning its application in programs of study.

THEORIES OF LEARNING AND AFFECTIVE EDUCATION

The vast majority of work in psychology has been concerned with cognitive development. Even though this may be considered fundamental to the understanding of behavior in general, it creates significant voids in attempts to understand the functioning of the whole person, and especially in any attempts to deal with affective development. Educational psychology has experienced a similar problem, especially in some earlier efforts to derive functional learning theories from studies of human behavior. In recent times, and especially since the early 1960's, the emphasis on affective development has become more clearly focused and consistent, with the result that formalized theories for affective learning have taken shape.

Educational psychology is built on the assumption that there is consistency in human behavior. Systematic observations of behavior provide the many hypotheses and generalizations used by psychologists and educators in the development of theories of learning. E.L. Thorndike conducted some of the earliest scientific experiments on behavior in his work with animals in 1898. During the first quarter of the 20th century he concentrated more seriously on learning in schools. Educational psychologists today tend to focus on observable human behavior. They depend primarily on the process of generating hypotheses (if . . . then assumptions), which are tested in appropriate experimental settings and evaluated. Theories of learning are then derived to provide some principles or laws to indicate conditions where learning may or may not take place.

When dealing with studies of human behavior in school settings, we must consider not only how a child develops and learns, but how the teacher perceives and instructs the child. The many variables that arise under these considerations create conditions wherein very few absolutes can be defined. It is extremely difficult to derive conclusions to fit every school situation. The best that might be hoped for is that teachers become familiar with as many theories of learning and instruction as possible to provide them with adequate resources for developing strategies to be used in teaching.

Virtually all of the scientifically-based theories of learning have been developed in the 20th century. It would be neither possible nor appropriate to review all of those theories and their underlying psychological principles in this text. What will be considered are the dominant theories in the psychology of learning which appear to have the greatest meaning and clearest implications for affective learning.

Learning Theory

Learning is most effectively defined in terms of the prominent factors that characterize it. Sahakian (1976) identifies those factors as (1) change—a relatively permanent behavioral alteration, (2) observability—where it is necessary to determine that something is taking place, (3) experience—where the individual finds meaning in what is learned. The first two of these characteristics would be most acceptable to traditional learning theorists and those persons identified as behaviorists, while the third is considered most acceptable to the group identified as humanists. Sahakian uses these three characteristics of learning in presenting what he refers to as an operational definition of learning: "Learning is a relatively permanent change in personality (including cognitive, affective, attitudinal, motivational, behavioral, experiential, and the like) and reflects a change in performance usually brought about by practice, although it may arise from insight or other factors, including memory" (p. 3). This definition is broad enough to account for virtually all of the major theories of learning. However, learning theorists may give greater or lesser emphasis to some factors in their individual theories. It is quite appropriate for reference in the discussions of affective learning used in this yearbook.

Theories for Consideration

William Sahakian, in one of his several books on psychology and theories of learning, offers an analysis of psychological theories that is quite helpful in establishing the bases for learning theories associated with affective learning. He uses a systems-oriented review of virtually every significant theory, hypothesis, or postulate in learning that has influenced thinking during the past one hundred years in his text *Introduction to the Psychology of Learning* (1979). Included are the following major theories and theorists:

Theory	*Theorists*
1. Association Psychology	
a. Classical Conditioning	Ivan P. Pavlov
b. Behaviorism	John Watson
c. Association by Continuity Theory of Learning	Edwin R. Guthrie
2. Reinforcement Theories of Learning	
a. Connectionism	Edward L. Thorndike
b. Operant Behaviorism	B.F. Skinner
3. Reinforcement by Drive Reduction	
a. Drive Reduction Theory of Learning	Clark L. Hull
b. Neo-Hullian Theory	Kenneth L. Spence
	Abram Amsel
	Frank A. Logan
4. The Cognitive Approach to Learning	
a. Cognitive Behaviorism	Edward C. Tolman
b. Neo-Tolmanism: Cognitive and Information Processing Theories	Martin E.P. Seligman
	John Garcia
c. Gestalt Learning Theory	Max Wertheimer
	Wolfgang Kohler
	Kurt Koffka
d. Neo-Gestalt Theory: Field Theoretical Approach	Kurt Lewin
e. Psychoanalytical Theory of Learning	Sigmund Freud
f. Cognitive Developmental Theory: Psychogenetic Epistemology	Jean Piaget
g. Neo-Piagetian Learning Theory	Jerome Bruner
	Daniel E. Berlyne
5. The Humanistic Approach to Learning	
a. Humanistic Theory of Learning	Abraham H. Maslow
b. Significant Learning Theory	Carl R. Rogers

A number of these theories are reviewed in the following pages in an effort to provide a historical as well as psychological perspective for understanding those which may have the greatest influence on affective education.

Associationist Theories. Psychologists from the time of Thorndike have attempted to show how their theories most satisfactorily apply in promoting classroom learning. Often theories of one psychologist have been built upon theories of others with appropriate modifications. Some in fact predate Thorndike, such as that of the English philosopher John Locke, who, in the seventeenth century proposed that the mind is blank (tabula rosa) at birth; it is impressionable; and the environment rather than heredity is the basis for learning. This early associationist theory was based on the idea that sense experience provided for the development of knowledge, morality, and values. Locke believed that through sense experience and internal reflection, complex ideas could be formulated and learning could take place.

Johann Herbart expanded Locke's position in the ninteenth-century with more clearly defined concepts of apperception, which is recognized as early associationism. This position focused on the relationships of newly perceived ideas to those already in the mind. He held that frequency and association were important factors in learning. Herbart believed that the more often ideas entered the consciousness, the greater the chance they would remain, and the combined strength of several ideas in the mind would determine the associations that subsequently enter the consciousness.

Herbart may have developed some of the earliest functional theories on learning of values, as he believed that a primary objective of education was morality. He developed a set of theoretical considerations intended to make children good. Those theories focused on two major points: (1) Ideas are learned only when perceived in the conscious mind and associated with other ideas, and (2) ideas are dynamic and moving, always struggling with one another for a place in the consciousness. These theories of apperception—also known as Herbartianism—had a great deal of influence on teacher education in the early 1900's.

S-R Theories. In the realm of stimulus-response theories, a tremendous amount of work was undertaken in the early 1900's, much of which was based on the pioneer efforts of E.L. Thorndike. The theory of connectionism acknowledged the relationship of stimulus (S) and response (R), and utilized some elements of associationistic psychology. In this early S-R theory learning was viewed as the formation of connections in the mind. Animal experiments involving puzzle boxes and the presentation of rewards, or satisfiers, for correct decisions resulted in three primary laws that Thorndike developed and refined over a period of thirty years: (1) the law of effect, (2) the law of readiness, and (3) the law of exercise. Eventually his theory of connectionism was modified to include only two major laws—the law of effect, which stated that rewards always strengthened connections, while punishment weakened it little or not at all, and the law of belonging-ness, which held that a connection could be more easily made if the stimulus and response belonged together in some natural or circumstantial order of things such as the formation of sentences from appropriately related words. The full sentence could be learned more readily if each successive word in the sentence fit in some logical way.

Contiguity Theories. Another major focus of learning research in the early 1900's involved the contiguity theories. The Russian physiologist I.R. Pavlov and the American psychologist J.B. Watson in 1914 prepared a modification of Thorndike's theory of connectionism. These contiguity theorists saw learning as a matter of habit-forming or pairing of stimulus and response, in much the way as connectionists. However, a key difference was in the meaning of timing. They held that learning occurs best when there is almost stimultaneous occurrence of the stimulus and response, and that a great deal of learning can take place from the individual doing something at the time an unrelated stimulus is provided. Habituated responses to the indirect stimulus can develop in this process. Pavlov's classical conditioning research involving dogs provided significant evidence for this learning theory.

Behavioral Theories. Early studies in behaviorism, which were initiated in the United States by J.B. Watson, reflected a refinement of Pavlov's theory, but involved human subjects. The major difference Watson maintained from Pavlov is found in the meaning of man's emotional responses to the learning process. Love, anger and fear, as existing innate responses, are important factors in conditioning patterns, and learning is a process of associating relevant stimuli to such innate responses. Watson's efforts represent one of the earliest attempts in dealing with feelings and emotions.

E.R. Guthrie developed Watson's theories even further in the 1930's and 1940's. His position was effectively a rejection of some of Thorndike's connectionist theories and the revision of earlier contiguity theories, and resulted in a single law of association: "A combination of stimuli which has accompanied a movement will on its recurrence tend to be followed by that movement." (Guthrie, 1952, p. 23) This says that when a conditioned stimulus and a conditioned response are paired, they are learned. Guthrie believed that an individual learns by doing and the best time to teach something is when the learner appears ready to learn. In a sense these positions represented an extension of earlier contiguity theories.

A third major group of S-R theories focused on the work of Clark Hull in the 1930's and 1940's. His connectionist position referred back to Thorndike's law of effect and became known as reinforcement theory. It focused on habit and stated that learning takes place through conditioning and reinforcement. Hull's habit-family hierarchy involved the ordering of a variety of probable responses (habits) that may occur with any given stimulus. It held that education consists of changing relative positions in a hierarchy of responses. The original or most likely behavior would not be lost, but would simply be displaced. "The original hierarchy of inherent responses is rearranged in relation to the reinforcement received in the course of life experiences, with those responses leading to reinforcement increasing in probability, and thus, gaining more strength on the hierarchy." (Thornburg, 1973, p. 12) Hull also emphasized that frequency of reinforcement is directly related to habit strength on the hierarchy.

Drive, cue, response and reinforcement (reward) were the four components of the learning process defined by John Dollard and Neal Miller (1941) from a simplified version of Hull's theory. Their position was that drive, which is a compulsion to act, elicits activity (readiness). A cue then provides the stimulus that creates a response, which in turn acts to reduce the drive. Reduction in the strength of the drive reinforces the response so that learning of the response results.

A review of learning theories, no matter how brief, would not be complete without considering the work of B.F. Skinner and his conditioning theories. Over a period of thirty years, Skinner developed and refined his theories on respondent and operant conditioning so that many present-day teachers now knowingly or otherwise employ them in their classrooms. During the period of the 1960's tremendous advances were made in developing teaching materials and instructional technology utilizing the principles of Skinnerian theory.

Skinner's respondent conditioning theory depended upon contiguity as a condition for learning. The emission of a response had to occur within the presence of a stimulus. His operant conditioning concept is based upon the person's response to his environment. No identifiable stimulus consistently elicits operant behavior, but rather individuals emit varying responses to various stimuli situations. Reinforcement is an important concept to Skinner, and learning, or recurring operant responses, results from appropriate reinforcements. That reinforcement (reward) can be presented to the learner through a number of sensory processes. In effect, the operant conditioning theories Skinner developed and refined have received the greatest attention in recent decades.

American psychologist Robert M. Gagné offered a more holistic description of learning based upon traditional S-R theories. He recognized the complexity and variety of human learning and developed a theory of hierarchical learning conditions as a response to these different states of the person. His focus is upon the prerequisite conditions of learning and the value of a hierarchy of learning types moving from simple to complex. Overall learning can be described in terms of cumulative and orderly effects. Gagné proposed eight types (levels) of learning, cumulative in nature; each more complex level depending on the prerequisite knowledge or learning in the lower level of performance:

> *Level 1, Signal Learning.* The individual learns to make a reflex- ive response to some external and specific, identifiable stimulus. The type of learning represented here is the same as Pavlov's classical conditioning and Skinner's respondent conditioning.

> *Level 2, Stimulus-Response Learning.* The learner discriminates among different stimuli and acquires a specific stimulus. The response is voluntary (unlike level 1) and is the same as Thorndike's S-R connection and Skinner's operant conditioning. This level may also be termed single discrimination learning.

> *Level 3, Motor Chaining.* The individual learns to combine a number of already acquired S-R connections into a sequential chain of psychomotor behaviors.

> *Level 4, Verbal Associations.* The learner acquires a chain of responses that are verbal. Basically, the conditions resemble those for chaining in motor learning (level 3). However, the presence of language makes this a special type of response because the facilitating links in learning the chain may be provided internally by the learner from his repertoire of language.

> *Level 5, Multiple Discrimination.* The individual learns to discriminate among—make differently identifying responses to— two or more different stimuli which have a similar appearance or similar characteristics.

> *Level 6, Concept Learning.* The learner acquires a capability of identifying and making a common response to an entire class of stimuli (objects or events) that may differ from each other widely in physical appearance. His understanding of the objects or events is based on the abstract properties of the stimuli and/or on verbal definitions.

> *Level 7, Rule Learning.* A rule is a chain of two or more previously learned concepts that are combined by the learner into a verbal principle that explains or determines behavior, events, or relationships. The learning of a rule always infers a capability to act on that rule. This type of learning must be carefully distinguished from learning the mere verbal statement of a rule which is a level 4 response (a chain of verbal responses).

> *Level 8, Problem Solving.* Two or more previously acquired rules are combined to produce a new, higher order rule which can be applied in resolving previously unencountered problems. (Thornburg, 1973, p. 16)

In his analysis and description of learning theories, from which much of the preceding was developed, Herschel Thornburg (1973) indicates that all of the psychologists included in this discussion derived their conclusions in part from the early efforts of Thorndike. Present-day reinforcement theory acknowledges with Thorndike, "(1) the necessity of reinforcement for learning, (2) the greater effect on learning that positive reinforcement (rewards, satisfiers, drive reduction) has over negative reinforcement (punishment, annoyers) and (3) the weakening of a response tendency if no reinforcement occurs." (p. 19) All of the learning theories reviewed here also emphasize the behaviorist point of view concerning learning and instruction.

Third Force Psychology

In some psychological circles, it is acknowledged that there are three major thrusts or forces upon which learning theories have been based (Winn, 1964). The first force, behaviorism, has been discussed in some detail in the preceding section. The second force is considered Freudianism or psychoanalysis and has not been given serious consideration in this review of learning theories. It is not believed that the objective of psychoanalysis, homeostasis, important as it may be to life, fits properly in this discussion of learning theories, and will not be given further consideration.

Third force Psychology was defined by Abraham Maslow and his allies in the 1960's as a reaction to reductionism, which tends to explain human qualities solely on a physical or animal basis. Maslow felt that both the behaviorists and psychoanalysts failed to recognize truly human qualities. This third force psychology, as explained by Sahakian (1976),

> ... relates to the philosophies of existentialism and humanism. The person-as-a-whole model, as the humanistic psychology model, emphasizes the person as postive, purposive, active, and involved in life experience. Humanistic education articulates a goal of growth, with the educational process continuing throughout life. Learning is characterized as experiential, its essence being freedom and its outcome one of healthy reform and revolt. (p. 380)

The "person-as-a-whole-model" provided the basis for a holistic approach to the study of human behavior espoused by Maslow. His reaction to what he viewed as the atomistic and reductionistic nature of behaviorism was to define a psychology that focused on developing healthy people—a psychology that emphasized self-actualization. In fact, self-actualization psychology is identified with Maslow. The term expresses the fundamental premise that people possess potentialities that become actualities through the process of wholesome growth. (p. 385) According to Sahakian:

Self-actualized people are well-integrated rather than conflict-ridden or anxiety-ridden; that is to say their id, ego, and superego are not in constant battle with each other. Furthermore, their cognitive, affective, conative, and motor aspects are also fairly well integrated. Self-actualizing people are blessed with peak experiences. While they cannot transcend all human problems, they cope better than other people with anxiety, conflict, sadness, frustration, hurt, and guilt. (p. 386)

It is in this context that a primary goal of learning in humanistic education becomes quite clear—to achieve self-actualization. Learning must lead to a realization of the satisfaction of basic emotional needs and be free from anxiety with respect to those needs. Learners must feel worthy of love, that they belong, that they are respected and wanted. It is through self-actualization that intrinsic learning becomes a reality, for the individual is learning to be a person, to change from within. In contrast, extrinsic learning is concerned with the process, with impersonal learning and with some impersonal skill or the mere acquisition of habits. A very large amount of teaching in schools today involves extrinsic learning processes.

Another form of humanistic theory is that defined by Carl Rogers in his book *Freedom to Learn* (1969). The major themes in Roger's discussions are "freedom" and "curiosity," and become what is described as "significant" or "experiential learning." It is, essentially, learning that is meaningful, experiential, and significant. Through experiential learning the student becomes self-reliant; the teacher becomes a resource for the learner and a facilitator of learning. (p. 401)

This yearbook proceeds in its discussion of affective learning in industrial arts from that psychological position. This is not to suggest that the position assumed by the yearbook authors is one which accepts humanistic psychology at the expense of behavioristic psychology, for a flavor of both will be noted in the chapters that follow. However, the authors agree that a central obligation of educators, including those in industrial arts, is to promote the development of the self-actualized person. This can be accomplished while applying some of the more rational behavioristic theories of learning. It is the obligation of the educator to choose which and how.

SUMMARY

In this chapter an attempt has been made to lay the groundwork for the discussion of affective learning that appears in the succeeding chapters. A review of central issues in education today indicated that the social, political and technological changes which have occurred during the past 40 years have had a dramatic and unsettling effect on the condition of schools and the lives of students. Pressures for more education and the acquisition of greater amounts of knowledge may force an unreasonable emphasis upon cognitive achievement at the expense of affective development. A major concern is for the loss of a vision for education that will promote the growth of the "whole" person.

Affective development is as critical to the process of educating as cognitive and psychomotor development. During times as these, when a tremendous amount of social and personal upheaval is disrupting the lives of so many students, it becomes essential that even greater consideration be given to those elements of affect that propel children and youth from day to day—their emotions, feelings, values, attitudes, and interests. The meaning in what they are directed to learn becomes of even greater importance to them as the basic institutions of society take on new forms.

Technological change is an equal partner among the forces creating a disturbance in traditional institutions and values today. Industrial arts educators face a major challenge in their efforts to interpret and describe that technology, for they have a very large obligation to recognize human values and attitudes that are influenced by technological activity. Students must find opportunities in industrial arts classrooms to deal with values issues.

A review of the psychological theories which have led to a greater interest in affective development reveals two divergent psychological positions—behavioristic and humanistic. Both of these positions acknowledge the presence of affect, but place different emphases upon its meaning and importance in the learning process. Teachers need to recognize the qualities in these psychological theories and their implications for teaching practices.

THE YEARBOOK CHAPTERS

The chapters that follow deal with several major aspects of affective learning. In Chapter 2, Louis Thayer addresses affective learning from the perspective of a person in a helping profession—guidance and counseling. His view of affective development emphasizes the "person-centered" approach to teaching and learning. He deals with many components of experiential learning and discusses its importance to the development of affect. Teacher as facilitator and student as learner are the major points of reference for Thayer's discussion of the classroom conditions and methodologies most appropriate for the achievement of affective development.

Chapter 3, by Lewis Kieft and Paul Kuwik, provides a set of examples for facilitating affective growth through industrial arts. Their concern for the self-actualized person speaks to the needs for a self-actualized teacher as well as student. Examples they offer for implementing affective experiences in industrial arts begin with general strategies for industrial arts classrooms. They then proceed to describe strategies for the elementary school, middle school, and senior high school grades to facilitate the development of skills for the process of valuing and decision-making.

In Chapter 4, H. James Rokusek considers the problem of evaluating affective behaviors. Quite often the reason given for not dealing with affective learning is that teachers view it as virtually impossible to assess affective behaviors. Rokusek emphasizes the importance of assessing affectivity and the necessity for stating affective objectives in behavioral terms. He discusses the purpose of the taxonomy for the affective domain in assessment, and some principles to be followed in assessing affectivity in industrial arts.

The role of industrial arts teacher education in affective learning is reviewed by Harold PaDelford in Chapter 5. The process of developing values and feelings in learners must be considered in industrial arts teacher education, for the acquisition of values is an unavoidable event. PaDelford describes the obligation faced by teachers and teacher educators in this process, and the qualities of value acquisition to be considered. He concludes with a description of teaching/learning strategies that can be used in industrial arts teacher education to promote a better understanding of value acquisition among students who are preparing to be teachers.

Chapter 6, by Gerald Jennings, offers an annotated bibliography of sources that may be helpful to the teacher or researcher who wants to become better acquainted with affective education and learning processes. It highlights some of the many sources referred to by yearbook authors, and provides a quick reference to some of those items which might be most useful to industrial arts teachers.

REFERENCES

Aspy, D.N. & Roebuck, F.N. Affective education: sound investment. *Educational Leadership*, April 1982, Vol. 39, pp. 488-493.

Aspy, D.N. *Toward a Technology for Humanizing Education*. Champaign, IL: Research Press, 1972.

Baier, K. & Rescher, N. (Eds.) *Values and the Future: The Impact of Technological Change on American Values*. New York: The Free Press, 1969.

Barber, W. *The Affective Domain.* Washington, D.C.: Gryphon House, 1972.

Beeler, K.D. Affective education: state of the field and source guide. *The School Psychology Digest,* Spring 1978, Vol. 7, pp. 8-11.

Berman, L.M. & Roderick, J.A. (Eds.) *Feeling, Valuing, and the Arts of Growing: Insights into the Affective.* (Yearbook) Washington, D.C.: Association for Supervision and Curriculum Development, 1977.

Birnie, H.H. Identifying affective goals in science education. *The Science Teacher,* December 1978, Vol. 45, pp. 29-33.

Bloom, B.S. (Ed.) *Taxonomy of Educational Objectives: Cognitive Domain.* New York: David McKay Company, Inc., 1956.

Bloom, B.S. Affective outcomes of school learning. *Phi Delta Kappan,* November 1977, Vol. 59, pp. 193-198.

Bloom, B.S. *Human Characteristics and Learning.* New York: McGraw-Hill, 1976.

Bloom, B.S.; Madeus, G.F. & Hastings, J.T. *Evaluation to Improve Learning.* New York: McGraw-Hill, 1981.

Blue, T.W. *The Teaching and Learning Process.* Washington, D.C.: National Education Association, 1981.

Botkin, J.; Dimancescu, D. & Strata, R. *Global Stakes.* Cambridge, MA: Ballinger Publishing Co., 1982.

Broudy, H.S. *The Real World of the Public Schools.* New York: Harcourt Brace Jovanovich, 1972.

Brown, G. The training of teachers for affective roles. In K. Ryan (Ed.) *Teacher Education.* Chicago: National Society for the Study of Education, 1975.

Burke, J.B. *Competency Designs for a More Human Education.* Paper presented at the Association for Education Data Systems Annual Convention, April 1973. New Orleans, LA.

Buscaglia, L. Affective education; a means to a beginning. *School Psychology,* Spring 1978, Digest 7: pp. 4-7.

Byrne, P.S. & Long, B.E.L. *Learning to Care: Person to Person.* Edinburgh, England: Churchill Livingstone, 1973.

Carkhuff, R.R. Affective education in the age of productivity, *Educational Leadership.* April, 1982, Vol. 39, pp. 484-487.

Combs, A.W. Affective education: or none at all. *Educational Leadership.* April 1982, Vol. 39, pp. 495-497.

Combs, A.W. *Perceiving, Behaving, Becoming: A New Focus for Education.* (1962 Yearbook) Washington, D.C.: Association for Supervision and Curriculum Development, 1962.

Costa, A.L. Affective education: the state of the art. *Educational Leadership.* January 1977, Vol. 34: pp. 260-263.

Divorky, D. Affective education: are we going too far? *The School Psychology Digest.* Spring 1978, Vol. 7, pp. 47-51.

Dollard, J. & Miller, N. *Social Learning and Imitation.* New Haven, CT: Yale University Press, 1941.

Eberle, B. & Hall, R.E. *Affective Education Guidebook.* Buffalo: D.O.K. Publishers, Inc., 1975.

Flynn, E.W. & LaFaso, J.F. *Designs in Affective Education.* New York: Paulist Press, 1974.

Forsyth, A.S., Jr. *Toward Affective Education: A Guide to Developing Affective Learning Objectives.* Columbus, OH: Batelle Memorial Institute, Center for Improved Education, 1973.

Gale, R.F. *Developmental Behavior: A Humanistic Approach.* New York: MacMillan, 1969.

Gilchrist, R.S. *Promising Ways to Humanize the Learning Environment.* Paper presented at the Annual Meeting of the American Association of School Administrators, 1976.

Guthrie, E.R. *The Psychology of Learning.* (rev. ed.) New York: Harper & Row, 1952.

Hamacheck, D.E. *The Self in Growth, Teaching and Learning.* Englewood Cliffs, NJ: Prentice-Hall, 1965.

Hanlon, J.M. *Administration and Education: Toward a Theory of Self-Actualization.* Belmont, CA: Wadsworth Pub. Co., 1968.

Harmin, M., et al. *Clarifying Values Through Subject Matter.* Minneapolis: Winston Press, 1973.

Hart, W.M. (Ed.) Editorial comment. *The School Psychology Digest.* Spring 1978, Vol. 7: 2, pp. 2-3.

Havighurst, R. *Developmental Tasks and Education.* (3rd ed.) New York: David McKay Co., 1972.

Hersch, R.H. Directions in values and moral education. *News, Notes, and Quotes. Phi Delta Kappa Newsletter.* July/August 1978, Vol. 22: 6, pp. 5-6.

Hurst, B. Integrated approach to the hierarchical order of the cognitive and affective domain. *Journal of Education Psychology.* 1980, Vol. 72: 3, pp. 293-303.

Kahn, S.B. & Weiss, J. The teaching of affective responses. In R.M.W. Travers (Ed.) *Second Handbook of Research on Teaching.* Chicago: Rand McNally and Company, 1973.

Kelley, E.C. *Humanizing the Education of Children.* Washington, D.C.: National Education Association, Department of Elementary/Kindergarten/Nursery Education, 1969.

Kirschenbaum, H. *Current Research in Values Education.* Sarasota Springs, NY: National Center for Humanistic Education, 1975.

Kniker, C.R. *You and Values Education.* Columbus, OH: Charles E. Merrill, 1977.

Kolesnik, W.B. *Humanism and/or Behaviorism in Education.* Boston: Allyn and Bacon, Inc., 1975.

Krathwohl, D.R.; Bloom, B.S. & Masia, B.B. *Taxonomy of Educational Objectives. The Classification of Educational Goals. Handbook II: Affective Domain.* New York: David McKay, 1964.

Lauda, D.P. & Ryan, R.D. *Advancing Technology.* Dubuque: Wm. C. Brown Co., Pub., 1971.

Lauda, D.P. Technology assessment: implications for industrial arts. *Industrial Arts and a Humane Technology for the Future.* Proceedings of the American Industrial Arts Association 36th Annual Convention, Seattle, 1974.

Leeper, R.R. (Ed.) *Humanizing Education: The Person in the Process.* 22nd Conference Addresses of the Association for Supervision and Curriculum Development, Washington, D.C.: The Association, 1967.

Lewis, M. & Rosenblum, L.A. *The Development of Affect.* New York: Plenum Press, 1978.

Mager, R.F. *Developing Attitude Toward Learning.* Belmont: Fearon Publishers/Lear Siegler, Inc., 1968.

Maley, D. & Lux, G. The development of selected contemporary industrial arts programs. In G.E. Martin (Ed.) *Industrial Education: Retrospect, Prospect,* (28th Yearbook of the American Council on Industrial Arts Teacher Education). Bloomington, IL: McKnight, 1979.

Maley, D. *Industrial Arts Puts the Whole Boy and Girl in the School in 1980.* College Park, MD: Maryland Vocational Curriculum Research and Development Center, 1980.

Martin, G.E. (Ed.) *Industrial Arts Education: Retrospect, Prospect* (28th Yearbook of the American Council on Industrial Arts Teacher Education). Bloomington, IL: McKnight Publishing Co., 1979.

Maslow, A.H. *Dominance, Self-Esteem, Self-Actualization: Germinal Papers of A.H. Maslow.* R.J. Lowry (Ed.) Monterey, CA: Brook/Cole Pub., Co., 1973.

Masters, J.; Borden, R. & Ford, M. Affective states, expressive behavior and learning in children. *Journal of Personality and Social Psychology.* (1979) Vol. 37, pp. 380-390.

Mesthene, E. *Technological Change: Its Impact on Man and Society.* Cambridge, MA: Harvard University Press, 1970.

Metcalf, L.E. (Ed.) *Values Education: Rationale, Strategies, and Procedures.* (41st Yearbook) Washington, D.C.: National Council for the Social Studies, 1971.

Monks, R. Values education in the '80's. *Education Digest.* (October 1980) Vol. 46, pp. 44-45.

Mosher, R. Education for human development. In R.H. Weller (Ed.) *Humanistic Education: Visions and Realities.* Berkeley, CA: McCutcheon Pub., Corp., 1977.

McPherson, W.H. Humanism in American education: a historical overview. In L.D. Anderson (Ed.) *Industrial Arts in the Open Access Classroom.* (27th Yearbook of American Council on Industrial Arts Teacher Education.) Bloomington, IL: McKnight, 1978.

Patterson, C.H. Insights about persons: psychological foundations of humanistic and affective education. In L.M. Berman & J.A. Roderick (Eds.) *Feeling, Valuing, and the Art of Growing: Insights into the Affective.* (1977 Yearbook) Washington, D.C.: Association for Supervision and Curriculum Development, 1977.

PaDelford, H.E. *Acquiring Psychomotor Skills.* Unpublished paper, 1983.

PaDelford, H.E. (in press) A conceptual model of the psychomotor domain. *Journal of Industrial Teacher Education.*

Piaget, J. *Intelligence and Affectivity: Their Relationship During Child Development.* Palo Alto, CA: Annual Reviews, Inc., 1981.

Ringness, T.A. *The Affective Domain in Education.* Boston: Little, Brown and Co., 1975.

Rogers, C. *Freedom to Learn.* Columbus, OH: Charles E. Merrill, 1969.

Sahakian, W.S. *Introduction to the Psychology of Learning.* Chicago: Rand McNally College Pub., Co., 1976.

Silver, M. *Values Education.* Washington, D.C.: National Education Association, 1976.

Simon, S. et al. *Values Clarification: Handbook of Procedures and Strategies for Teachers and Students.* New York: Hart Publishing Co., 1972.

Simpson, E.L. *Humanistic Education: An Interpretation.* Cambridge, MA: Ballinger Publishing Co., 1976.

Smalley, L.H. & Lauda D.P. *The Future: A Challenge to Industrial Arts.* Monograph of the American Council on Industrial Arts Teacher Education (1975) No. 5.

Smith, W.H. *The Maryland Plan: A Study of Technology and Industry with Their Implications for Man and Society.* College Park, MD: University of Maryland, 1970.

Sonnier, I.L. Holistic education: teaching in the affective domain. *Education.* (Fall 1982) Vol. 103: pp. 11-14.

Stanley, M. *The Technological Conscience: Survival and Dignity in an Age of Expertise.* New York: The Free Press, 1978

Starkweather, K. AIAA: pioneering leadership in industrial arts/industrial technology. *Man/Society/Technology* (May, June 1983) Vol. 42:8, pp. 8-12.

Strom, R.D. & Torrance, E.P. (Eds.) *Education for Affective Achievement.* Chicago: Rand McNally and Company, 1973.

Superka, D. et al. *Values Education Sourcebook.* Boulder, CO: Social Science Education Consortium, Inc., 1976.

Timmermann, T. & Ballard, J. *Yearbook in Humanistic Education.* Amherst, MA: Mandala, 1976.

Timmermann, T. & Ballard, J. *Strategies in Humanistic Education.* Amherst, MA: Mandala, 1978.

Toffler, A. *Future Shock.* New York: Bantam, 1970.

Thornburg, H.D. *School Learning and Instruction.* Monterey, CA: Brooks/Cole Pub. Co., 1973.

Tryon, C. & Lilienthal, J.W. III. Developmental tasks: I. the concept and its importance. In *Fostering Mental Health in Our Schools.* (1950 Yearbook of the Association for Supervision and Curriculum Development) Washington, D.C.: The Association.

Tyler, R. Dynamic response in a time of decline. *Phi Delta Kappan.* (June 1982) Vol. 63: 10, pp. 655-658.

Tyler, R. A place called school. *Phi Delta Kappan.* (March 1983) Vol. 64: 7, pp. 462-470.

Valett, R.E. *Affective-Humanistic Education: Goals, Programs and Learning Activities.* Belmont: Fearon, Pub., 1974.

Valett, R.E. *Humanistic Education: Developing the Total Person.* St. Louis: The C.V. Mosley Co., 1977.

Valett, R.E. *Self-Actualization: A Guide to Happiness and Self-Determination.* Niles, IL: Argus Communications, 1974.

Waetjen, W. *The Exploratory Function of Industrial Arts Education.* An address at the American Industrial Arts Association Annual Convention. Los Angeles, March, 1954.

Waetjen, W. Psychological theories. In C. Gerbracht & G.O. Wilber (Eds.). *A Sourcebook of Readings in Education for Use in Industrial Arts and Industrial Arts Teacher Education.* (6th Yearbook of American Council of Industrial Arts Teacher Education.) Bloomington, IL: McKnight and McKnight Pub. Co., 1957.

Waetjen, W.B. Peer society—industrial arts education—their relation. *The Industrial Arts Teacher.* (April 1953) Vol. 12: 4.

Watkins, B.O. & Meador, R. *Technology and Human Values: Collision and Solution.* Ann Arbor: Ann Arbor Science Publishers, 1977.

Weiler, H.H. Education, public confidence, and the legitimacy of the modern state: do we have a crisis? *Phi Delta Kappan* (September 1982), Vol. 64: 1, pp. 9-14.

Weinburg, C. *Humanistic Foundations of Education.* Englewood Cliffs, NJ: Prentice-Hall, Inc., 1972.

Weinstein, G. & Fantini, M.D. (Eds.) *Toward Humanistic Education: A Curriculum of Affect.* New York: Praeger Publishers, 1970.

Weller, R.H. (Ed.). *Humanistic Education: Visions and Realities.* (Phi Delta Kappa Symposium on Educational Research). Berkeley, CA: McCutcheon Publishing Corp., 1977.

Wilber, G. *Industrial Arts in General Education.* Scranton, PA: The Haddon Craftsmen, Inc., 1954.

Winn, T.W. (Ed.) *Behaviorism and Phenomenology: Contrasting Bases for Modern Psychology.* Chicago: University of Chicago Press, 1964.

Zahorik, J.A. & Brubaker, D.L. *Toward More Humanistic Instruction.* Dubuque, IA: Wm. C. Brown Co., 1972.

Chapter 2

On Person-Centered Experiential Learning and Affective Development

Louis Thayer, Ed.D.
Professor
Department of Leadership and Counseling
Eastern Michigan University
Ypsilanti, Michigan

. . . It is in fact nothing short of a miracle that the modern methods of instruction have not yet entirely strangled the holy curiosity of inquiry; for this delicate little plant, aside from stimulation, stands mainly in need of freedom; without this it goes to wrack and ruin without fail.

Albert Einstein

INTRODUCTION

There have been many contributors to the writings, teachings, and research on affective components of learning. In the last forty years, there has been a marked increase in the focus on the feelings of learners as persons and the relationship of these feelings to learning. In essence, a "person" centered approach to the facilitation of learning has evolved. Several labels have been attached to various parts of this movement: humanistic education, affective education, confluent education, values clarification, individualized instruction, student-centered teaching, learner-centered teaching, person-centered approach, and others.

Personally, the term "person-centered" seems appropriate as it encompasses the "whole" of the individual — emotions, values, attitudes, behaviors, experiences, meanings, etc. The cognitive and affective components of learning are not separate. They are intertwined, each affecting the other. Each belongs to the whole person. It is a more holistic approach to learning and education.

For me, this chapter is somewhat of a reflection on my search for a path, a personal approach to the facilitation of learning in others and in myself. What I describe will be views that are based on my values, my goals, my experiences, my learnings, and my studies. I seek to be a learner among learners as well as a facilitator of learning.*

What are these directions then? First, the emphasis is on the person and his or her tremendous inner potential and tendency to actualize the "self." The facilitator holds great respect for the person's ability to learn, to develop, and to change. The facilitator seeks to establish a positive climate for a learning process in which the person is the focus — a person-centered learning approach.

It is the attitudes and behavior of the facilitator that create a climate for optimum learning. If the facilitator is genuine and real in the learning situation, unconditionally prizes and respects the learners, and demonstrates an understanding of the learners' realities, then a relationship can develop between the learners and the facilitator which can enhance the discoveries of inner potentials for learning and development. The perceptions and feelings of the learners are central in the motivation of learning and achievement. The facilitative climate gives learners the confidence to release their inner potentials and abilities in order to take increased responsibility for their own learning directions.

The process of learning becomes more experiential when many of the concepts to be learned are actually experienced in the situation. The learners learn what they experience. Learning outcomes reflect more personally relevant accomplishments, higher achievements, increased creativity, and greater productivity. Because of the inward-directed nature of the learning process, learners experience heightened self-awareness, self-direction in learning, and self-confidence. Their self-concepts are enhanced.

------

*The terms facilitator and learner have been used in this chapter rather than teacher and student.

With a person-centered experiential learning approach, the process moves from a facilitator-directed process to a facilitator-learner directed process to a more learner-directed process of learning. Learners develop trust in their own abilities to be responsible, to be risk takers, and to be independent as learners. Facilitators discover that learners can be trusted with their own curiosities and questions.

KEY CONTRIBUTORS

Who are some of the people who have provided foundations for the development of learning approaches that are person-centered and humanistic in nature? Numerous people have contributed to these foundations and have used different emphases to make a contribution. All contributors cannot be mentioned because of space. The following are representative of those dedicated persons. The sources used in this section are those which are applicable to the development of the theme.

To begin with, the United States has been a rich environment in which individuals can develop. The tenets of democracy foster individualism, self-reliance, personal creativeness, and responsibility to oneself and others. The person and her or his inner potentials hold the answers to the future of the nation. So, individuals receive dignity and respect for their humanness, their creativity, their abilities to be responsible, and their desires to be independent.

John Dewey (1938) was certainly one of the early leaders with his emphasis on experience, experimentation, purposeful learning, and freedom. Without a doubt, Carl Rogers (1961, 1974, 1983) stands out as an international educator and psychologist for the past forty years with his theory and research on therapy, education, and interpersonal relationships. In Rogers' writings and in his encounters with people, he has shown the deepest respect for the person and his/her inner potentials for self-determined development and change. Abraham Maslow (1968, 1973) had no small effect on the humanistic movement with his hierarchy of needs, emphasis on self-actualization, and views on the "taoistic" teacher. Stephen Corey (1944) encouraged teachers to understand the perceptions, feelings, and realities of the learner. Arthur Jersild (1955) noted how important it is for teachers to understand and accept themselves in order to help learners know themselves and to develop healthy attitudes of self-acceptance. Arthur Combs (1959, 1969) has been involved significantly for over thirty years in helping to humanize learning environments, prepare teachers for dealing with their own perceptions of learners, and aid the teachers in seeing themselves as the critical instruments in the learning situation

— the self-as-instrument. He has also conducted research on the perceptual organizations of effective helpers. Combs (1979) proposed the notion that affective education is a myth. He says that all learning is affective. Teachers must deal with both cognition and emotion simultaneously because they are inseparable. Combs, Avila, and Purkey (1978) also made an important contribution with their book, *Helping Relationships*.

Thomas Gordon (1970, 1974) has written extensively, provided models, and offered training sessions on effective and humanistic parent-child and teacher-child relationships. The Association for Supervision and Curriculum Development (1962) published one of the key books on a humanistic view of learning and development with Earl Kelly, Carl Rogers, Abraham Maslow, and Arthur Combs as the main contributors. ASCD (1967) contributed another fine book on the person as the center of the learning process. Dinkmeyer and Dreikurs (1963) published their views on approaching the learning situation with a most positive encouraging process. In 1964, Krathwohl, Bloom, and Masia developed a *Taxonomy of Educational Objectives* for the affective domain. And while Clark Moustakes (1966) has written much on freeing people to learn and develop, his revision of an earlier book focused heavily on listening to the emotional expressions of learners and being authentic in relationships with them.

Haim Ginott (1965, 1972) continued the themes of listening to children and learners while also helping parents and teachers to be more genuine and communicative in their relationship with children. Raths, Harmin, and Simon (1966) focused on the importance of teaching for value clarity and brought forth a method on values clarification. Additional books on *Values Clarification* came from Simon, Howe, and Kirschenbaum (1972) as well as Harmin, Kirschenbaum, and Simon (1973) on *Clarifying Values Through Subject Matter*. Casteel and Stahl (1975) also prepared a comprehensive book on the rationale of value clarification and provided activities for the classroom. Sprinthall and Mosher (1978) expressed their belief that moral/ethical value development is the aim of education.

William Glasser (1969) has made numerous speeches and written a book stressing the need for learners to experience success, not failure, in schools in order to enhance their full development as persons and citizens. He has refined the idea of classroom meetings for learning and problem-solving. Another development in 1969 saw William Pfeiffer and John Jones publish the first volume of *Structured Experiences for Human Relations Training*. The publishing company which they founded, University Associates, has become a leader in the publication of professional materials on experiential learning and human resource development. Also, W. Limbacher (1970) presented his *Dimensions in Personality* series that was a graded program in affective education. It was group-centered and activity-oriented. While exploring the more subjective dimensions of teaching, Herbert Greenberg (1969) examined the feelings and needs of teachers and how these feelings and needs affected the teachers' approaches in their classrooms. Weinstein and Fantini (1970) presented a model for a curriculum of affect, and Terry Borton (1970) described an attempt to ". . . reach students at basic personality levels, touch them as individual human beings, and yet teach them in an organized fashion" (p. vii). He developed a curriculum based on student concerns and feelings, and wrote about how to handle these concerns and feelings effectively. Norman Newberg was also involved with Terry Borton in the development of an affective education project in the Philadelphia Public Schools.

George Brown (1971) stressed the need to have affective components intertwined with cognitive objectives, hence confluent education. Brown wanted to bring the two components into focus for a humanizing process. Gloria Castillo (1978) developed her personal approach to confluent education by preparing a set of activities integrating affective and cognitive components. And a very sensitive book, *Learning to Feel — Feeling to Learn* was written by an ex-military officer, Harold Lyon, Jr. (1971) on the significance of emotions and the development of the person, regardless of the situation. Alschuler, Tabor, and McIntyre (1971) advanced their theory on achievement motivation and the place of feelings in psychological education. Leo Buscaglia (1972) shared one of his key books, *Love,* and the relationship of love to learning and living. And in 1973, C. H. Patterson wrote a comprehensive book on *Humanizing Education.* He also stressed the need for changes in teacher preparation programs. Sidney Jourard (1971, 1974) demonstrated a deep concern for the individual with his emphasis on the development of the healthy personality and related concepts. Alfred Gorman (1974) presented a view on the "interactive process of education" and ways to facilitate that method.

In 1974, Louis Thayer and Kent Beeler (1974, 1975, & 1977) edited the first of their three handbooks of affective tools and techniques for educators. These handbooks were supported by the Special Interest Group on Affective Education (American Educational Research Association). Louis Thayer (1976, 1981a) edited two books of strategies for experiential learning emphasizing a person-centered approach. These two books have a number of activities that deal with right-brain learning. Robert Carkhuff and his associates have done much research on the skills and processes of helping, and Carkhuff, Berenson, and Pierce (1976) published the *Skills of Teaching* which offered the Carkhuff model for preparing teachers in the art of developing human relationships for learning. Jack Canfield and Harold Wells (1976) provided a whole book of structured activities for enhancing self-concept in the classroom. Gerald Pine and Angelo Boy (1977) prepared a very thorough book on *Learner-Centered Teaching* that includes a list of resources for putting theory into practice — books, kits, curriculums, tapes, films, organizations, directories, and guides. William Purkey (1978) outlined his views on invitational education and how it relates to learner successes and the development of positive self-concepts in learners.

Persons who have done considerable research in the area of humanizing learning environments are David Aspy and Flora Roebuck (1974, 1977), (Aspy, 1972). They have researched the key components of the facilitation of the learning climate and the effects upon learner achievement, classroom interaction, and other learning variables. Their research has most promising results for learner achievements, learner self-concepts, and teacher preparation programs.

More recently, Lee and Pulvino (1978) have highlighted a dichotomy in the development of the total person by focusing on the forgotten part of the brain — the right hemisphere. This hemisphere is related more with spatial perception, perceptual insight, tactile sensation, and visualization. While the left hemisphere of the brain specializes more in logical-analytical thought and verbalization, the right hemisphere emphasizes being more intuitive, creative, and holistic. The book describes structured activities in five topical areas of right hemisphere domain — visualization, concentration, memory, creativity, and personal well being. For additional reading on the topic, Ornstein's (1972) book is a good introduction.

In 1979, Bob Eberle and Rosie Hall prepared a book on affective directions with a strong emphasis on aesthetic sensitivity, interpersonal relations, moral-ethical development, and self-knowledge. The book showed facilitators how to integrate content, strategies, and processes.

Additional developments in the 1970's came in the form of sequentially arranged, affectively oriented kits which fit into a year long curriculum. American Guidance Services of Circle Pines, Minnesota published several excellent resources. Of special note are the *DUSO* kits. *DUSO* stands for *Developing Understanding of Self and Others*. The authors, Don Dinkmeyer and Don Dinkmeyer, Jr. (1982a, 1982b) have revised both kits — *DUSO I,* grades K-2 and *DUSO II,* grades 3-4. The first *DUSO I* kit came out in 1970 with personal and social development as a key goal for the activities, songs, and other materials. Dinkmeyer and McKay (1976) developed the STEP (*Systematic Training for Effective Parenting*) program which teaches about parent-child relationships that enhance responsibility, self-initiative, respect, and self-worth. Dinkmeyer, McKay, and Dinkmeyer (1980) have also developed a kit, *Systematic Training for Effective Teaching,* based on Adlerian principles. Dupont, Gardner, and Brody (1974) created a program for grades 3-6 that provides lessons in affective development. The kit (*Toward Affective Development* — TAD) uses innovative materials, actively involving the total class in games, simulations, role playing, acting out, modeling, imitating, brainstorming, and group discussion. Dupont and Dupont (1979) have another kit called *Transition* which focuses on the social and emotional development of learners aged 12-15. All of these kits had extensive field testing and refinement before they were published.

Also of special note are the *Magic Circle* materials prepared at the Human Development Training Institute. These program materials were prepared by Uvaldo Palomares, Harold Bessell, Geraldine Ball, and others (1976). There are many other people who have been actively writing and contributing to the humanistic education movement (Ashton-Warner, 1963; Leonard, 1968; Mager, 1968; Postman & Weingartner, 1969; Zathorick & Brubaker, 1972; Thatcher, 1973; Seaberg, 1974; Wittmer & Myrick, 1974; Chase, 1975; Ringness, 1975; Read & Simon, 1975; Valett, 1977; Smith & Lusterman, 1979; Steinaker & Baker, 1979; and Anderson, 1981).

Additional resources on the affective domain will be covered in other chapters of this book.

CONCEPTS OF THE APPROACH

What Are Several of the Basic Concepts Associated with Affective Development and Experiential Learning?

The following concepts have gone through a refinement process and are described in Rogers' (1959, pp. 194-212) chapter on "Therapy, Personality and Interpersonal Relationships." The chapter provides an extended discussion of the concepts.

These concepts have appeared frequently in the literature.

1. *Actualizing Tendency.* "This is the inherent tendency of the organism to develop all its capacities in ways which serve to maintain or enhance the organism" (p. 96). It is a forward moving process which reaches for autonomy in its environment. Basic needs are a part of this concept.

2. *Self, Concept of Self, Self-Structure.* "These terms refer to the organized, consistent conceptual gestalt composed of perceptions of the characteristics of the 'I' or 'me' and the perceptions of the relationships of the 'I' or 'me' to others and to various aspects of life, together with the values attached to these perceptions" (p. 200). This gestalt has a fluid and changing nature.

3. *Tendency Toward Self-Actualization.* "Following the development of the self-structure, this general tendency toward actualization expresses itself also in the actualization of that portion of the experience of the organism which is symbolized in the self" (p. 196-197).

4. *Experience (noun).* This concept includes "all that is going on within the envelope of the organism at any given moment which is potentially available to awareness." The concept is a psychological one that "includes events of which the individual is unaware, as well as all phenomena which are in consciousness." Rogers has used other terms to give an understanding of this concept such as "sensory and visceral experiences," "organic experiences," "experiential field," or Combs and Snygg's (1959) term of "phenomenal field" (p. 197).

5. *Experience (verb).* "To experience means simply to receive in the organism the impact of the sensory or physiological events which are happening at the moment ... 'To experience in awareness' means to symbolize in some accurate form at the conscious levels the above sensory or visceral events" (p. 197).

6. *Feeling, Experiencing a Feeling.* This concept means "an emotionally tinged experience, together with its personal meaning." The "cognitive content of the meaning of that emotion in its experiential context" is included in the concept. "Experiencing a feeling fully" is noted when a person is "congruent in his experience (of the feeling), his awareness (of it), and his expression (of it)" (p. 198).

7. *Awareness, Symbolization, Consciousness.* The three terms are seen as "the symbolic representation (not necessarily in verbal terms) of some portion of our experience" (p. 198).

8. *Perceive, Perception.* It is noted that "a perception is a hypothesis or prognosis for action which comes into being in awareness when stimuli impinge on the organism. Synonymous terms are awareness and perception; however, perception emphasizes the stimulus in the process, while awareness is the "symbolizations and meanings which arise from such purely internal stimuli as memory traces, visceral changes, and the like, as well as external stimuli" (p. 199).

9. *Congruence, Congruence of Self and Experience.* "The individual appears to be revising his concept of self to bring it into congruence with his experience, accurately symbolized." Synonymous terms are genuine, real, whole, and integrated. (p. 200)

10. *Openness to Experience.* "When the individual is in no way threatened, then he is open to his experience. To be open to experience is the polar opposite of defensiveness . . . It signifies that every stimulus, whether originating within the organism or in the environment, is freely relayed through the nervous system without being distorted or channeled off by any defensive mechanism" (p. 206).

11. *Unconditional Positive Regard.* This is a key concept developed by Standel (1954). "If the self-experiences of another are perceived by me in such a way that no self-experience can be discriminated as more or less worthy of positive regard than any other, then I am experiencing unconditional positive regard for this individual." It means "to value a person, irrespective of the differential values which one might place on his specific behaviors." One might also use the term acceptance. Rogers likes John Dewey's term to "prize." (p. 208)

12. *Empathy.* This is "to perceive the internal frame of reference of another with accuracy, and with the emotional components and meanings which pertain thereto, as if one were the other person, but without ever losing the 'as if' condition . . . If this 'as if' quality is lost, then the state is one of identification" (pp. 210-211).

13. *Locus of Evaluation.* "This term is used to indicate the source of evidence as to values. Thus the internal locus of evaluation, within the individual himself, means that he is the center of

the valuing process, the evidence being supplied by his own senses. When the locus of evaluation resides in others, their judgment as to the value of an object or experience becomes the criterion of value for the individual" (p. 210).

14. *Formative Tendency.* Rogers' most recent concept focuses on the creative, building energy in the universe. "There is a formative directional tendency in the universe, which can be traced and observed in stellar space, in crystals, in microorganisms, in more complex organic life, and in human beings. This is an evolutionary tendency toward greater order, greater complexity, greater interrelatedness. In humankind, this tendency exhibits itself as the individual moves from a single-cell origin to complex functioning, to knowing and sensing below the level of consciousness, to a conscious awareness of the organism and the external world, to a transcendent awareness of the harmony and unity of the cosmic system, including humankind" (Rogers, 1980, p. 133).

15. *Polarity, Polarization.* The concept points out that there are two opposite qualities, tendencies, or powers. In this chapter, polarity signifies the affective-cognitive, internal (self)-external world splits that affect much of what is done in learning situations. Integration of these conceptualized polarities is a key goal in the facilitation of learning (Simkin, 1979).

How Does a Person Recognize an Approach
Which Is Not Humanistic In Nature?

One way of approaching this topic is to ask several questions that aid a person in examining various aspects of learning environments, processes, outcomes, and facilitators.

First, is the facilitator concerned at all with her or his own "self" development? The notion is that positive changes in the facilitator's behavior and attitudes bring about greater changes in student learning and behavior. The effective facilitator seeks an understanding of her or his "self" and how her or his behaviors and attitudes affect learners.

What is most valued by the facilitator regarding the learning situation? By reviewing the values of the facilitator, a person can determine whether or not the focus will be on the *person* in the learning process or if the focus will be on strictly cognitive content and a related teaching style. The humanistic approach involves the subjective world of the learner as well as the cognitive content. An open communication process is valued as it can relate the subjective world of the learner to the content.

What is the facilitator's view.on the nature of learners? Some facilitators believe that learning must be totally structured and directed because learners are not disciplined and cannot accept responsibility, while others believe in the abilities of learners to accept responsibilities for aspects of the learning process. The assumptions that facilitators hold with regard to learners affect everything that they do in the situation.

What are the psychological conditions that are necessary in order for positive cognitive and affective learnings to occur? The effective facilitator needs to build positive interpersonal relationships with learners. Good relationships with learners are crucial to the development of a healthy psychological climate.

How does the learning process unfold? The facilitator has much power in determining whether the learning will actually be process oriented or whether all activities will focus on outcomes and external standards. Humanistic facilitators emphasize the "here and now" in the process and provide for learning concepts through experience.

Is there an effort on the part of the facilitator to use operant conditioning principles to manipulate, coerce, or force the learner into learning selected knowledge and behaviors? Often, the facilitator may be attempting to motivate the learner to know or behave in ways that the facilitator or system deems appropriate. Humanistic facilitators establish ways and means to understand learner needs, feelings, and perceptions. Learners are brought into the decision-making process.

What are the most visible outcomes of learning? In the humanistic situation, enhanced learner self-concepts rank high. Processes are present that highlight the internal processes (e.g., feelings, meanings, immediate experiencing) of learners. The process movement of the situation shows the learners moving away from not being responsible towards being more responsible and self-directed.

Finally, to what extent is the learning situation facilitator/teacher centered as versus learner/person centered? The emphasis needs to be on learning rather than teaching with a key goal of helping people learn how, what, when, and where to learn.

APPLICATIONS

Areas for Which Person-Centered Experiential Learning and Affective Development Are Applicable

Most people in our society spend years in various types of learning situations. With the movement towards lifelong learning, learners need to understand their own feelings, values, perceptions, attitudes, and behaviors related to learning. They need to have psychologically healthy learning environments. Because of the nature of most learning situations, this person-centered approach can have meaning where numerous interpersonal relationships are present.

Learning situations have many variables — the group as individuals, the learning development of persons, facilitator attitudes and behaviors, teacher self-development as a facilitator, physical facilities, the subject of study, administrative support, etc. The areas which are covered here are not meant to be all inclusive; however, they provide key examples of areas for which this approach can be of help. Perhaps, facilitators could compare the differences and similarities with their own approaches.

Being genuine in learning relationships. Often learners believe that they become more vulnerable in situations when they express their true thoughts, feelings, and perceptions on learning events. There is a fear of loss. The learners may lose self-esteem, caring of the facilitator and peers, and a place in the group. Learners seem to be hampered within the learning environment from being themselves and from establishing genuine psychological contact with peers and the facilitator.

Learners pose these questions: "Can I share my true thoughts and feelings here?" "Can I trust peers and the facilitator with my real self?" "Is this a situation that can be lived on a real basis?" Learners have found from experience that some situations are *threatening*. So, they sense a need to be defensive and protect their inner selves. When defensiveness is present in learners, there is an incongruence "within" some and this incongruence is reflected "between" learners/persons in interpersonal relationships. A lack of genuineness stymies learning.

Expressing feelings in the learning situation — toward affective awareness and development. The expression of innermost feelings is essentially part of being real or congruent in interpersonal relationships. Can facilitators be sensitive to the learners' intense feelings of anger, desperation, annoyance, tenderness, joy, jealousy, resentment, love, fearfulness, hate? Learners must not have to hide feelings from peers and facilitators. What will be the cost of hiding feelings? What are learners' fears of expressing feelings? If there is the constant question of whether or not others will accept persons and their feelings, how can learners be encouraged to accept their own feelings, let alone understand the emotions of others? Expressing positive feelings can be as much of a problem as expressing negative feelings. When feelings are suppressed, learners may decrease their trust in their own experiencing. They may not learn to be sensitive to their own experiencing and feelings as they listen to others tell them how to interpret experiences. Often, learners have denied their feelings for so long that they are not fully aware of their feelings toward the subject, people, and events in the learning situation.

Learners may interpret their interpersonal relationships according to what someone else believes is right rather than what they believe is right. The nonverbal communication of learners carries many of the feelings which need to be expressed. With feelings as key motivators of behavior, the place of feelings in learning processes is significant.

Accepting learners as unique individuals and persons. At times, learners believe that they are not viewed as unique with their own ideas and potentials. In the learning situation, they may not be viewed as separate persons. Consequently, they are not perceived so much as individuals as they are perceived to be a group. The notion that each individual can give direction to his or her learning process and direction is subsumed under another's master plan for the time.

The roles and role expectations of facilitators are often not the same as those of the learner. Occasionally, facilitators try to mold learners according to their views of life and living. Facilitators' expectations, with no input from learners, can be a problem. When learners are held at a distance from their own inner curiosities, potentials, discoveries, and expectations, they fail to develop confidence and a more positive concept of self. They are not developing a greater acceptance of self and its uniqueness. Their learnings, directed by others, may suffer from lack of personal meaning and relevance to their lives.

Each learner is unique and a resource in the learning situation. Can facilitators help learners identify with the learning group and yet maintain individuality and separateness? Can individuals listen to their own feelings and share them? Do learners have a right to share their expectations with the facilitator and peers? Can learners listen to the facilitator and peers and still maintain a sense of self-identity?

Listening and fostering two-way/group communication. When there is no process for or a breakdown in communication, learners perceive that they are not heard and certainly not understood. Then, they believe that peers and facilitators do not understand their experiences in learning and in the world. Are they valued as persons? The process of communication may be only a one-way avenue with the facilitator giving out requirements, decisions, values to follow, and guidelines for learning.

To resolve conflicts, facilitator power and authority are used. Learners are not allowed to develop or maintain any sense of personal power. Since there is little mutual listening, acceptance of the views of others is minimal. Learners' views may not be respected. Authority may reside with the facilitator.

Enhancing the development of personal power. As learners trust their own thoughts, feelings, and perceptions more, they can also learn not to "give up" power to others in determining their directions regarding life behaviors and attitudes. With learners being more congruent in terms of experiencing, awareness, and communication, they can, with greater self-trust, become more self-directing, independent, responsible, and assertive.

Unleashing learner creativity. With the facilitator making every attempt to understand learners, the individuals, with a uniqueness of their own, unleash the tremendous variance in the ways the world and its activities have been experienced and perceived. Facilitators encourage this uniqueness and the special "stream of images" which accompanies each person's sharing. The expression of these images and their concommitant feelings and thoughts are related to the world through the media/subject matter which the facilitator and learners dream up. They are creating new views, symbols, and ideas from their experiences.

Exploring and trusting personal knowledge. The facilitator is aiding learners in bringing to awareness those life experiences which have personal meaning and from which knowledge can be gleaned. It is part of a process that causes learners to examine life experiences and place greater trust in themselves for knowing some of the principles which are written in books by experts. Learners can compare their personal knowledge with that knowledge presented by experts after years of research. As a part of this process, facilitators can help learners discover when they need to seek outside resources and information.

Clarifying controversial and societal issues. The learning situation can offer a place and a process for "thinking the priorities." It can be a place to examine and discuss controversial issues of our time which have major effects on our society, our personal lives, and our learning processes. The situation can offer the opportunity to express intense feelings about external events that affect our survival. The learning members can become a group that supports its members in handling the demands of careers, peers, television, wars, relationships, families, societal influences, and world events. Is that expecting too much of learning situations?

Learning what, how, when, where, and with whom to learn. In most respects, this point is what education is for. The movement through our educational system can be one which is both an inward journey and an exploration of the world about us. Too often, the journey into the self is neglected; yet, it is the more important process. The facilitator has the task of understanding learning and its facilitation (Rogers, 1969) to its fullest. The person's "will to learn" is tapped and sets a course or direction for personal learnings. The facilitator aids by listening and encouraging the learner in developing what, how, when, where, and with whom to learn. The facilitator is a resource person. The situation is a place for exploration and experimentation. In some areas of study, selecting a good facilitator/teacher is often more significant than the content being studied.

Using an experience-based learning approach. Without a doubt, many facilitators utilize this style with no fanfare. They see that experiencing of key concepts is crucial to the process. Learners are involved in experiencing. Lesson plans are prepared which involve the learner in "doing" in order to gain an understanding of concepts and related information. Often, plans are prepared for a step-by-step process to bring personal awareness and understanding of the concepts. Experiencing helps make the situation real and alive because the learner's self is involved.

Establishing a process for change in learners, in group cohesiveness, and in problem-solving. The learning situation can become a place in which situational issues and problems can be resolved. Too often, no process for group development or problem-solving exists. Situational problems are either left to the facilitator to solve or they are ignored. With no process in place, the development of a positive learning atmosphere is hindered.

Learners bring with them definitions of the "learning situation." Based on previous experiences, the definition usually includes expectations of the facilitator, rules for learning, and roles for learners. Without the establishment of a process, these attitudes and expectations of learners are never explored with the facilitator. Some learners may have never verbalized these inner attitudes about learning, roles, and facilitators. This definitional set certainly affects learning dynamics and development.

Is there an opportunity within the process to discuss values and their relationship to the cognitive content and to living? How does a learner gain values and a sense of clarity of values? The learner is more than a receptacle for the values of others. Learners need opportunities for values exploration and clarification.

A process can also provide learners with an opportunity to participate in decision making. People learn about making decisions and democratic processes by being involved and having some ownership of the process. Must the facilitator always be the final authority?

A group process with sharing can serve learners by giving them a chance to integrate their experiences. The process provides for a periodic meeting of the minds.

What Are Some of the Key Values Held by a Facilitator with This Approach?

In examining a person's values for being a facilitator of learning, several questions come to mind that may be helpful in clarifying these values. These "questions I ask myself" may help a facilitator examine the learning climate and process which he or she establishes for others. A facilitator could begin by asking: How do I learn best? Under what psychological conditions do I learn best? What have I learned best? What learning has been most personal, meaningful, and lasting? Where have I learned best? When have I learned best? Have relationships with teachers/facilitators affected my learning?

The following list of valued aspects of learning and facilitation might be considered by facilitators.

1. The "whole" person (right brain/left brain, emotion/cognition, mind/body, strengths/weaknesses, etc.) is valued more than the subject matter.

2. There is a deep caring and respect for learners as persons and persons as learners.

3. A healthy psychological climate for learning which is non-threatening and enhances emotional well-being is critical.

4. Feelings of the learners and the facilitators are valued as they are key motivators of learning behavior and a significant part of our humanness.

5. The inner world of learners is valued with the unique richness of potentials, experiences, perceptions, feelings, and thoughts.

6. Experience is valued as a key to learning about ourselves, others, and the world. We learn by doing/experiencing. We learn what is lived in the learning situation.

7. Positive interpersonal relationships with learners make learning a human process. We build people with people.

8. A process with movement towards self-directed learning goals, processes, and outcomes develops a freedom in which learners can be responsible and part of a democracy.

9. Personal knowledge of learners is respected and brings numerous resources to the learning situation. These sources can be trusted. They bring an inner wisdom to the learning process.

10. Listening and understanding oneself and others is crucial to learning about life.

11. Self-assessment is encouraged rather than leaving all evaluation to the facilitator.

12. Feedback in an honest and constructive manner is rated above praise.
13. Genuineness and realness in the situation are valued to encourage emotionally healthy, integrated individuals. Polarities within the person are explored.
14. The clarification of values, attitudes, and behaviors is a precursor to stating goals and taking actions in life.
15. Learning is valued more than teaching.

It is helpful for effective facilitators to develop their own list of values and then to begin experimenting and developing ways of implementing the values.

What Are the Goals or Directions for the Learning Environment?

In beginning this section, it seems appropriate that facilitators pause a few moments to examine their own philosophies on facilitation and their goals for a healthy learning climate. The effective facilitator is involved in an ever-present self-assessment process. Here are several questions to aid in that process.

— How have I come to be in my current situation?
— What are my "here and now" reasons for being in the situation I am?
— What are my thoughts and feelings about the situation in which I am?
— What mental images (present and future) accompany my thoughts and feelings about my learning environment, my learning group, my supervisors, my _____?
— What significant learnings have affected my style of facilitation?
— How would I like to change my facilitation of learning in my current environment?
— What kind of a person do I wish to be in my situation?
— Am I as much of a learner as I expect others to be?
— What are my goals for being a facilitator of learning?
— Am I worthy of being chosen as a mentor by some special person?

It may be beneficial for the facilitator to select a significant person and to share responses to the questions. Hopefully, it is a person who can be trusted and who offers acceptance. As the significant other person listens to the responses, have that person relate his or her understandings of you and perceptions about you and your behaviors/attitudes towards the facilitation of learning.

Centering the learning process within the person. The key point is to center the learning *within* the person and keep focus on the person rather than focus on the cognitive content. A goal is to let the content, plans, process, and resources revolve around the inner world of the learner as the facilitator attempts to meet learner needs and personalize the situation. In many instances during the process, the "self" of the learner is the key source of content or an important complement to the cognitive aspects. Learning which is experiential involves all the feelings, creative ideas, curiosities, and potentials of the learners. The learners' inherent capacities for development are endless, and the facilitator can challenge these capacities.

Effective facilitators have a positive view about persons and their capacities for change. They are not afraid to enter interpersonal relationships in order to be able to see inside the person and recognize talents at the same time as the learners are looking inward. Facilitators hold a respect for learners as persons and as unique individuals. A goal of facilitators becomes one of helping learners actualize the "self." And in building positive relationships with persons, a positive climate is developing for everyone. When threat to each individual is reduced, greater learning strides are made.

Facilitators attempt to understand feelings, thoughts, and meanings, especially in terms of learning and living right now. Feelings are of particular importance as they affect future behavior. In that sense, feelings are keys to motivation. When facilitators demonstrate empathy by listening to the feelings of learners, learner energies are released for achievement and creativity. The learners know that their inner processes are valued and respected. When learners perceive that they are being understood, they know that they can be more themselves in the situation. And learners also begin to pay attention to the feelings of peers.

With threat to the self of the learner lowered, then the facilitator can communicate efficiently about the meaning that the subject matter has to the learner. Learners explore their feelings on the subject matter and look for the personal relevance of the content. The exploration of feelings and attitudes towards the subject matter and learning processes aids both facilitators and learners in plotting course directions. Facilitators can help learners become aware of the influence and impact of their feelings and attitudes on learning processes, living, and the future. What they value in terms of study is explored. So, concurrently, learners pursue a deeper understanding of themselves and the interactive components of cause, effect, and circumstance.

Each learner arrives in a situation at a different developmental point. The facilitator has to be able to understand their developmental processes in order to invite them into a process that offers expectations and projects in line with their needs, aspirations, and future directions. Learners may have unique ways of studying and experiencing the subject. In the absence of a threatening learning climate, they can express their inner perceptions and readiness on the subject matter. The facilitator can help personalize the process and the creative directions of learners. What is set in motion is a process of "actualizing the self" which can be a lifelong endeavor. The facilitator's goal fosters an inward journey of understanding oneself and developing one's inherent potentials as well as learning about a specific content area at the same time. It is an exciting adventure in which inherent potentials within a person are emerging into actualization. What an exciting process it is!

Establishing a healthy psychological learning climate. The components of a facilitative learning process are critical. The facilitator is a significant person in this respect. She or he demonstrates qualities that may affect variables in the learning process — communication, respect for the learner, optimism about actualizing potentials, understanding of self and others, self-confidence as a facilitator, congruence as a person, belief and trust in the learner, etc. Rogers' (1983) ideas on the qualities necessary for person-centered experiential learning and affective development are incorporated into this discussion.

The first quality and, perhaps, one of the most crucial is that of *congruence*. Other terms such as genuineness and realness have been used to describe this quality. Congruence means that the facilitator attempts to be whole in the learning relationship. What the facilitator is experiencing is present in his or her awareness and is available for communication. In essence, the facilitator is integrated, all in one piece. When the facilitator is congruent, she or he is *fully present* in the relationship and, in most ways, is transparent to the learner in terms of the here and now. The learners can also see into the heart of the facilitator. Actually, the facilitator moves away from playing roles or presenting a facade in the situation. The facilitator is viewed as a person with a certain set of competencies and knowledge — and as a learner, too. Although the responsibilities of facilitators and learners differ in some ways, both are viewed as persons with feelings, thoughts, ideas, loves, etc.

The second quality is *unconditional positive regard*. This quality is one which the facilitator experiences toward the learner. The facilitator has a deep respect and caring for the individual both as a learner and as a person. There is an acceptance of the person with all of her or his weaknesses, strengths, idiosyncrasies, and possibilities. Another word that is commonly used is that of "prizing" the learner. And there are no conditions attached to this caring. The facilitator experiences a tremendous respect for the dignity and integrity of each person. Will the facilitator like all of the behaviors of each learner? Perhaps not, but the respect is still present for the person.

The third quality is *empathic understanding*. This quality has received the most attention from the helping professions — teaching, counseling, health care, pastoral counseling, crisis center work, parenting, etc. It seems to be a quality that has been difficult for some people to develop. Empathy is being able to listen to what learners communicate, verbally and nonverbally; understand the feelings, thoughts, and meanings; and then put these understandings in one's own words and communicate these understandings to the learner. When the learners perceive themselves as being heard and understood, they explore their inner worlds more deeply. The effective facilitator is not trying to tell learners the meanings of their worlds but she or he is attempting to "walk in their shoes" to understand the learners. The facilitator seeks to understand what their needs are, what their wants are, what their joys are, what their disappointments are, what their views of learning are, what their hates are, what their perceptions of the world are, what their concepts of themselves (self-concepts) are, what their sorrows are, what their directions in learning are, what their dreams are, and on and on. But is there time for this kind of understanding? The facilitator who seeks to help learners needs to set aside the time in order to know them. Persons develop with "person help." Enough time must be spent with learners.

Having a facilitative interpersonal relationship. When the three qualities or core conditions are met, a facilitative learning climate emerges that has at its core helping interpersonal relationships. Because the facilitator seeks to be congruent in the learning situation, to experience an unconditional positive regard for learners, and to demonstrate empathic understanding with learners, learners begin to emulate these qualities in learning relationships with the facilitator and with peers. The qualities are contagious. Now learners and the facilitator can move towards the development of their inner potentials in an environment that has caring, trust, congruence, communication, risk taking, feedback, cognition, and a lack of threat. Under these circumstances, the facilitator does not have to worry about the achievement or productivity of learners. They will learn cognitive content rapidly and achieve closer to what they are capable of achieving. The learners and the facilitator have made a commitment to themselves, to each other, and to learning. Learners become responsible because they have ownership in the process and have retrieved their responsibilities — their own learning and development. It is a more holistic form of self-development which includes the affective, cognitive, and psychomotor domains. The process is alive, exciting, and challenging. Learners are, with the facilitator's aid, unlocking their inherent potentials to learn, to create new ideas and products, to achieve, to be resources for each other, and to be fully human in the process. It is an experience based on good interpersonal relationships.

Developing competencies for facilitation. The competencies to be developed are the core qualities reflected in behavior. The reflection of the qualities in behavior is a process movement of integration and congruence on the part of the facilitator. *If* the facilitator has the qualities and experiences them internally, *then* the qualities need to be demonstrated in the daily interactive process with learners. These qualities are ones which facilitators hold for themselves. They are persons, too. The behavioral competencies to be worked on are reflections of these qualties: a goal of being congruent in interpersonal relationships in the learning setting; a sincere caring and acceptance of learners as persons; and, a willingness to listen and understand the feelings, perceptions, and realities of learners.

Thayer (1977) has described an effective step-by-step experiential learning process for the development of these competencies. He has also outlined several of the key competencies (Thayer, 1981a, pp. 13-15) in his book on strategies for experiential learning. A summary of Thayer's competencies plus three additional ones follows.

1. *Being attentive* signals one's intent or willingness to engage in communication with the other person. Attentiveness communicates a readiness on the facilitator's part to focus on the other person and what this person is saying and feeling. In essence, the facilitator is ready to pay attention to all that the person is experiencing and communicating. The facilitator's body reflects this intent to be attentive. Good eye contact is maintained, but the facilitator does not stare. The facilitator's physical posture is turned toward the person to show interest in what is being communicated. Furthermore, the facilitator generally allows the other person to select the topical content; communication is encouraged by helping the person talk about

the topics that he or she has chosen. The focus is on the other person; the facilitator follows the person's expressions of thoughts, feelings, and meanings. (p. 13)

2. *Being relaxed* aids in attentiveness to the other person and to the process. The muscles in the facilitator's body should not be overly tense; such tenseness often indicates that other conditions or events, such as uneasiness about the current situation or personal concerns, are distracting the facilitator. Not being relaxed can affect the facilitator's ability to be focused on the other person. Taking several deep breaths helps in becoming more relaxed. Tensing the body muscles several times for five to seven seconds and then releasing the tightness also aids in relaxing the muscles. (p. 13)

3. *Sensing and communicating an understanding of thoughts* (verbal messages) means that the facilitator is able to hear the other person's message and to state in his or her own words what the person is saying. Such a statement communicates to the person what is heard and allows for an accuracy check by that person. The facilitator's communication helps to assure the person that someone is really trying to understand his or her ways of viewing life experiences. The intent is to follow the person's leads in order to understand the person and then, in turn, to communicate this understanding to the person. Questions are used infrequently since they often represent the facilitator's curiosity and desire to direct the process. Instead, the facilitator encourages the person to direct the flow of communication because the person knows what the concern is. Practice helps in attempting to state accurately what the other person has just said. (p.13)

4. *Sensing and communicating an understanding of feelings and meanings* (verbal and nonverbal messages) is an effort on the facilitator's part to grasp the other person's entire communication, both verbal and nonverbal, and then to let the other person hear what is understood of his or her feelings in relation to events and experiences. The facilitator listens carefully for feeling words and observes the simultaneous nonverbal messages in the voice and physical expressions. Responding to feelings and meanings is a key skill that can communicate understanding of the person's world to that person. Feelings are communicated in both verbal and nonverbal ways. The facilitator must be particularly sensitive to the nonverbal messages because they are not always the same as the verbal messages. A difference between the verbal and the nonverbal message may signal that the person is not completely aware of his or her experiencing; the person may be in a state of incongruence. Some research

psychologists believe that over 65 percent of the feeling and meaning of a message is communicated nonverbally. This research indicates that the facilitator needs to be aware of facial expressions, voice tones, eye contact, hand gestures, body movements, and so forth. In addition to the skill training in responding to a person's feelings, thoughts, and meanings, the facilitator may practice helping another person talk when only nonverbal cues are exhibited. (pp. 13-14)

5. *Being aware of personal (facilitator) experiencing and express-ing related thoughts and feelings* is another area on which to work. The facilitator is encouraged to be in touch with his or her own thoughts and feelings concerning the current moment of experiencing. In other words, the facilitator tries to pay atten-tion to his or her own inner self and any internal dialogue. He or she focuses inward to be aware of feelings and thoughts and then practices expressing these feelings and thoughts in "I" messages. Using "I" indicates that the facilitator owns these messages and is responsible for them. Expressing inner feel-ings and thoughts helps the facilitator become more honest and direct in interactions with others, more congruent as a person. (p. 14)

6. *Experiencing positive regard and appreciation for learners as persons and showing respect for others and for oneself* is reflec-tive of an attitude of caring and concern for people. The facilitator is encouraged to take a moment to consider the feel-ings and thoughts of others as well as his or her own rights as a person in learning situations. In essence, the facilitator should attempt to demonstrate to the other person that "I prize you as a person and as a learner." People will acknowledge care and concern for them. When respect for learners is shown, learners gain more self-respect and also view their own human potentials as worthwhile and as resources worth tapping. (p.14)

7. *Trusting and expressing intuitive hunches* can often be more valuable than relying on intellect. The facilitator who remains open with all senses will, at one point or another, experience a very real "gut" sensation about the other person and what that person may be experiencing. Such a feeling may begin in the pit of the stomach and eventually flow over the entire body. This intuitive hunch, often perceived only minimally by the facilitator, can become a very accurate perception and a useful tool in the helping/learning process. The facilitator may wish to test the accuracy of intuitive hunches to be able to place more trust in them. (pp. 14-15)

8. *Recognizing and responding to that personal material which is most conspicuous by its absence* is a competency of facilitation. Occasionally, learners will communicate an amount of information which reveals some component of feelings, thoughts, or information that is conspicuously absent. With sensitivity, the facilitator may choose to respond depending on what the missing component might be. Take, for example, a teenager who talked of sports, school, his mother, siblings, grades, and teachers. The component that seemed obviously missing was talk of his father. Upon responding to the absent information, the facilitator learned that the boy's father had died several months earlier and that it was difficult for the boy to accept his father's death. In this case, the situation was sensitive. The facilitator had to respond with care. But much can be learned by understanding what a learner is speaking about and what is conspicuously absent in the themes of communication.

9. *Paying attention to personal (facilitator) mental images* that are based upon stimulus statements and communication from the learner provides a rich source of data for understanding the world of the learner. At times, concurrent feelings and thoughts will be generated in the facilitator that bring him or her closer to the visual/perceptual world of a learner. In addition to understanding the learner, the facilitator can help the learner to develop imaginative ideas, explore fears and blocks to learning, project risks and consequences of desired actions, and others. Paralleling the visualizations from the eye of the learner's mind can make for greater empathic understanding and personal relevancy of learning. It is a doorway to unlock the creative process.

10. *Recognizing polarities and helping learners integrate* these apparent splits is a challenge for facilitators. Perhaps, in terms of this chapter, the split of emotion and cognition is worthy of integration, not only within the learner, but also within the learning/education system as a whole. Often, in learning situations, cognitive or affective domains are dealt with separately when they belong together as one. Too often, learners have been caused to deny feelings and their relationship to the total process of learning. The facilitator has an exciting adventure ahead if he or she can help learners accept the polarities that exist, integrate the affective and cognitive aspects of learning, stop denying the affective part, and recognize that the result will be a whole, fuller process of learning, greater than the sum of the two parts. While we are at it, why don't we add the psychomotor domain?

What Are Some of the Functions of the Facilitator?

Again, asking four questions of facilitators serves as a way to open this brief discussion (Thayer, 1981a).

— What are the ideals to be sought by the facilitator in the current learning process?
— What are the responsibilities of the facilitator in the current learning process?
— What are the roles of the facilitator in the current learning process?
— What are the rights and privileges of the facilitator in the current learning process?

It is the process of examining these questions which aids the facilitator. Absolute answers may not be the most desirable result. The process is to illuminate the thinking of the facilitator regarding his or her directions in the facilitation of learning.

The following functions of facilitators (Thayer, 1981b) are integrated with learner input as the process moves from facilitator-directed to learner-directed. These, of course, will vary from facilitator to facilitator. Although these are not all of the functions, here are examples:

— being a person and a learner in the group
— creating a healthy learning climate
— identifying learner needs and talents
— selecting with learner input appropriate cognitive concepts, information, and skills along with the complementary affective components
— designing learning strategies and experiences to meet learner needs, talents, and educational prescriptions
— clarifying personal learner values through the study of subject matter, the self, and others
— helping learners discover their own curiosities and motivation to learn
— developing, locating, and having learning resources
— having trust in learners and placing responsibility in their hands

— helping learners develop communication proficiencies and learn effective, constructive means of giving and receiving feedback
— reducing threat and, consequently, stress on oneself and learners
— establishing cooperative assessment and self-assessment procedures for achievement and learning processes
— resolving conflicts through use of group processes
— developing assertive responses in learners (genuineness/congruence)
— inviting learner participation in decision-making
— extending the learning process beyond the two covers of a book and the four walls of a learning situation.

Because constructive feedback is such a crucial component of successful facilitation, eleven feedback principles (Johnson, 1972, pp. 16-17) are provided here for review. Also, for learners to become good resource people for peers, they have to develop effective and caring methods of feedback. Focusing on learner strengths as much or more than weaknesses is helpful in building a positive learning climate.

1. Focus feedback on behavior rather than on persons.
2. Focus feedback on observations rather than on inferences.
3. Focus feedback on description rather than on judgment.
4. Focus feedback on descriptions of behavior which are in terms of "more or less" rather than in terms of "either-or."
5. Focus feedback on behavior related to a specific situation, preferably in the "here-and-now," rather than on behavior in the abstract, placing it in the "there-and-then."
6. Focus feedback on the sharing of ideas and information rather than on giving advice.
7. Focus feedback on exploration of alternatives rather than on answers or solutions.
8. Focus feedback on the value it may have to the receiver, not on the value of "release" that it provides the person giving the feedback.
9. Focus feedback on the amount of information that the person receiving it can use, rather than on the amount that you have which you might like to give.

10. Focus feedback on time and place so that personal data can be shared at appropriate times.
11. Focus feedback on *what* is said rather than *why* it is said.

(Johnson, 1972, pp. 16-17)

What Are the Responsibilities of Learners in the Learning Situation?

The notion of the responsibility of learners is one which has been discussed endlessly. A many faceted question is appropriate for learners, too. "What are the ideals to be sought, the responsibilities of, the roles of, the rights of, and the privileges of learners in the learning process?" Some believe learners do and should always look to teachers for directions, goals, standards, and amounts of time to study. But the effective facilitator believes in the learners and respects their abilities, strengths, and potentials to use the learning process to clarify issues and to gain knowledge of self, life, and the world. They can assume more responsibility and initiative for their own learning and development. They can accept responsibility for their own goals, decisions, actions, and consequences.

Yet, often learners have not been given responsibility to learn about responsibility. They have been told exactly what, when, and where to study.

When facilitators give more responsibility to learners, it is an experiment for both as they share the joys and growing pains of learning. Some learners do not seek responsibility, independence, or freedom to learn. Many learners are amazed to see that a facilitator openly recognizes and believes in their abilities to move toward self-direction, to use a facilitative psychological climate to learn about ideas and feelings, to develop their talents, to confront controversial issues, and to understand others. Learners can accept the changing focus of evaluation as it moves towards resting in the learners, not outside of them.

Learners need to examine their own reasons for being in the situation and understand the effects that these reasons will have on their learning attitudes, behaviors, and accomplishments. The commitment to the learning process rests with the individual learners. They determine their investments, actions, and consequences/outcomes in learning. What are their personal motivations to learn? And have they developed a discipline for learning?

Learners need to review their own expectations for the learning process, the facilitator, and for themselves. And it is appropriate to discuss these with the facilitator as she or he shares expectations, too.

Learners need to participate more in the exploration part of the process and identify components for study. The facilitator, through experimentation, relinquishes more and more control of the structure so that the process becomes one of mutual ownership and shared power in decision making. Learners can take a large part in determining what cognitive and affective directions are appropriate, what the current needs and wants of the group are, and how and where various components can be experienced/studied. The facilitator serves as a guide, a key resource person. Even learners serve as resource people. After the process has evolved to some degree, learners and the facilitator are involved in self-assessment and process assessment. Are we reaching the goals and standards that we have set for ourselves?

In the movement towards a person-centered experiential learning approach, persons learn to accept responsibility for their own directions and learnings. The risks as well as the rewards, changes, and disappointments belong to the learners. Learners find that they have an ownership in the process. The process and the learnings have personal meaning for life and living in these United States.

What Are Some Marking Points of the Process as well as Outcomes of Learning?

Perhaps a story (Shah, 1972, pp. 26-27) could mark the beginning of the process. It is one that is used with learners to stimulate their thinking and feeling about their own search.

There Is More Light Here

A man saw Nasrudin searching for something on the ground.

"What have you lost, Mulla?" he asked.

"My key," said the Mulla.

So the man went down on his knees too, and they both looked for it.

After a time, the other man asked: "Where exactly did you drop it?"

"In my own house."

"Then why are you looking here?"

"There is more light here than inside my own house."

(pp. 26-27)

Although each learning situation is somewhat unique, several common themes of traditional, standard processes are mentioned here to draw a bit of a contrast with the discussion of the process/outcome section. Usually, situations begin with a teacher preparing a syllabus, developing materials for an entire course, and explaining requirements for reading, projects, class activities, and evaluation. Then, a process occurs with the teacher lecturing and conducting discussion sessions, assigning new materials for reading, and giving examinations on lectures and readings. This process repeats itself until the prescribed cognitive content is covered or the semester ends. The teacher sets all or most goals and reading requirements. The class is mostly directed by the teacher with little or no input from students concerning feelings about the subject matter, course goals, class projects, classroom process, classroom physical arrangements, or evaluation methods. Primarily, the subject matter is the focus and the teacher is the center of the instructional process. It is a teacher-directed process where students are perceived to need lots of guidance for learning. Teaching is emphasized. There is little emphasis or concern with what is occurring "within" the student or "between" members of the learning groups. Desks are in rows with the teacher's desk in the front of the class. The teacher is the expert, the authority.

Of course, Rogers (1961) has a somewhat different view when he says "It seems to me that anything that can be taught to another is relatively inconsequential, and has little or no significant influence on behavior" (p. 277).

Here are some observations concerning a person-centered process which may also be viewed as outcomes of learning. If the facilitative conditions of unconditional positive regard, congruence, and empathic understanding are present, then a person-centered process of self-experience and affective development will *inevitably* evolve in the learning situation. Because of the evolutionary nature of this kind of process, all of the outcomes are not predictable. Of course, each and every learning group will be unique, based on the specific facilitator and the learners. Each learning group's process will have a sequential, logical order of its own based on the complexities of the group interactions, the potentials of the learners, and the self-development of the facilitator. And the process will be experience-based.

First of all, when the three facilitative qualities are present in the facilitator and a positive learning climate is developing, then some changes begin to occur within most learners. When learners perceive a genuineness and congruence on the part of the facilitator, they enter a process which promotes genuineness in their own interactions with the facilitator and peers. They are more open to the learning experience and more aware of their own immediacy of experiencing in terms of the "here and now." There is a greater awareness of the total self with all its configurations and complexities. As they are more in tune with their own feelings, thoughts, and meanings, they are able to use this increased awareness in their communication. As a result of increased attention to inner processes and experiencing, learners are more integrated or whole, and they are able to bring together the polarity of emotion and cognition as it should be in learning. It is a more holistic approach to learning as they consider all aspects of their humanness. Because the facilitator places more trust in their experiencing, individuals learn to trust their own inner processes. While being more themselves, they are more assertive.

If learners perceive that the facilitator has an unconditional positive regard for them, they will come to prize themselves more. When someone else, such as the facilitator, can accept them with all their strengths and weaknesses, they become more accepting of all that is going on inside themselves. Self-acceptance affects their personal views of themselves and what they have to contribute. They are worthwhile. Learners who have an increased acceptance of themselves also show an increased acceptance and prizing of others. Acceptance of oneself seems to be a beginning to change — change in relationships with others, in energy for learning, in developing potentials, and in refining humanness. Of special importance here is the movement away from an alienation of self and others towards an acceptance and understanding of self. It is an exhilarating feeling to see the positive changes in self-concept and self-confidence — "I can, I will . . ."

If learners find that the facilitator listens and demonstrates an understanding of their world of hopes, dreams, and feelings, they will begin a process of listening to themselves more and seek an understanding of their own inner realities. As they listen to themselves more, they develop an empathic ability to be better listeners with others. They have a sensitivity for the feelings, thoughts, and inner experiencing of others. Learning for them becomes more personal and relevant as they understand their "paths" in life better.

The facilitative conditions have an effect on each person as they go about the task of actualizing the self and their potentials. Self-esteem of the person is enhanced because new qualities of the self emerge. An openness to inner processes, learning, and experiencing leads to risk taking on the part of the person. The learner becomes more fully functioning as a person and goes beyond the "me" focus to having a respect for the dignity and integrity of others. Of course this respect, listening, and congruence affects the resources in the learning situation. The resources are multiplied with affective and cognitive components intertwined.

The observer can perceive a subtle and continuing emergence of changes in who directs the process and in the exchange of responsibility and power. As the process evolves, learners receive more responsibility for directions in the process. This change involves increased power over what, how, when, and where to learn. Essentially, there are three general phases observed. Initially, the process is more facilitator directed with learners receiving more responsibilities on special projects and lessons. As learners are encouraged and trusted, the process takes on a structure which demonstrates that it is facilitator-learner directed. The process finally moves to be learner directed. The last phase is not achieved by every facilitator and group of learners. Learners enter learning situations with different competencies and developmental levels of responsibility. Facilitators and situations are different in terms of the experimentation with learner freedom and situational boundaries.

When learners move to be more self-directing, they set more of their own expectations for the total learning process. Learners do not wait for the facilitator to lay out all the expectations of the learning situation. Usually, but not always, learner self-expectations, in terms of energy and effort expended, go beyond what is expected by a facilitator.

The process develops with the learners having a more internal frame of reference. They look inside themselves more for perceptions, questions, feelings, and goals. Learners use external sources when they have exhausted an internal search. In this same respect, learners tend to have the locus of assessment within themselves as versus outside of themselves. They are much more involved in setting their own standards, assessing their own progress, and determining what their next steps are in learning. When they seek external assessments, they ask for constructive feedback from experts who can help them develop specific competencies. Learners take back the control of responsibility for their own learning progress along with the consequences.

The process has a more "here and now" connotation. Learners are involved in a developmental phase which calls for personal relevance of learning or an appreciation of the content in the scheme of their own development. They move away from the learning expectations of others and toward their own self-expectations and directions. The meaning is that learners must understand for themselves the relevance of what is offered for consumption. Knowledge and experiences must be relative and current.

In a person-centered process, what is amazing is the direction of the journey with regards to the self. There is an increased acceptance of the self and its value in learning. The learner is able to clarify values in relation to the self, the subject matter, future directions, and the world. The learner is not always looking outside the self for approval and recognition. As a result, the person and learner becomes much more self-accepting, self-confident, and self-worthy. Greater self-esteem leads to an enhanced self-concept which produces more quality accomplishments. And as the individual learners gain a view of worthiness on their own parts, they tend to see other learners as worthy and acceptable persons. It is contagious. So, while you have a process that is developing *within* each individual learner, you also have a group process which is evolving *between* learners. The interpersonal relationships between learners even change as they move from more negative exchanges to a view of "everyone in the learning situation is in some way a rich resource." Feelings are shared. Communication is the rule, not the exception. The effect on the positiveness of the situation is tremendous in terms of shared resources, achievements, and standards. The outcomes have both quality and quantity.

EXAMPLES OF WAYS TO FACILITATE EXPERIENTIAL LEARNING AND AFFECTIVE DEVELOPMENT

This section provides several examples of the more practical side of my interpretation of a person-centered approach. To me, it is most stimulating to see how professionals vary the ways and means in which they implement a similar set of principles in the learning process. My highlights include discussions on the use of experience-based learning strategies, a method of personalizing the process with learner-planned experiences, the use of self-assessment activities, and a personal writing experience entitled, The Last Paper.

Using strategies for experiential learning. These strategies can be used to integrate experience-based learning with cognitive and affective components of a selected topical area of study. The main goal is to structure a step-by-step process in which the learners will experience the key concepts to be learned and will have opportunities to discuss their own related feelings, meanings, and perceptions. The learners are directly involved in the process. The focus is on the learners and their experiencing as the facilitator makes the process more humanistic.

The experience-based strategies are usually ideas that have been developed, field-tested, and refined by facilitators. The aim of the facilitators is to make sure that the experiential process relates especially well to the goals of the strategy. When these strategies are prepared by facilitators for sharing with other professionals, they are prepared in a somewhat standard format which includes the goals, group size, time required, physical setting, materials, step-by-step process, variations, commentary, suggested readings, references, and any necessary minilectures, worksheets, or instruments. Facilitators need to give careful consideration to the goals, step-by-step process, and variations.

Thayer's (1976, 1981a) books provide especially well defined strategies and offer a variety of experiential activities which focus on such areas as learner strengths, affective education, self-awareness, perception, identity, career development, interpersonal relationships, feedback, helping/teaching concepts and skills, self-assessments, imagery awareness, interactive-communication dynamics and group processes, value clarification, learning environments, and creativity. Several other books which contain affectively oriented learning activities that were not mentioned earlier also provide excellent ideas and plans for facilitators (Schrank, 1972; Hamlin, 1975; Hendricks & Wills, 1975; Howe & Howe, 1975; Hawley & Hawley, 1975; Hendricks & Roberts, 1977; Thompson & Poppen, 1979; and Hendricks & Carlson, 1982).

When selecting experience-based strategies, it is important to assess the needs of the individuals in the group. Involving the learners in selecting the experiences adds significantly to their feelings of ownership in the process. Facilitators may find the following points (Thayer, 1981a) helpful in picking strategies for use.

1. Assess the developmental stage of the learning group.
2. Consider the affective and cognitive needs of learners.
3. Examine the readiness for experiential learning of the learners and the facilitator.
4. Note the needed facilitator competencies.
5. Review the goal for which a particular strategy is planned.
6. Complement other learning activities and the overall direction of the learning process.
7. Set aside adequate time for experiencing and processing the feelings and thoughts generated by the experience.
8. Modify the strategy or select one of the variations in order to meet the goals of the learning group.
9. Evaluate the results of using the strategy.
10. Make sure that learners have important others/resource people with whom they can process any remaining feelings after the strategy has been completed.

Often, the facilitator may wish to plan a sequence in which strategies can be used to accomplish learning goals. Consideration may be given to a sequence which flows from experiences of a relatively simple nature to ones of increasing complexity in terms of subject matter concepts, values, attitudes, and group process. At the same time, facilitators can also consider the movement from more facilitator-structured activities to facilitator-learner-structured activities to learner-structured processes. The latter may even require less pre-planned structure with a more spontaneous structure always emerging.

It is critical that facilitators modify strategies for experiential learning to meet the needs of learning group members. Occasionally, the variations will be appropriate; however, the facilitators may choose to write their own variations of the process, alter the timing, require different materials, or process the results in new imaginative ways. It is helpful to view each strategy as a well-developed idea which worked in one unique setting but may need modification for other settings.

Most strategies for experiential learning have a suggested step-by-step process. But Jones and Pfeiffer (1975) have outlined five steps of the experiential model in which all have a significant part. They see the steps as these: experiencing, publishing, processing, generalizing, and applying. Of course, the last step begins the cycle again with a new experience.

The assessment of the step-by-step process is as important as the experiencing part of the activity. The assessment part can serve as a stimulus to future goal setting and personal behavior change in and out of the learning group. The facilitator must make sure that there is appropriate time allotted for processing learners' feelings, thoughts, perceptions, and meanings of the experience. The lack of proper processing can lead to an aborted activity. If a learner seems to be experiencing unusual difficulty in processing his or her feelings and perceptions, it is appropriate to speak with the learner, listen to his or her concerns, and help the learner select a resource person such as a counselor who could offer professional help.

Several forms of grouping participants may be useful in the assessment phase (Thayer, 1973). The facilitator may wish to use one of these forms: self-assessment, one-to-one sharing/feedback; small group (8-15 people) sharing; or large group sessions. The facilitator also could use one of several other assessment aids such as: the expert or panel of observers; group-on-group observation; written stimulus questions; audio- or video-taped playback sessions; assignments for homework; image recall procedures; or brief fantasy views of the process. The facilitator helps the learners integrate new principles and personal knowledge. The activity can be a very worthwhile endeavor.

An example of one strategy (Thayer, 1976, pp. 83-86) with the goals, step-by-step process, and worksheet is provided here:

Goal
To help teacher and counselor trainees become sensitive to the hazards of labeling students and predicting student potential without thorough and careful study.

Step-By-Step Process
   I. The facilitator asks the students to write a short anecdotal report based on their observations of a child under the age of sixteen. The statement, limited to sixty words or less, should consist of descriptive phrases and adjectives. Only a fictitious name should be mentioned in the description. The facilitator offers several examples of behavioral descriptions that might be used in the anecdotal statements. He asks the students to prepare the assignment for the next class meeting.

   II. Before the class is dismissed, the facilitator asks four to six people to stay after class. He asks these students to write the assignment based on their own childhood and in terms of how significant others may have perceived them before the age of sixteen. The facilitator cautions these students *not* to reveal their assignment to the other students.

   III. At the designated class period, the facilitator divides the students into small groups of six to eight persons to discuss their anecdotal statements.

   IV. He collects the papers from each group and distributes them to another group.

   V. Each person reads the paper he receives to the others in his group. Then the other group members try to predict each child's future development. For example, in five years, will each child be designated as gifted, average/normal, psychotic, neurotic, delinquent, or mentally deficient? The facilitator encourages the students to discuss the cases and to keep individual records of their predictions. One person in each group may keep a tally of the group consensus on each child.

   VI. After the groups complete their discussions and predictions, the facilitator distributes copies of the Labeling Students Case Sheet, Figure 2-1. Each group discusses each case and reaches group consensus on predicting the child's future development.

VII. Each group shares with the total class some of the comments that were made as the group predicted each child's future development.

VIII. The facilitator reads the names of the people who were described on the case sheet:

Case 1: Eleanor Roosevelt

Case 2: Albert Einstein

Case 3: Thomas Edison

He emphasizes how hasty judgments based on incomplete evidence can affect people's lives.

IX: The facilitator reveals that a number of the anecdotal statements reviewed earlier were written about actual members of the class. He may ask the students to attempt to identify the classmates who were described.

X. The facilitator asks each person who wrote about himself to read his anecdotal report and to discuss briefly some of the perceptions held by significant others in his life. Discussion can continue according to level of interest and time limitations.

Figure 2-1. Labeling Students Case Sheet

In five years, will each of the following children be designated as gifted, average/normal, psychotic, neurotic, delinquent, or mentally deficient?

Case 1

Girl, age sixteen, orphaned, willed to custody of grandmother by mother, who was separated from alcoholic husband, now deceased. Mother rejected the homely child, who has been proven to lie and to steal sweets. Swallowed penny to attract attention at five. Father was fond of child. Child lived in fantasy as the mistress of father's household for years. Four young uncles and aunts in household cannot be managed by the grandmother, who is widowed. Young uncle drinks; has left home without telling the grandmother his destination. Aunt, emotional over love affair, locks self in room. Grandmother resolves to be more strict with granddaughter since she fears she has failed with own children. Dresses granddaughter oddly. Refused to let her have playmates, put her in braces to keep back straight. Did not send her to grade school. Aunt on paternal side of family crippled; uncle asthmatic.

Case 2

Boy, senior year secondary school, has obtained certificate from physician stating that nervous breakdown makes it necessary for him to leave school for six months. Boy not a good all-around student; has no friends — teachers find him a problem — spoke late — father ashamed of son's lack of athletic ability — poor adjustment to school. Boy has odd mannerisms, makes up own religion, chants hymns to himself — parents regard him as "different."

Case 3

Boy, age six; head large at birth. Thought to have had brain fever. Three siblings died before his birth. Mother does not agree with relatives and neighbors that child is probably abnormal. Child sent to school — diagnosed as mentally ill by teacher. Mother is angry — withdraws child from school, says she will teach him herself.

These cases are reprinted from V. Goertzel & M.G. Goertzel, *Cradles of Eminence*, Boston: Little, Brown & Co., 1962, pp. xii-xiii.

As an immediate follow-up to the activity, the film *Cipher In The Snow* (1973) gives additional realness to the activity. Learners will not soon forget who Cliff Evans is.

Personalizing the learning process with the experience module. In my several years of teaching/learning experience, there has been no other single assignment which has been so fruitful and amazing as the Experience Module (EM). The purpose of the module is to have learners design an experience which will help them develop and change as well as bring a meaningful experience into their lives.

Many learners come to the learning situation with the expectation that the facilitator will have almost total control over what they learn, how they learn, under what conditions they will learn, and how the learning will be evaluated. With the EM, they are given a gentle, but firm push from the usual other-directed learning stance toward a more self-directed learning experience. It is one step which calls for a greater commitment of time and energy to self-planned, experiential learning and, perhaps, higher levels of personal risk-taking.

The goal of the facilitator is to help learners actively design, plan, complete, and assess a learning experience. Learners are trusted to prepare personally relevant experiences. When threat is lowered and learners are helped to focus on themselves, they often know best about their needed learning topics, learning processes, areas of strength and weakness, and the circumstances under which they learn best. And they are encouraged to trust their own perceptions, explore the dimensions, and understand the different meanings of the EM. They are challenged to develop and put in order the *personal knowledge* that can be gleaned from the experience. Then learners are aided in comparing their personal knowledge with the knowledge of experts. The facilitator serves as a resource person for the comparisons.

The self-life experience may directly or indirectly complement some aspect of the course. Learners are asked to determine and submit in written form their own goals, the nature of the process, the level of risk, any necessary materials and conditions, the setting, the time commitment, how they will report the experience, and how they will process and assess the significant and insignificant *affective and cognitive* learning outcomes. They determine the parameters and process for the experience. The facilitator serves as a resource person to assist in whatever way possible: listening, brainstorming for ideas, exploring possible consequences, facilitating decision making, securing materials, providing information, etc.

The facilitator does not accept or reject any proposal, but tries to help learners explore, clarify, and develop their ideas specifically on the basis of what they, the learners, need and want to accomplish/experience. The EM is usually part of a contract style grading approach because of the difficulty in grading such personal learning experiences, and the facilitator seeks to encourage more "response-ability." Learners experience the joy of their learnings and accept the disappointments, too. They have ownership in their own learning.

Although each experience module is different, several examples are provided here.

1. Re-establish feeling level communication with my wife in order to enhance our relationship.
2. Complete some "unfinished business" with my father because he is dying of cancer.
3. Assemble a furniture kit with my husband in order to increase our time together and enhance our communication.
4. Prepare a set of lessons on values, feelings, and behavior for my eighth grade class.

5. Locate a successful blind teacher and interview her or him about teaching style, relating to learners, being an effective facilitator, etc. because I want to be a helping teacher and I am blind.

6. Regain my self-confidence to dive from the high diving board. Since my diving accident, I have not dived in competition.

7. Interview several unemployed people about their perceptions of themselves, work, and society. Then I will proceed through the steps of applying for welfare.

8. Complete the Last Paper on Interpersonal Relationships: Marriage, Partners, and Alternatives. This is especially meaningful because of my divorce last year.

9. Participate in the training sessions for becoming a volunteer at the local community crisis center.

10. Attend several counseling sessions as a client to explore and understand my own career directions better. My goal is to make some decisions about graduate study.

It is an exciting process to observe and hear about the special outcomes, awareness, and personal development that accompany self-appropriated experiences. Rogers (1961) believes that "... the only learning which significantly influences behavior is self-discovered, self-appropriated learning" (p. 276).

Learners find unique ways of processing their feelings, thoughts, and perceptions by the use of journals/diaries, short books, poems, booklets with pictures, audiotaped presentations with music, films, special skits, and regular written reports. Often, learners are willing to relate to the learning group their perceptions and feelings on the life experience. The sharing sessions are quite amazing and offer excellent examples of learner "openness to learning and experience." The facilitator helps individuals and the group process the experiences for the significant outcomes.

The Experience Module can be used to complement ordinary classroom work and personalize aspects of the process. It is a step towards self-directed learning.

Providing self-assessment activities. One way to facilitate a more self-directed learning stance is by using self-assessment activities. Learners are involved in assessing their own progress toward specific objectives in the learning experience. Then learners are encouraged to take more responsibility in the assessment process by the use of a self-assessment inventory.

A self-assessment inventory is prepared for use with learners, often with their input. The inventory may consist of 25 to 35 stimulus items. Each item is an "I" statement which calls for learner ownership in the process. The items relate specifically to the current learning experience (e.g., subject matter, learning style, group process, attitudes/behaviors on learning). Here is an example of one such statement: "I demonstrate empathy by understanding what another person is saying and I communicate to her/him what it is I understand." Learners are asked to rate themselves on a scale from one to five. One means that they *never* demonstrate empathy while a five on the scale indicates a *regular or frequent* use of empathy in responding to others. Learners are also asked to clarify their own rating by commenting on their response to each stimulus item. The inventory may or may not be completed during the learning session.

After learners have completed the inventory, they are asked to review the items and select three personal strengths and three personal weaknesses in terms of the course activities and their attitudes/behaviors. Then they are asked to select a person with whom they will share their inventory. The partners exchange inventories. Each carefully reviews the other's inventory and writes a brief profile of what that person is like as a learner/achiever in the course. After the profiles are written, the partners focus on one person at a time and discuss the profile of the person along with his or her own list of three strengths and three weaknesses. The partners are encouraged to identify one strength which can be utilized more and one weakness on which they will establish specific objectives for work. The completed inventories also serve as an ideal discussion aid for learner-facilitator conferences on learner progress, classroom activities, and learning style.

In using the inventory, learners are not asked to arrive at a score which categorizes them in some way. The self-assessment inventory is used as an aid to encourage learners to take more responsibility for their own learning processes and outcomes. The movement is away from labeling them as good or poor learners toward helping them to assess their own strengths and weaknesses and then find a way to do something about these strengths and weaknesses.

Figure 2-2 shows several examples of stimulus items which may be useful in helping learners look at their own attitudes and behaviors toward learning.

It is interesting and challenging for facilitators to enlist the input of learners and write a 25-item self-assessment inventory which focuses on learners and their learning situations. The process can be enhancing for the situation. The self-disclosure is healthy.

1. I search diligently for all available resources to facilitate my learning.
   Never   1   2   3   4   5   Regularly
   Comments: _____

2. I establish realistic learning goals.
   Never   1   2   3   4   5   Regularly
   Comments: _____

3. I have accepted full responsibility for my learning goals, process, progress, and change.
   Never   1   2   3   4   5   Regularly
   Comments: _____

4. I respect myself as a learner.
   Never   1   2   3   4   5   Regularly
   Comments: _____

5. There are situations in which I must force myself to learn.
   Never   1   2   3   4   5   Regularly
   Comments: _____

6. Threat from teachers has little effect on my learning style.
   Never   1   2   3   4   5   Regularly
   Comments: _____

7. I work hard to please my teachers.
   Never   1   2   3   4   5   Regularly
   Comments: _____

8. I look to significant others to help me assess and explain the meaning of my learning experiences.
   Never   1   2   3   4   5   Regularly
   Comments: _____

9. I seek sufficient information on which to base my decisions and behavior.
   Never   1   2   3   4   5   Regularly
   Comments: _____

10. Recent new learnings have increased by competencies for my career position.
    Never   1   2   3   4   5   Regularly
    Comments: _____

Figure 2-2.

The Last Paper: A Writing Experience. The Last Paper is an optional assignment that can be offered to learners who are seeking ways to explore their career development and to establish new career directions. The self-assessment task becomes a very personal process. Therefore, no evaluation or judgment from the facilitator accompanies the task. The papers vary from learner to learner, but people find that they can be responsible for their own review process. Often, through the self-assessment process of The Last Paper, learners examine and establish life goals on which they wish to work. Many find that the paper is in large measure a form of self-disclosure. Jourard (1971) believes that self-disclosure is a process that produces positive mental health.

At this point, three Last Paper assignments have been developed — a review of personal learnings, interpersonal relationships (marriage, partners, and alternatives), and career development. The assignment sheet for The Last Paper: Career Development (Thayer, 1981a, pp. 52-53) is presented here as Figure 2-3.

Figure 2-3. The Last Paper: Career Development

The area of career development is receiving much attention throughout our country. A prerequisite for setting new career directions is the assessment of the development of current attitudes, behaviors, and learnings that pertain to work.

Because this task focuses on self-assessment, it is highly personal and difficult to evaluate. Consequently, it must be undertaken on a strictly voluntary basis; no evaluation or judgment accompanies the task.

The Task

If, for some unknown reason, this were to be your last paper ever written concerning your career development (professional field), try to write a paper in which you would assess and specify your significant learnings up to this point. Through reading this paper, a person could come to know you, gain a clearer understanding of your career development, your philosophy of work, your significant learnings gained from work, and the new directions (goals) you plan to pursue in your work.

When you are preparing this paper, give consideration to the following questions:

— How have I come to have the career I have?

— How have I come to have my present thoughts and feelings on this career?

— What images accompany my thoughts and feelings regarding my career?

— How have I come to be the person I am at work?

— How can I use my potential to achieve the kind of career I want?

Expectations on the Task

The following statements are the facilitator's expectations concerning the paper and the process.

1. If you choose to complete the task, you need an appropriate amount of time and energy to spend on the task.

2. The length of the paper is self-determined.

3. The paper will not be evaluated or judged. Any course grade involved will be affected only insofar as the paper is part of a contractual agreement for a grade.

4. The paper need not be handed in as part of the contractual agreement as long as the facilitator knows that the paper has been completed.

5. It is very beneficial for you to share your paper with a significant other person in your life. The person should be someone whom you can trust and respect. After the person reviews your paper, have him or her relate to you some of his or her perceptions about you and your behavior in relation to your career/work.

6. *If you choose to allow* the facilitator to read your personal paper, it signifies a trust in him or her. Ask the facilitator to give you honest perceptual feedback concerning his or her perceptions of your paper.

7. It would be most interesting to save your paper for reading at some future date to note your changes and personal growth.

(pp. 52-53)

EVALUATION

Research and evaluation of affective education will be covered in another chapter of this book; however, it seems appropriate to call attention to some key research. Combs and Soper (1963) found that both good and poor teachers know what an effective helping relationship ought to be like; yet, the teachers might not be putting that knowledge into practice. They also reviewed all of the research on being able to discriminate between good and poor teachers on the basis of the methods that teachers used. They found no research to show that methods of teaching could be linked to good or poor teaching. So, ". . . the key to the nature of effective helping relationships is not to be found in what the helper knows or in the methods he(she) uses" (Combs, 1969, p. 9).

Arthur Combs was stimulated to be the catalyst for a series of research studies that covered a period of ten years at the University of Florida. He believed that it was the helper's unique "self" which was the instrument in helping others. Combs (1969) and his colleagues studied the perceptual organizations of effective and ineffective helpers — counselors, teachers, Episcopal pastors, student nurses, and college teachers. They made inferences on the perceptual organizations of helpers from observations of the helpers' behavior. They postulated that the teachers' beliefs have an organizing effect upon further perceptions and affect their behaviors. They found that effective and ineffective teachers have characteristically different perceptual organizations. *Effective teachers* can be described in terms of their perceptual organizations (Gooding, 1969, pp. 32-33) in these areas:

A. The general frame of reference of effective teachers tends to be one which emphasizes:
1. An internal rather than an external frame of reference.
2. Concern with people rather than things.
3. Concern with perceptual meanings rather than facts and events.
4. An immediate rather than a historical view of causes of behavior.

B. Effective teachers tend to perceive other people and their behavior as:
1. Able rather than unable.
2. Friendly rather than unfriendly.
3. Worthy rather than unworthy.
4. Internally rather than externally motivated.
5. Dependable rather than undependable.
6. Helpful rather than hindering.

C. Effective teachers tend to perceive themselves as:
1. With people rather than apart from people.
2. Able rather than unable.
3. Dependable rather than undependable.
4. Worthy rather than unworthy.
5. Wanted rather than unwanted.

D. Effective teachers tend to perceive the teaching task as:
1. Freeing rather than controlling.
2. Larger rather than smaller.
3. *Revealing rather than concealing.*
4. *Involved rather than uninvolved.*
5 *Encouraging process* rather than achieving goals.

(pp. 32-33)

Aspy and Roebuck (1974) partially summarized an extended period of research that offered some remarkable results. They wanted to find out whether or not being human in the classroom had any measurable effects and, if so, what these were. They were also interested in whether or not teachers could change their attitudes to become more effective. They expressed a belief of many people that "... mankind, both collectively and individually, has a potential to grow healthfully" (p. 164).

A key hypothesis was to test Carl Rogers' formulations that empathic understanding, congruence, and unconditional positive regard are the necessary and sufficient conditions for constructive personality change. The hypothesis was: "People who received high levels of Empathy, Congruence, and Positive Regard (E, C, PR) would attain more growth than those who had been given low levels of them" (Aspy & Roebuck, 1974, p. 164).

Here are major results of their studies.

1. Rogers' definitions of Empathy, Congruence, and Positive Regard (E, C, PR) were sufficiently sharp to permit them to be translated into process scales which could be applied to classroom interaction for research purposes.

2. The process scales for the facilitative conditions (E, C, PR) identified variables which related significantly and positively to students' (a) academic achievement, (b) attendance, (c) cognitive processes, and (d) intelligence measures.

3. According to the results of our work with the process scales, there appears to be a general level of interpersonal functioning. That is, the level was not significantly related to sex, race or geographical area of the United States.

4. The measures obtained from the process scales were generally supported by anecdotal evidence and other scales, i.e., Flanders' Interaction Analysis, Self-Disclosure and Inferred Self-Concept.

5. The process scales could be successfully employed in a didactic-experiential model to enhance classroom teachers' levels of interpersonal skills.

6. The most effective trainers of teachers were those who exhibited the facilitative conditions at their highest levels.

7. Audio-tape recordings of classroom teaching were satisfactory methods of obtaining data about the teachers' levels of inter-personal functioning. They were logistically feasible, and their results identified significant variables in the classroom interactions.

8. Relatively naive undergraduate and graduate students could be trained to apply the process scales at high levels of inter-rater and intra-rater reliabilities (.90 plus) across a two-year time span. The evaluation process was sufficiently stable to allow serious investigation.

(p. 169)

There are some additional points of interest in their studies. First, teachers who provide low levels of empathy, congruence, and positive regard may retard students' learning. This means that *teaching may be a "for better or for worse" situation.* Second, elementary school teachers are better at interpersonal relationships than secondary school teachers. And elementary teachers are more receptive to train-ing in interpersonal relationship skills. Third, a principal who offers high levels of E, C, and PR can account for a lot of the variability of a school's level of effectiveness — lower absences, higher achieve-ment, more parent involvement, fewer discipline problems, etc. Finally, it is significant that good facilitative interpersonal conditions, as postulated by Rogers, are positively related to the enhancement of learners' classroom performance and that facilitators can be trained to improve their levels of interpersonal functioning.

With Whom Should A Person Study?

Is the old adage true that "you gotta have a good model for being a humanistic facilitator"? Perhaps this idea is true. If one is attempt-ing to develop a personal facilitative style that is effective with learners, then the idea seems plausible that a person should study with the best. But is the person you might pick a person who can help you bring out what is *within* you as a creative and imaginative facilitator, a helper of persons? Will your friend who is helping you allow you "to experience" his or her every movement in helping others? Polanyi (1962) states that the master who provides a skillful performance does so by observing a set of rules of which she or he is not completely aware. Can it be that the master facilitator of learning is not com-pletely aware of the ingredients which make up a masterful perfor-mance? Polanyi (1962) says that the master's performance goes beyond a set of specified particulars. The "whole" performance is greater than the set of particulars, more than the sum of the parts. Facilitation is an art? All of the attitudes and behaviors are unspecifiable.

Do you truly wish to be a master of facilitation of learning in others? A person needs to answer the question first. If the answer is yes, then begin a search for what you wish to be. Who has more of what you wish to learn? You need to find that person. Study with the best! Then, a person can request to be in her or his presence. Stand beside this person, a master, and watch and watch and experience and watch and experience and perhaps, just perhaps, if you are open to experience, you will have "it" too, something which even you will not be able to define fully. You will know when you have "it" because soon others will seek you out to be by your side.

SUMMARY

The focus of this chapter has been on an experiential learning process that views the person, the learner, as the center. It is a process in which individuals learn what they experience. The facilitator serves as a guardian of individuality and strives to give the learners a sense of dignity and respect. The facilitator seeks to offer positive psychological learning conditions of empathic understanding, congruence, and unconditional positive regard. The continually emerging process is the lesson, and the movement is away from a separate view of cognition and emotion in education to one that is more "holistic" in nature. In that sense, affective education is not to be separated from cognitive education. The process shows a movement away from facilitator-established goals towards learner-directed experiences, ones in which the learners have responsibility and ownership. Significant personal learnings that influence behavior can be the rule, rather than the exception. The learning place is an exciting place "to be" with learners as they search for a "path with heart." There is no finality in a true learning process.

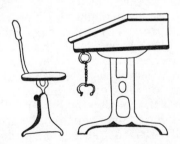

REFERENCES

Alschuler, A. S., Tabor, D., & McIntyre, J. *Teaching Achievement Motivation: Theory and Practice in Psychological Education.* Middletown, CT: Education Ventures, Inc., 1971.

Anderson, L. W. *Assessing Affective Characteristics in the Schools.* Boston: Allyn and Bacon, Inc., 1981.

Ashton-Warner, S. *Teacher.* New York: Simon and Schuster, 1963.

Aspy, D. N. *Toward a Technology for Humanizing Education.* Champaign, IL: Research Press Company, 1972.

Aspy, D. N., & Roebuck, F. N. From humane ideas to humane technology and back again many times. *Education,* 1974, *95,* 163-171.

Aspy, D. N., & Roebuck, F. N. *Kids Don't Learn from People They Don't Like.* Amherst, MA: Human Resource Development Press, 1977.

Association for Supervision and Curriculum Development. *Humanizing Education: The Person in the Process.* Washington, D.C.: ASCD, A department of the National Education Association, 1967.

Association for Supervision and Curriculum Development. *Perceiving Behaving Becoming: A New Focus in Education* (Yearbook). Washington, D.C.: ASCD, A department of the National Education Association, 1962.

Borton, T. *Reach, Touch, and Teach: Student Concerns and Process Education.* New York: McGraw-Hill Book Company, 1970.

Brown, G. I. *Human Teaching for Human Learning: An Introduction to Confluent Education.* New York: The Viking Press, 1971.

Buscaglia, L. F. *Love.* Thorofare, NJ: Charles B. Slack, Inc., 1972.

Canfield, J., & Wells, H. C. *100 Ways to Enhance Self-Concept in the Classroom: A Handbook for Teachers and Parents.* Englewood Cliffs, NJ: Prentice-Hall, Inc., 1976.

Carkhuff, R. R., Berenson, D. H., & Pierce, R. M. *The Skills of Teaching: Interpersonal Skills.* Amherst, MA: Human Resource Development Press, 1976.

Casteel, J. D., & Stahl, R. J. *Value Clarification in the Classroom: A Primer.* Pacific Palisades, CA: Goodyear Publishing Company, Inc., 1975.

Castillo, G. A. *Left-Handed Teaching: Lessons in Affective Education* (2nd ed.). New York: Holt, Rinehart and Winston, 1978.

Chase, L. *The Other Side of the Report Card: A How-to-do-it Program for Affective Education.* Pacific Palisades, CA: Goodyear Publishing Company, 1975.

Cipher in the Snow. Provo, UT: Brigham Young University, Media Marketing, W-STAD, 1973.

Combs, A. W. *Myths in Education: Beliefs that Hinder Progress and Their Alternatives.* Boston: Allyn and Bacon, Inc., 1979.

Combs, A. W., Avila, D. L., & Purkey, W. W. *Helping Relationships: Basic Concepts for the Helping Professions* (2nd ed.). Boston: Allyn and Bacon, Inc. 1978.

Combs, A. W. (Ed.). *Florida Studies in the Helping Professions* (Social Sciences Monograph No. 37). Gainesville: University of Florida Press, 1969.

Combs, A. W., & Snygg, D. *Individual Behavior: A Perceptual Approach to Behavior* (rev. ed.). New York: Harper & Row, Publishers, 1959.

Combs, A. W., & Soper, D. W. The helping relationship as described by "good" and "poor" teachers. *Journal of Teacher Education,* 1963, *14,* 64-67.

Corey, S. M. A poor scholar's soliloquy. *Childhood Education,* 1944, *20*(5).

Dewey, J. *Experience and Education.* New York: Collier Books, 1938.

Dinkmeyer, D., & Dinkmeyer, D., Jr. *DUSO-1: Developing Understanding of Self and Others* (rev. ed.). Circle Pines, MN: American Guidance Services, Inc., 1982. (a)

Dinkmeyer, D., & Dinkmeyer, D., Jr. *DUSO-2: Developing Understanding of Self and Others* (rev. ed.). Circle Pines, MN: American Guidance Services, Inc., 1982.

Dinkmeyer, D., & Dreikurs, R. *Encouraging Children to Learn: The Encouragement Process.* Englewood Cliffs, NJ: Prentice-Hall, Inc., 1963.

Dinkmeyer, D., McKay, G. D., & Dinkmeyer, D., Jr. *Systematic Training for Effective Teaching.* Circle Pines, MN: American Guidance Services, Inc., 1980.

Dinkmeyer, D., & McKay, G. D. *Systematic Training for Effective Parenting.* Circle Pines, MN: American Guidance Services, Inc., 1976.

Dupont, H., & Dupont, C. *Transition.* Circle Pines, MN: American Guidance Services, Inc., 1979.

Dupont, H., Gardner, O. S., & Brody, D. S. *Toward Affective Development — TAD.* Circle Pines, MN: American Guidance Services, Inc., 1974.

Eberle, B., & Hall, R. *Affective Direction: Planning and Teaching for Thinking & Feeling.* Buffalo, NY: D.O.K. Publishers, Inc., 1979.

Ginott, H. G. *Between Parent and Child: New Solutions to Old Problems.* New York: Avon Books, 1965.

Ginott, H. G. *Teacher and Child: A Book for Parents and Teachers.* New York: Avon Books, 1972.

Glasser, W. *Schools Without Failure.* New York: Harper & Row, Publishers, 1969.

Goertzel, V., & Goertzel, M. G. *Cradles of Eminence.* Boston: Little, Brown & Company, 1962.

Gooding, C. T. The perceptual organization of effective teachers. In A. W. Combs (Ed.), *Florida Studies in the Helping Professions* (Social Sciences Monograph No. 37), Gainesville: University of Florida Press, 1969.

Gordon, T. *Parent Effectiveness Training: The "No-Lose" Program for Raising Responsible Children.* New York: Peter H. Wyden, Publisher, 1970.

Gordon, T. with N. Burch. *T.E.T.: Teacher Effectiveness Training.* New York: Peter H. Wyden, Publishers, 1974.

Gorman, A. H. *Teachers and Learners: The Interactive Process of Education* (2nd ed.). Boston: Allyn and Bacon, Inc., 1974.

Greenberg, H. M. *Teaching with Feeling: Compassion and Self-Awareness in the Classroom Today.* New York: Pegasus, 1969.

Hamlin, B. *Awareness Experiences for School Use.* Dayton, OH: Pflaum Publishing, 1975.

Harmin, M., Kirschenbaum, H., & Simon, S. B. *Clarifying Values through Subject Matter: Applications for the Classroom.* Minneapolis: Winston Press, Inc., 1973.

Hawley, R. C., & Hawley, I. L. *Human Values in the Classroom: A Handbook for Teachers.* New York: Hart Publishing Company, Inc., 1975.

Hendricks, G., & Carlson, J. *The Centered Athlete: A Conditioning Program for Your Mind.* Englewood Cliffs, NJ: Prentice-Hall, Inc., 1982.

Hendricks, G., & Roberts, T. B. *The Second Centering Book: More Awareness Activities for Children, Parents, and Teachers.* Englewood Cliffs, NJ: Prentice-Hall, Inc., 1977.

Hendricks, G., & Wills, R. *The Centering Book: Awareness Activities for Children, Parents, and Teachers.* Englewood Cliffs, NJ: Prentice-Hall, Inc., 1975.

Howe, L. W., & Howe, M. M. *Personalizing Education: Values Clarification and Beyond.* New York: A&W Visual Library, 1975.

Jersild, A. T. *When Teachers Face Themselves*. New York: Teachers College Press, Columbia University, 1955.

Johnson, D. *Reaching Out: Interpersonal Effectiveness and Self-Actualization*. Englewood Cliffs, NJ: Prentice-Hall, Inc., 1972.

Jones, J. E., & Pfeiffer, J. W. (Eds.). *The 1975 Annual Handbook for Group Facilitators*. San Diego: University Associates, Inc., 1975.

Jourard, S. M. *Healthy Personality: An Approach from the Viewpoint of Humanistic Psychology*. New York: Macmillan Publishing Co., Inc., 1974.

Jourard, S. M. *The Transparent Self* (rev. ed.). New York: Van Nostrand Reinhold, 1971.

Krathwohl, D. R., Bloom, B. S., & Masia, B. B. *Taxonomy of Educational Objectives — The Classification of Educational Goals — Handbook II: Affective Domain*. New York: David McKay, Inc., 1964.

Lee, J. L., & Pulvino, C. J. *Educating the Forgotten Half: Structured Activities for Learning*. Dubuque, IA: Kendall/Hunt Publishing Company, 1978.

Leonard, G. B. *Education and Ecstasy*. New York: Dell Publishing Co., Inc., 1968.

Limbacher, W. J. *Dimensions of Personality Series*. Dayton, OH: Geo. A. Pflaum, Publisher, 1970.

Lyon, H. C., Jr. *Learning to Feel — Feeling to Learn: Humanistic Education for the Whole Man*. Columbus, OH: Charles E. Merrill Publishing Company, 1971.

Mager, R. F. *Developing Attitude toward Learning*. Palo Alto, CA: Fearon Publishers, 1968.

Maslow, A. H. *Toward a Psychology of Being* (2nd ed.). New York: Van Nostrand Reinhold, 1968.

Maslow, A. H. What is a taoistic teacher? In L. J. Rubin (Ed.), *Facts and Feelings in the Classroom: Views on the Role of the Emotions in Successful Learning* (pp. 149-170). New York: The Viking Press, 1973.

Moustakes, C. *The Authentic Teacher: Sensitivity and Awareness in the Classroom*. Cambridge, MA: Howard A. Doyle Publishing Company, 1966.

Ornstein, R. E. *The Psychology of Consciousness*. San Francisco: W. H. Freeman and Company, 1972.

Palomares, U., Ball, G., & Bessell, H. *"The Magic Circle": Methods in Human Development-Theory Manual* (rev. ed.). LaMesa, CA: Human Development Training Institute, 1976.

Patterson, C. H. *Humanistic Education*. Englewood Cliffs, NJ: Prentice-Hall, Inc., 1973.

Pfeiffer, J. W. & Jones, J. E. (Eds.). *A Handbook of Structured Experiences for Human Relations Training — Vol. 1*. San Diego: University Associates, Inc., 1969.

Pine, G. J., & Boy, A. V. *Learner Centered Teaching: A Humanistic View*. Denver: Love Publishing Company, 1977.

Polanyi, M. *Personal Knowledge: Towards a Post-Critical Philosophy*. New York: Harper Torchbooks, 1962.

Postman, N., & Weingartner, C. *Teaching as a Subversive Activity*. New York: Delacorte Press, 1969.

Purkey, W. W. *Inviting School Success: A Self-Concept Approach to Teaching and Learning*. Belmont, CA: Woodsworth Publishing Company, Inc., 1978.

Raths, L. E., Harmin, M., & Simon, S. B. *Values and Teaching: Working With Values in the Classroom*. Columbus, OH: Charles E. Merrill Publishing Co., 1966.

Read, D. A., & Simon, S. B. (Eds.). *Humanistic Education Sourcebook*. Englewood Cliffs, NJ: Prentice-Hall, Inc., 1975.

Ringness, T. A. *The Affective Domain in Education*. Boston: Little, Brown and Company, 1975.

Rogers, C. R. A theory of therapy, personality, and interpersonal relationships, as developed in the client-centered framework. In S. Koch (Ed.), *Psychology: A Study of a Science, Vol III. Formulations of the Person and the Social Context* (pp. 184-256). New York: McGraw Hill, 1959.

Rogers, C. R. *A Way of Being*. Boston: Houghton Mifflin Company, 1980.

Rogers, C. R. Can learning encompass both ideas and feelings? *Education*, 1974, 95, 103-114.

Rogers, C. R. *Freedom to Learn*. Columbus, OH: Charles E. Merrill Publishing Company, 1969.

Rogers, C. R. *Freedom to Learn for the 80's* (rev. ed.). Columbus, OH: Charles E. Merrill Publishing Company, 1983.

Rogers, C. R. *On Becoming a Person*. Boston: Houghton Mifflin Company, 1961.

Schrank, J. *Teaching Human Beings: 101 Subversive Activities for the Classroom*. Boston: Beacon Press, 1972.

Seaberg, D. I. *The Four Faces of Teaching: The Role of the Teacher in Humanizing Education*. Santa Monica, CA: Goodyear Publishing Company, Inc., 1974.

Shah, I. *The Exploits of the Incomparable Mulla Nasrudin*. New York: E. P. Dutton & Co., Inc., 1972.

Simkin, J. S. Gestalt therapy. In R. J. Corsini (Ed.), *Current Psychotherapies* (2nd ed.), (pp. 273-301). Itasca, IL: F. E. Peacock Publishers, Inc., 1979.

Simon, S. B., Howe, L. W., & Kirschenbaum, H. *Values Clarification: A Handbook of Practical Strategies for Teachers and Students*. New York: Hart Publishing Company, Inc., 1972.

Smith, J. M., & Lusterman, D. D. *The Teacher as Learning Facilitator: Psychology and the Educational Process*. Belmont, CA: Wadsworth Publishing Company, Inc., 1979.

Sprinthall, N. A., & Mosher, R. L. (Eds.). *Value Development . . . As the Aim of Education*. New York: Character Research Press, 1978.

Standal, S. *The Need for Positive Regard: A Contribution to Client-Centered Theory*. Unpublished doctoral dissertation, University of Chicago, Chicago, 1954.

Steinaker, N. W., & Bell, M. R. *The Experiential Taxonomy: A New Approach to Teaching and Learning*. New York: Academic Press, 1979.

Thatcher, D. A. *Teaching, Loving, and Self-Directed Learning*. Pacific Palisades, CA: Goodyear Publishing Company, Inc., 1973.

Thayer, L. C. An experiential approach to learning skills. *The Humanist Educator*, 1977, 15, 132-139.

Thayer, L. C., & Beeler, K. D. (Eds.). *Activities and Exercises for Affective Education*. Ypsilanti, MI: The Special Interest Group: Affective Aspects of Education (American Educational Research Association), 1975.

Thayer, L. C., & Beeler, K. D. (Eds.). *Affective Education: Innovations for Learning*. Ypsilanti, MI: The Special Interest Group: Affective Education (American Educational Research Association), 1977.

Thayer, L. C., & Beeler, K. D. (Eds.). *Handbook of Affective Tools and Techniques for the Educator*. Ypsilanti, MI: The Special Interest Group: Affective Aspects of Education (American Educational Research Association), 1974.

Thayer, L. C. (Ed.). *50 Strategies for Experiential Learning: Book One*. San Diego: University Associates, Inc., 1976.

Thayer, L. C. (Ed.) *50 Strategies for Experiential Learning: Book Two.* San Diego: University Associates, Inc., 1981. (a)

Thayer, L. C. *Process Assessment as a Learning Strategy.* Paper presented at the meeting of the American Educational Research Association, Special Interest Group: Affective Aspects of Education, New Orleans, LA, March, 1973.

Thayer, L. C. Toward a more person-centered approach in teacher education. *Education,* 1981, *101,* 322-329. (b)

Thompson, C. L., & Poppen, W. A. *Guidance Activities for Counselors and Teachers.* Monterey, CA: Brooks/Cole Publishing Company, 1979.

Valett, R. E. *Humanistic Education: Developing the Total Person.* St. Louis: The C. V. Mosby Company, 1977.

Weinstein, G., & Fantini, M. D. (Eds.). *Toward Humanistic Education: A Curriculum of Affect.* New York: Praeger Publishers, 1970.

Wittmer, J., & Myrick, R. D. *Facilitative Teaching: Theory and Practice.* Pacific Palisades, CA: Goodyear Publishing Company, Inc., 1974.

Zahorik, J. A., & Brubaker, D. L. *Toward More Humanistic Instruction.* Dubuque, IA: Wm. C. Brown Company Publishers, 1972.

Chapter 3

The Implications of Affective Learning for Industrial Arts Education

Lewis D. Kieft, Ph.D.
Associate Professor
Department of Business and Industrial Education
Eastern Michigan University
Ypsilanti, Michigan

and

Paul D. Kuwik, Ph.D.
Professor and Head
Department of Inter-Disciplinary Technology
Eastern Michigan University
Ypsilanti, Michigan

This chapter illustrates, with examples, the application of the concepts and philosophies of affective behavior as presented by the author in Chapter 2. In addition, it presents the premise that before affective behavior can be treated in the classroom or laboratory, the instructor must be self-actualized; that is, the individual must understand his/her own system of values, and the process of valuing. It is recognized that if a program is to be successful, the teacher must be an integral part of the process. This necessitates that the teacher have or be aware of the many attitudes, values, and feelings represented by students. The procedure for assisting a teacher to become a self-actualized person should include both self-evaluation and peer-evaluation.

The affective growth of students may be facilitated by participating in a variety of activities. This chapter describes and illustrates the role of the teacher as an important aspect of facilitating teaching methods which will enhance the student's affective learning. The chapter also presents a number of activities which may be useful to the teacher to facilitate affective growth in students.

THE NEED FOR TEACHER SELF-ACTUALIZATION

The cognitive, affective and psychomotor domains have long been given philosophical treatment by teacher educators at institutions of higher education throughout the country. In practice, however, the emphasis in the industrial arts laboratory has been primarily in the cognitive and psychomotor domains. Affective education, although philosophically treated with a high level of importance, has seldom received an overt emphasis in the instructional process. The need for affective education in industrial arts is critical for a twenty-first century society which will be bombarded by new technologies and the impact these technologies will have upon social change, values, and economics. For a teacher in an industrial arts laboratory to effectively implement affective learning into the instructional process, he or she needs first to be self-actualized. Teacher self-actualization is an awareness of the various elements or components which tend to modify affective behavior. All teachers should realize that everyone the student comes in contact with in the school may serve as a role-model and have some influence on shaping attitudes and values of the student. For some students, the industrial arts teacher may serve as a strong role-model. For example, if the industrial arts teacher is admired and respected by students, and the teacher is consistent in following safety rules in the laboratory, then some students will begin to follow this example. If this teacher is well organized, deals fairly with students, and carefully communicates his expectations to students, many students may respond to this example. Unfortunately, this incidental transfer of values and expectations could also be detrimental in some cases. If the teacher is often late arriving to class, some students may follow this example. Teachers can and do "set the example" in many situations. In addition to this type of incidental affective learning, industrial arts teachers can also establish realistic goals and learning situations in the classroom which will promote specific aspects of affective learning.

Each teacher in the instructional process must understand that he or she brings to the teaching environment a knowledge base and a set of values uniquely different in most cases from that of the students. This knowledge base and set of values has usually been developed because the teacher has completed extensive years of higher education and has reached a level of maturity well beyond that of the students. Each classroom teacher also brings to the instructional environment a set of cultural attitudes and a knowledge of cultural heritage which may or may not be appropriate to the students or parallel to their needs. Quite often cultural bias and cultural differences do much to impact the affective behavior of the student groups the teacher serves. Classroom teachers come from a specific social system and often bring the values associated with that social system to the beliefs and values which they profess in the teaching environment. These values and social systems are quite often different from those of the students they teach. Finally, a classroom teacher quite often comes from an economic environment which may differ significantly from the economic environment of the students he or she serves. It is imperative in the instructional environment that teachers recognize the knowledge base, cultural attitudes, social systems, values, and economic environment that have an impact on students' development and values and the affective behavior they exhibit in a classroom. These attitudes and values, although appropriate to their individual value system, must be recognized as a set of personal values and may not be the values appropriate for all learners in an educational setting. However, some values and attitudes may be deemed appropriate for all learners. Therefore, teachers must carefully examine their reasons for attempting to change a student's values or attitudes.

THE PROCESS FOR TEACHER SELF-ACTUALIZATION

In any educational environment the process of teacher self-actualization is critical if faculty are to relate to the students they serve. Once a faculty member recognizes the unique differences between his or her established value system and that of the students they are teaching, it is important that he or she begins to establish an environment whereby other viewpoints and other value systems can be accepted and dealt with in the educational setting. This environment can be accomplished by having teachers identify the values of their adult culture and specifically of the social and economic systems which are common to their adult lives. After this value system has been identified, it is important that teachers work with peers and also with students to identify the values of the students' culture. Where there are differences between the adult values and the student values a teacher must be willing to identify strategies for dealing with the imposed differences. In doing this a teacher must first have a positive view of his or her own self-concept. In addition, he or she must have an open mind to accepting others for their own unique cultural and attitudinal differences. The teacher must also understand that self-actualization is a life-long process of development. Differences in individual traits between the teacher and the learner may require the development of a profile of the differences between students and teachers for analysis and diagnostic purposes. It is important to understand that individual attitudes and values are constantly changing. It is important also to realize that value differences between adult teachers and adolescent learners cannot be developed into a taxonomy which will remain constant, but rather that value differences result from a process based upon changes in society and the development of the individual.

CHARACTERISTICS OF THE SELF-ACTUALIZED INSTRUCTIONAL PROCESS

Self-actualized instruction is a process of experiential teaching and learning which employs the significant use of problem-solving, decision-making, and goal-setting activities. The self-actualized instructional process integrates the domains of cognitive, affective, and psychomotor behavior into a unified whole as the instructional processes also transform industry and technology content that is relevant and understandable to the learner. It is important for teachers and students to realize that decision-making can be taught in an instructional environment by affective use of the problem-solving method. Students begin to develop skills in decision-making by identifying the elements of the decision-making process. These elements include gathering information from relevant sources both external and internal, and learning to utilize the collected information to make informed reasonable decisions about the technology they are studying. It is important, therefore, that experiential learning systems be identified in every study of industry and technology. Students should begin to accept responsibilities of problem-solving and, therefore, accept the responsibilities for making their own choices, for managing their own resources, and for directing the future course of their responsibilities in the industrial arts laboratory and hopefully the future of their own lives. In doing this students must examine their own values, attitudes, and social systems and develop skills in identifying goals for their learning process. In addition to setting goals for their instructional activities, they must develop monitoring systems to identify how well they are reaching their goals, and also modification systems for altering goals, wherever necessary. Self-actualized instruction should teach students the impact of divergent value, social, and attitudinal systems upon decision-making and goal setting. Students must learn the potential impact of affective behavior in modern society, and of the necessity of being able to project themselves into future social systems which deal with various cultural differences. It is important for students to understand differences in affective behavior and to promote this in an experiential learning environment early in their development, if they are to have the skills necessary to deal with these affective differences in their adult lives.

REALITIES OF AFFECTIVE DEVELOPMENT FOR STUDENTS

It would be comforting to know that all students leaving school had participated in affective learning processes and had shown substantial progress in becoming self-actualized. That is, they had developed a good understanding of their feelings; they had established a system of value clarification; and they were capable and willing to apply their values to solve personal problems in their daily living. It would be good to know that all students could rely on their own decision-making and goal-setting techniques to resolve personal conflicts and to provide a positive direction to their lives. But these accomplishments are unrealistic expectations because self-actualization is a life-long process, and because most students have not yet had the opportunity to adequately clarify their values or to develop special decision-making skills.

In many circumstances, students are given little or no direction in developing value systems or decision-making skills. This is inappropriate because the student's value system, which continues to develop, may happen haphazardly with too much influence from inappropriate sources. Too often, students' values and decisions are shaped and influenced by peer pressure, propaganda, TV, movies, selfish desires, or false information. Sometimes a student's value system may cause the student to reject people or agencies which are designed to assist in helping people understand values and decision-making processes. Students provided with little or no guidance in developing values and decision-making skills will most likely experience a great deal of trouble and conflict. Often their trouble or conflict may be more extensive than need be because of their own inappropriate behavior or decisions.

Too much or too little guidance in helping students make decisions and develop a set of values can provide difficulties for them in the future. "Most young people do not need adults running their lives for them, but they do want and need help." (Simon, Kirschenbaum, Howe, 1972, p. 17) Although some efforts to provide students with affective education are made by parents, the school, the church, and other institutions and organizations, the help given is often not sufficient and sometimes not appropriate.

This is not to suggest that students haven't already started developing a value system or that they cannot make decisions. There is a great range of abilities of students to clarify values. Some students will be quite capable of using a valuing system to make decisions. Others will sometimes display attitudes or behaviors which are unacceptable in the home, classroom, or community, or which appear to be detrimental to themselves or others. These students may have used their valuing and decision-making skills appropriately and, by free choice, have decided to accept the consequences of their actions. However, this may also be an indication that their value systems or decision-making processes are either faulty or undeveloped and that the students need some help.

TRADITIONAL VALUE DEVELOPMENT

One approach to value development, which has been used considerably, is to focus on helping students develop specific values which appear to be generally accepted by society. (Krathwohl, 1964) In many situations, the value systems of students are primarily shaped by the people in their environment. Adults attempt to modify behavior and perhaps values through convincing arguments, persuasion, appeals, rules and regulations, example setting, and cultural or religious dogma. (Raths, 1966, p. 39) Most influential will be parents, other family members, friends, teachers, and others whom the student admires. The assumption is made that most students do not have the experiences, knowledge, or abilities to establish values and behaviors which would conform to society if left on their own.

At least two major criticisms of the traditional value development approach exist. First, some parents may be overly protective and/or domineering with their children. They impose a system of values, demand certain behavior, and give the student little or no responsibility or opportunity for making major decisions on their own. In time, the student's values and behavior become molded, but students are heavily dependent upon their parents for any decisions. When they eventually move from the protective custody of the parents and their associated value system, they are not prepared to think and act for themselves. They have not learned how to make decisions for themselves and have not had opportunity to formulate their own set of values. They may become confused and reluctant to make any choices or decisions, or may make inappropriate ones.

A second criticism of this approach relates to some attempts to persuade all students to develop a particular set of values or to make certain "pre-determined" decisions. Students and their situations are unique. Therefore, it would be unreasonable to expect to teach all students to hold the same values, to set the same goals, or to make the same decisions.

VALUING — ANOTHER APPROACH

A second approach to affective learning which has become very popular among educators places emphasis on the process of valuing rather than resulting in any particular value. (Rath, 1966; Simon, 1972) A major aspect of this approach is to allow the student a free-choice to clarify values and make choices. This process of developing a value involves the following seven elements:

1. Choosing freely,
2. Choosing from among alternatives,
3. Choosing after thoughtful consideration of the consequences of each alternative,
4. Prizing and cherishing,
5. Affirming,
6. Acting upon choices,
7. Repeating the action with consistency. (Raths, p. 28)

All seven criteria must occur before the value is formed. In this method, educators may be involved by helping students determine their actual values through a series of unbiased questioning techniques, but may not attempt to change the student's views or values in any way. This approach has great potential for preparing students to become independent and to think and solve problems for themselves. It places great confidence in the student's ability to reason and to accept responsibility.

However, this approach also has some criticism. There is the feeling that a belief may fit all seven criteria mentioned above and still not be a value. The one important element missing from the seven listed is a rational and analytical examination of the value. This includes a values analysis which deals with the source of values, their consistency within a values framework, and their dependence upon varying conditions. (Bell, Bennett, Fallace, 1982, p. 99)

Another concern of the valuing approach to affective learning is its apparent rejection of all suggestions, opinions or recommendations which teachers might give students concerning the development of specific values. Educators assisting students in the valuing process are encouraged to exclude all attempts at giving the student any of their values, moralizing, or providing any hints of "good," "right," or "acceptable," or their opposites for fear of intimidating the students' free choice. (Raths, 1966, p. 53) Yet, students must have ample information concerning the consequences of their choices. They should also know how others feel about an issue and why they feel that way. If students are denied information concerning public views or parental values or feelings, their decision may be diminished by the lack of that information. Also, many students want and seek some type of confirmation, input, or advice from their parents when they are pondering a major decision. Receiving information from mom or dad or a teacher about what they think about an issue appears to be contrary to this approach.

A final concern regarding the valuing approach relates to its apparently limited application to those issues in a student's life where he/she will have opportunity to make free choices. Advocates of this approach indicate that if students are to develop values, they must develop them out of personal choices and real experiences. (Raths, 1966, p. 36) Yet, for most people, opportunities do not exist to "experience" before making many decisions and most decisions made will be influenced in some way by some other person. It appears that if the valuing approach were the only method used to help students shape values, it would have only limited use. This approach appears to work better for some issues than for others.

USING BOTH APPROACHES IN THE CLASSROOM

Both approaches have merit, but neither approach seems to be appropriate by itself for all students and all situations. Certainly we do not wish to make students so dependent upon adults for values and decisions that they can not think and act for themselves when they become adults. Nor would we expect students to develop values through experience and to make intelligent decisions about most issues without relying at all on advice, opinions, or suggestions from adults.

Students could not avoid receiving some indoctrination from adults on most issues, even if they wanted to avoid it.

Perhaps this topic (the formation of student values) would be an appropriate issue to begin discussing with students. A "Values Continuum" could be established. After the teacher draws a line on the board, two contrasting positions on the issue of how students values are developed are placed at the opposite ends of the line as shown below.

Students should rely completely on advice and suggestions from . . . . adults to develop values.

Students should not rely at all on advice and suggestions from adults.

How do you believe student values are presently being developed?
Ideally, how should student values be developed?

Students are asked to indicate where they stand on this issue and to briefly describe their position. Students should be allowed to pass if they wish. Some students may select a position far to the left and indicate that young students have few experiences to rely on and need a great amount of guidance from adults. Rules, regulations, and laws already exist to serve as guidelines and students need guidance from adults to help understand and obey them. Other students may indicate their position far to the right believing that all students are entitled to their own views, values, and actions. They may indicate that in the past, they have been forced to act in a manner which is in opposition to their beliefs or values. They may want much more control of their lives.

Regardless of their position on the continuum, many students may suggest that as students grow older and have more experiences, they should be allowed to assume more responsibility to develop their own values and to make decisions. Perhaps only two conclusions will be made by students after the activity and discussion are completed. Students may conclude that everyone is entitled to the views and values that he/she holds and that people hold many different views about the same issue. This activity may also prompt some students to begin thinking about the process of clarifying values and making decisions.

Ultimately, it is the student's actions and behavior which teachers are concerned about. Will students act in the best interests of themselves and others when they are given the opportunity to do so?

A combination of the two approaches discussed above will probably be necessary to insure that students are ready to assume this responsibility and are capable of accomplishing it. In many situations, adults should make known their values, opinions, and suggestions (without being overbearing or indoctrinating) and yet attempt to allow the student as much opportunity as reasonable for making choices and clarifying values. As students gain skill, experience and confidence, they should be encouraged to become more involved in the valuing process.

Regardless of whether a student's behavior is restricted or not, industrial arts teachers can still use elements of the valuing process to assist students in developing values and making decisions. To facilitate this, teachers may use various teaching strategies which focus on elements of the valuing process. These elements may serve as a guide to insure that all aspects of valuing are covered. The following guide may be used by industrial arts teachers to help students pursue affective learning. This guide is a modification of Rath's (1966) description of skills needed to complete the process of value clarification. To become self-actualized students should:

1. Become aware of one's own feelings, attitudes, preferences, abilities, and values.
2. Become skillful in problem solving. This includes identifying problems, seeking alternative solutions, analyzing the consequences of each alternative, and making a decision.
3. Prepare for the probable consequences of a choice and initiate action on one's choices and preferences.
4. Cherish one's values and act with a pattern and consistency which reflects one's values.

A variety of teaching strategies may be employed which will assist students in developing valuing skills in each of these areas.

GOALS FOR AFFECTIVE LEARNING IN THE INDUSTRIAL ARTS CLASSROOM

There are no goals relating to affective education which are unique to industrial arts education. The affective education goals incorporated into the industrial arts classroom or laboratory are the same as general education goals which might be taught or reinforced in any subject area of the school. In some cases, such as the following example from West Virginia, state educational goals relating to affective learning have been directly included in the State Industrial Arts Curriculum Guide:

- develop creative talents;
- develop and maintain the ability to form ideas, to seek out answers, to reason and shall have a positive attitude towards learning;
- acquire the ability to develop basic values and ethical principles and apply them to life;
- recognize personal responsiblity for the quality of the environment;
- acquire the skills, understanding and appreciation necessary for relating to and working with other people;
- acquire the knowledge, habits, and attitudes of a responsible citizen;
- improve his/her capacity to respond to the needs and responsibilities which occur in daily living. (*Industrial Arts/Technology in West Virginia Schools*, p. i.)

However, even though many of the same goals may be pursued in different subject areas, the nature of industrial arts offers additional opportunities for the teacher to incorporate affective learning into the classroom. "The uniqueness of industrial arts lies in the fact that its activities can provide a greater variety of elements that enhance the learning process than any other single discipline." (ACESIA Monograph 5, p. 23). In industrial arts, a variety of topics can be discussed and a multitude of activities incorporated which help to bring about desired affective learning. As a result of these activities, students can develop self-awareness, clarify values, and develop social skills. They can be provided with learning situations which will help them develop and test decision-making skills relating to realistic situations. A variety of activities may offer students opportunity to experience feelings which are relevant to developing values and attitudes.

INDUSTRIAL ARTS AND AFFECTIVE LEARNING AT DIFFERENT GRADE LEVELS

The opportunity to use industrial arts to develop affective learning starts at the elementary school level. Elementary teachers may use industrial arts activities for such purposes as: enhancing self-awareness, developing social skills, promoting good working habits, generating enthusiasm, solving problems, making decisions and exploring characteristics of various careers.

At the middle school level, students may experience much more independence in the industrial arts laboratory. They are likely to be given more opportunity to make more decisions and solve more problems, such as selecting and designing their own projects. They will be expected to rely more on their own problem-solving skills and should be challenged to stimulate their thinking and reasoning processes. They will also be given opportunities to accept more responsibility and to demonstrate behavior which reflects a maturing value system.

At the senior high level, industrial arts students should be given opportunities to implement actions which relate to the attainment of goals which, hopefully, were made by sound decisions on their part. Each student's basic value system and skill in decision-making should be already established and involved in his or her life. The student's attitudes and behavior should reflect this value system.

At the elementary level, the value systems and decision-making skills are only developing and children may need to rely a great deal on adults. At the senior high level, students should be relying on their own values, judgments, and decisions. The industrial arts activities provided may also be used to evaluate the progress of students in their affective learning development.

SELECTING ISSUES FOR AFFECTIVE LEARNING IN INDUSTRIAL ARTS EDUCATION

Although the teacher's main focus on affective learning may be on the method of valuing, specific issues and decisions will be a part of every teaching strategy. During the process of developing valuing skills, students will become involved in confronting specific issues and problems for which appropriate decisions must be made. If the issues and problems selected for study by the teacher have some significance to the lives of the students, the process will be more meaningful. Most teachers will have an unlimited number of topics they can choose from to serve as examples in teaching and the process of value clarification. Since industrial arts students are already involved in a study of industry and technology, this content area may serve as a large source of examples of issues and problems which can be related to the lives of the students. These examples can be used to help students develop a valuing process and, at the same time, help students gain insights into values held and decisions made by others regarding industry and technology. Decisions about many aspects of our industrial world are based upon the values which people hold concerning technology. Clarifying values regarding technology will help prepare students for future decisions they may face and reinforce the valuing and decision making process.

Following are examples of controversial topics regarding the use of industrial technology which may be presented for industrial arts student discussion and consideration.

1. Should corporations or companies be allowed to seek raw materials in state forests and other recreational areas?
2. Should corporations produce and sell products which might someday be used as weapons?
3. Should laws be made to force certain products to be recycled?
4. If a consumer is injured using a product, should the company or corporation which made the product be held responsible?
5. Should the government regulate more closely imports of products from other countries?
6. Should companies be allowed to charge whatever they want to for their products?
7. Should companies and corporations be forced by law to clean up all of the pollution and waste products caused by their corporation?
8. Should women and minority workers hold more high-level positions in large corporations?
9. Are products of today as durable as they were in the past?
10. What criteria should be used to determine how much a worker in an industry gets paid?
11. Do unions benefit workers?
12. Would you like to someday work in an industry? What type of work would you like to do? Why do you hold these feelings or values?

Many of these issues will have only indirect effect on the students' lives. However, many other issues which students encounter will have direct and immediate effect upon their lives. In many classrooms, teachers will strongly encourage students to act or behave in a certain manner. This encouragement may be to assist students in complying with school rules and regulations, or it may be to help the students use more of their potential. The attitudes and values of the student may or may not coincide with the requested behaviors. If it is evident that there is conflict between attitudes or values and behavior, it often becomes the responsibility of the teacher to attempt to change attitudes. In many industrial arts classrooms, the teacher may have a professional responsibility to focus on specific values and attempt to help mold specific value outcomes. This is especially true regarding values associated with performance and behavior in the laboratory. "Industrial arts teachers have long recognized the teaching of positive attitudes, such as good work habits, cooperation on the job, and pride in workmanship, as part of their mission." (*Wisconsin Value and Attitude Handbook*, 1980, p. 7) In many industrial arts laboratories, specific types of behavior are required of students by state law or by school rules. Since behavior is closely related to attitudes and values, it becomes the responsibility of the industrial arts teacher to assist students in developing a specific (and often predetermined) set of values regarding an issue which will result in the desired behavior. Teachers are cautioned, however, against attempting to impose a specific set of values on students if there is no legal or professional requirement to do so.

Following is a list of examples of behaviors often discussed in industrial arts laboratories. They relate to the affective utilization of the laboratory by a group of students and to individual safety and performance. Students can be assisted in developing a value regarding each of these issues. Hopefully, the value developed also will be appropriate for application by the student to many other aspects of the student's life beyond the classroom.

1. Following safety rules
2. Following clean-up procedures
3. Following directions
4. Conserving materials
5. Maintaining tools and equipment properly
6. Showing respect for others
7. Being organized
8. Assuming responsibility
9. Showing initiative
10. Developing confidence and self-worth
11. Taking pride in personal appearance and in hygiene
12. Being honest
13. Being punctual
14. Being precise and demonstrating workmanship

Many other personal daily living and social skills may be discussed in the industrial arts classroom. However, they usually are introduced only as a result of some incident, some aspect of the laboratory operation, or as part of some aspect of the content of technology being studied. Careful consideration should be given by the teacher in selecting examples of personal values to be clarified. Even though the teacher may be interested mainly in developing the process of value clarification, some values may be objectionable to students, parents, or other groups in the community. Some issues may be so sensitive to student discussion that teachers should not attempt to help students clarify a relating value unless they have had special training.

TECHNIQUES AND STRATEGIES FOR INFUSING AFFECTIVE EDUCATION INTO THE INDUSTRIAL ARTS CLASSROOM

A large number of techniques and strategies are available to the industrial arts teacher for infusing affective education into a classroom or laboratory. Teachers may also modify existing strategies or may design their own. Most of these strategies are not unique to industrial arts. However, because industrial arts activities are usually practical, exciting, and action oriented, they often provide greater opportunity for infusing affective learning into the student's education. Following are some laboratory activities which provide opportunities for affective learning. These activities are unique to only a few subject areas in the school, including industrial arts.

Students may become involved in:

1. Designing a project to be constructed
2. Solving problems of design of a product
3. Testing and evaluating a product
4. Constructing a project
5. Simulating occupations relating to industry
6. Diagnosing problems relating to a product
7. Disassembling, repairing, and assembling a product
8. Providing preventive maintenance for a product

Most teaching strategies for affective learning can be easily integrated into the daily lessons without disruption of existing content areas. Teachers should first analyze their courses to identify areas where affective learning activities could and should be used. The number and type of strategies used will depend upon such considerations as the time available, receptiveness of the students, and evaluation of the use of previous strategies by the teacher. Each group of students may respond somewhat differently and it may take several years for a teacher to identify the appropriate types and number of strategies which are the most effective for their teaching situation.

Some teaching strategies for affective learning are planned, and if successful, they may eventually become part of a unit or activity.

Their initial selection may be dependent upon helping students develop a particular element of the valuing process. Other strategies may be spontaneous, arising from an incident, event, or some experience involving students. Some teaching strategies will be used with groups of students, while others may be for individuals.

Some teachers may wish to alter their classes considerably to accommodate various aspects of affective education. Such approaches can be very effective, but usually require additional planning and preparation on the part of the teacher. Teachers who are considerably involved should be cautioned against replacing valued subject content with affective education and against over-emphasizing specific values to the extent that students begin to react in a negative manner.

Affective education teaching strategies should relate to some aspect of exploring emotions, attitudes, or feelings; molding value systems; or developing sound decision-making processes. These aspects are interrelated and if students are to understand and develop skills in the affective domain, these aspects should be taught in a correlated manner rather than studied separately. However, single comments from the teacher, a class discussion, or an involved activity can all contribute to the student's overall affective development.

MATCHING TEACHING STRATEGIES WITH DESIRED OUTCOMES

Assume that an industrial arts teacher in a middle school adopts the four-part model described earlier as a guide for teaching affective learning concepts. There are many teaching techniques and strategies which could be used to assist in the development of each of the four skill areas mentioned. A single teaching strategy used by itself is not likely to achieve the affective education goal that is desired. It is more realistic to expect that a series of experiences over a considerable time will be needed by each student to develop the necessary understanding, skills and value clarification.

In the following paragraphs, several teaching strategies are presented which may be effective in reinforcing one or more of the special skills noted in the model. A brief description of the purpose of the strategy is provided. Variations of each of these strategies are common as different teachers desire to alter the strategies to suit their own teaching situations. Although these teaching strategies have been arranged to show application to a specific part of the model, they could be used in any part of the model. Although only one reference has been provided for each strategy listed, all of these strategies are common and a description of their use can be found in various references.

Immediately following each suggested teaching strategy is an example of an application of that strategy to help industrial arts students become aware of feelings, attitudes and values, and to help them develop skills relating to affective learning. These applications relate to a variety of issues common to industrial arts at the middle and senior high school levels.

Values Voting

This strategy is sometimes used as a starting point for the discussion of feelings, value clarification, or decision-making. The teacher introduces an issue by asking the students a question and having them respond as if they were voting. This strategy helps students realize that others may see issues the same or quite differently from themselves. It also is used very effectively as a guide for feedback or evaluation by the teacher. (*Values and Attitude Handbook*, 1980, p. 48.)

Application to Industrial Arts: At a middle school, the teacher initiates an activity or unit by asking industrial arts students to respond to several questions by a show of hands. The teacher starts each question with the words, "How many of you . . .?" Each of the first three questions relates to issues concerning content which might be studied in industrial arts. The remaining three questions relate to issues concerning the industrial arts laboratory which most teachers feel a need to discuss. Additional questions for discussion purposes are also provided.

"How many of you . . .

1. feel that most people waste energy?"
   "What types of energy do they waste?"
   "How could they be more conservative?"

2. feel that many new products are not safe for our use?"
   "What products aren't safe?"
   "How could they be improved?"

3. feel that you would like to some day work in industry?"
   "What type of job would you select?"
   "Why would you like to do that type of work?"

4. feel that safety glasses should be worn at all times in the laboratory?"
   "How often do you wear your safety glasses?"
   "What alternatives exist which would still result in a safe working environment?"

5. feel proud of the results of the assignment you have just completed?"

"What makes you feel that way?"

"What things would you like to change about your performance on your assignment?"

6. believe that all people should clean up their own work areas when they have finished working?"

"Are there any situations where you shouldn't be expected to clean up your work area?"

"Do you check your work area each time you leave to see if you have left any tools or materials out?"

Strongly Agree/Strongly Disagree

This technique forces students to examine the strength of their feelings about certain issues. Students are asked to indicate their reaction to a given statement. This technique usually allows the student five options from which to choose. This technique also helps students and others assess their feelings toward a particular value. (Simon, Howe, Kirschenbaum, 1972, p. 252)

Application to Industrial Arts: Students are given the following sentence to read: "Everyone should become computer literate." Students are then given an opportunity to consider their feelings about this statement and mark accordingly on a continuum. The five most common responses included on a continuum are "Strongly Agree," "Agree," "Undecided," "Disagree," and "Strongly Disagree." Several questions regarding the same issue may be responded to by students. After the responses have been completed, volunteers may be selected to explain their views and choices.

Values Continuum

This technique helps students identify opposing viewpoints on a given issue. It also helps students identify the strength and direction of their own feeling about the issue involved. Students usually select a number on a continuum to indicate how closely their feelings or values are relating to the two opposing alternatives. This technique also helps students begin to understand that the solutions to many problems and issues are not "one" or the "other," but rather a compromise somewhere between the two. (Simon, Howe, Kirschenbaum, 1972, p. 116)

Application to Industrial Arts: The industrial arts teacher has identified "Product Quality" as an important issue for discussion in the classroom. In this strategy, students first identify several views cerning the quality of American products when compared to similar products from other countries. Two views are selected to be placed at opposite ends of the continuum as shown below:

"How would you rate American products in comparison to products from foreign countries?"

American products are . . . . Foreign products
much better.   are much better.

Each student places a mark on the continuum to indicate his or her position on the issue. Individual student responses can be later transferred to a class chart which will allow each student to assess his or her feelings in relation to the feelings of the entire class. Many other questions can be posed to generate additional discussion.

I Learned . . . Statements

This strategy is used after students have participated in a values activity discussion. Students are asked the question "What did you learn about yourself or your values as a result of the activity?" Students are given an opportunity to think of their answers and then are asked to respond either verbally or in writing. This technique helps students clarify and reinforce values and provides feedback to the teacher. Similar questions may also be used effectively. (Simon, Howe, Kirschenbaum, 1972, p. 163)

Application to Industrial Arts: Industrial arts students have just returned from a field trip to a small industry. Prior to going on the field trip the students had been requested to observe the working conditions, safety precautions, and the job characteristics during the visit. Students are asked to respond in writing to the question "What did you learn or realize about working conditions, safety, or job characteristics from this field trip?" After responding individually, students will form small groups to compare and discuss their responses.

TEACHING STRATEGIES
FOR PROBLEM-SOLVING SKILLS

The following teaching strategies have been selected as being effective in helping students in the industrial arts classroom develop problem solving skills.

Brainstorming

In this teaching strategy, students are asked to use their imaginations to provide as many solutions to a given problem as possible. This encourages students to think about the problem and to search for alternatives. (Simon, Howe, Kirschenbaum, 1972, p. 204)

Application to Industrial Arts: Industrial arts students may be asked to think of as many ways as possible in which students could conserve materials in the classroom. A similar question might ask students to think of ways to encourage students to clean up after working in the laboratory. Responses from the students may not solve the problem but may bring about a student awareness of the problem.

Alternative Action Search

This strategy encourages students to consider alternatives for action in specific situations. The teacher initiates the activity by describing a situation which calls for some proposed action. Each student writes down what he would do in the given situation and the responses are discussed in small groups to see if one action can be selected as most desirable. (Simon, Howe, Kirschenbaum, 1972, p. 198)

Application to Industrial Arts: The teacher presents the following situation to a group of industrial arts students. "In an industrial arts laboratory a safety rule exists which states that 'All students must wear safety glasses while operating machines.' You see one of your classmates operating a machine without safety glasses. The teacher does not see the student, but the teacher has already reprimanded the student on two previous occasions for not wearing safety glasses." What would you do? After responding individually and in small groups, the discussion may be opened to the entire class.

Consequence Search

In this teaching strategy, students are asked to identify many possible consequences if a certain action were taken or avoided. This is designed as a follow-up activity to the "Alternative Search" strategy and it encourages students to consider the consequences of each alternative they consider. (Simon, Howe, Kirschenbaum, 1972, p. 207)

Application in Industrial Arts: Industrial arts students are asked to identify as many consequences as possible which might happen if a person decides not to perform the recommended maintenance on a product or piece of equipment. The responses may be recorded on the chalkboard or a chart and may include both immediate and secondary consequences. The probability of the consequence happening may also be assessed.

The Free Choice Game

This game is usually played in small groups with one person relating a problem in his life which requires a decision. The problem may be real or simulated. Others in the group ask questions to gain information and clarify the problems; to explore alternatives and consequences; and to explore feelings about the choice. This game helps both the individual student and the group members insure that a systematic approach is used in solving the problem. It also helps students to clarify values concerning the issue.

Application to Industrial Arts: The industrial arts class is divided into groups of four or five students in each group. In one group Alan, a student, outlines the following problem regarding the purchase of safety glasses. "Alan's school announced that all students participating in industrial arts classes must purchase a particular type of safety glasses. Alan did not have the money himself to purchase the glasses, so he asked his father for the money. His father refused to give him the money indicating that he felt the glasses were overpriced and that for the types of things they were going to be doing in the industrial arts laboratory, safety glasses weren't really necessary." After hearing the story, students are to question Alan in an effort to help him clarify his feelings and values and to make an appropriate decision regarding the situation.

TEACHING STRATEGIES FOR ANTICIPATING DECISION CONSEQUENCES

The following strategies can be used in helping students prepare for the probable consequences of a decision and in initiating action on one's choice regarding various issues.

Pattern Searches

In this strategy, students identify as many patterns of their actions as possible. They may determine which of these patterns they wish to keep and which they wish to stop. Their decision should reflect some thought and possible discussion regarding their attitudes and values. (Simon, Howe, Kirschenbaum, 1972, p. 214)

Application to Industrial Arts: Several weeks after classes have started, students are asked to list as many "patterns" as they can think of which they use in the industrial arts laboratory. Each student is then asked to consider each pattern and determine if they should continue it, halt it, or modify it. Some students may wish to develop new patterns. Hopefully, the patterns which are beneficial to the students can be continued in other aspects of their lives.

Public Affirmation/Testimony

This strategy involves students in making a public affirmation about one of their values. This might be done in writing or verbally. Students may be asked to present "what they believe" and "why they hold that belief."

Application to Industrial Arts: The industrial arts teacher asks for student volunteers to tell the class about a recent dangerous incident involving a product or a piece of equipment. The students will also be encouraged to relate their feelings about the incident and to share any resolutions they have made as a result of their experience. After each student has related to the incident, questions and/or discussions may follow. This strategy may also be used if an unexpected incident happens in the industrial arts laboratory.

Record Keeping For Self-Evaluation

Accurate information obtained from records can be valuable in helping students assess their behavior. They may use information from records to identify future goals and they may also use records to determine their progress in obtaining these goals. Students involved in some form of record keeping are also reminded of the objective each time they record information (Simon, Howe, Kirschenbaum, 1972, p. 388)

Application in Industrial Arts: Jack, an industrial arts student, always seems to be behind on his class assignments. The teacher suggests that maybe he would do better if he budgeted his time. The teacher encourages Jack to keep a record for one week noting how he used his time in the laboratory. Categories for time entries might include: Getting tools and materials out; Talking to others; Problem solving; Constructing the project; and Cleaning the work area. After the time estimates have been recorded, Jack and the teacher review the results to determine if time is being wasted in any areas and what might be done to prevent this from happening. Even if no conclusions can be made from these records, the activity will help Jack become more conscious of his use of time in the laboratory. Jack may also wish to repeat the activity again at the end of the course and compare the records to determine if he has been able to use his time more efficiently.

Information Search

Making good decisions and clarifying values both depend upon having adequate information. Too often students make decisions or develop values without having adequate and accurate information. This strategy directs students to obtain additional information which will be used in their decision making or value clarification. A variety of assignments may be given to help students achieve this objective.

Application to Industrial Arts: Industrial arts students are given the assignment to contact a worker in an industry (parent, relative, friend) and ask this person to provide certain information about his or her job. Questions asked by the students might include: "What do you like best about your job?" "What do you like least about your job?" "What is the salary or wage for your job?" "How would you describe the working conditions of your job?" The questions selected for the interviews can be determined by the students. Information gathered can be placed on a chart to allow some comparisons. Students are asked to identify which jobs seem most appealing to them, and to identify the reasons for that selection.

STRATEGIES FOR TEACHING PATTERN AND CONSISTENCY

The following strategies can be used in helping students in industrial arts act with pattern and consistency concerning specific issues.

Goal/Objective Setting

After students have identified some goals they would like to achieve, they are given the opportunity to identify objectives which will accomplish that goal. Students may also be asked to consider the criteria for completing each objective. (*Values and Attitude Handbook,* 1980, p. 70)

Application to Industrial Arts: The industrial arts teacher provides all students with goal sheets and requests that students identify several goals which they would like to achieve during the course. Goals may be written for safety, personal behavior, work skills, completion of projects, and quality of work. Students are then asked to identify several objectives which relate to the accomplishment of each goal. The teacher has an individual conference with each student to discuss the goals and objectives and to possibly advise.

Role-playing

In this strategy students are asked to assume the roles of people in a hypothetical situation involving some type of perceived issues or conflict. Students act out a solution, and later discussion may be used to determine the appropriateness of student decisions and behavior.

Application to Industrial Arts: Students in an industrial arts classroom have been discussing employability and job interviewing skills. The teacher outlines for the class a job interview setting which could be role-played. Volunteer students are selected to play the roles of a receptionist, an employee doing the interviewing, and an employee seeking a job. After the role-playing episode is completed, the participants may verbally express their feelings. Students may raise questions concerning some of the actions or behavior. Recommendations for improving the technique of interviewing may be made. The teacher may recommend that another group of students role-play the same situation so that a comparison of techniques can be discussed.

Reaction Statements

A thought-provoking statement is placed somewhere in the classroom by the teacher. After students have had ample opportunity to read it and think about it, the teacher asks students to react to it by making statements or by asking questions.

Application in Industrial Arts: An industrial arts teacher places a large sign next to one of the machines in the laboratory. It reads "This machine can hurt you." Several days later, the teacher asks for volunteers to react to that statement. Several dangerous aspects of the machine may be mentioned. Several safety rules may also be mentioned. This strategy will start students thinking about an issue or problem and the sign may serve as a constant reminder.

APPLICATION OF SELECTED TEACHING STRATEGIES TO REINFORCE AFFECTIVE LEARNING IN INDUSTRIAL ARTS AT DIFFERENT GRADE LEVELS

Following are three examples of incorporating an emphasis on affective education in industrial arts. The first example relates to an industrial arts activity at the elementary grade level. The second example relates to a ten-week industrial arts course at the middle school level; and the third example relates to an industrial arts class at the senior high level. A brief description of the unit or course activities, content and objectives are provided at the beginning of each example. Examples of various teaching strategies are then presented to demonstrate how a teacher might assist students in becoming aware of their feelings, attitudes, developing values and goal setting skills, and responsible behavior.

INFUSING AFFECTIVE EDUCATION INTO ELEMENTARY SCHOOL INDUSTRIAL ARTS

At the elementary level, industrial arts is often included as part of an integrated teaching unit. A motivational topic is selected by the teacher which often relates to social studies, science, or technology. A variety of content areas relating to the main topic are integrated into the unit through various activities. Opportunities for including affective education are numerous in any unit of this nature.

The following example of an integrated teaching unit is designed for the fourth grade level. The title of the unit is "Manufacturing." The main goals of the unit are to help children:

— Gain an understanding of the processes of manufacturing;
— Gain insights into the role of manufacturing in our society;
— Reinforce basic skills such as math and language arts;
— Have opportunity for self-awareness and career exploration;
— Develop and/or reinforce social and basic work skills.

Subject areas pursued during this unit will include: math, science, language arts, industrial arts, and career education. The main activity will involve students in simulated roles as workers in a manufacturing industry. The fourth grade students will first simulate the formation of two classroom manufacturing companies. Students in each of these companies will design or select a simple product which will be mass produced on an assembly line. These classroom assembly lines will be engineered, constructed, and operated by student workers. Students will also be involved in the sale of the product after it has been produced. Activities of this nature (simulations) have been successfully implemented with a number of fourth grade classes in the Ypsilanti, Michigan area.

Students participating in this unit will achieve to varying degrees the goals listed above and most will consider their experiences to be very enjoyable and memorable. In addition, with a conscious effort by the teacher, the students can have valuable experiences relating to affective learning. If career education becomes a major focus of this unit, aspects of affective education will already be included in the forms of self-awareness and decision-making activities.

The remaining part of this sample unit does not go into detail concerning the structure of subject matter or activities. What is provided in the following pages are samples of teaching strategies designed to pursue affective learning. The children are asked to think about their feelings and attitudes during the activity. They will be given opportunity to develop techniques for making good decisions, and involved in making decisions which will relate either to their own personal involvement in the activity or to the operation of the company. The children will also have opportunity to implement most of the decisions which are made. Some of the decisions will be made by the entire class, some by groups of students, and some by individuals. Decisions which appear to the teacher to be inappropriate will be discussed to insure that the procedure for reaching the conclusion was appropriate and valid.

The teaching strategies listed below are appropriate for use in assisting children to develop an awareness of the role and processes of manufacturing and to become aware of their own feelings and attitudes experienced during the activities.

1. Brainstorming — uses of products
2. Career Exploration — learning about work associated with manufacturing
3. Likes/Dislikes — identification of enjoyable tasks and student strengths
4. Role-playing — role-playing employment or employee problems
5. Decision-making — based upon valuing and including a consequence search for alternatives
6. Record Keeping — keeping records for personal consideration
7. Feelings Analysis — identification of strong feelings experienced during the activity
8. Self and Peer Evaluation — evaluating performances

Additional information about the use of each teaching strategy in the unit is provided in the following paragraphs.

Brainstorming

Brainstorming techniques will be used on several occasions to introduce different topics and concepts. Usually the elementary teacher will ask a question, allow the students a brief opportunity to think about responses, and then ask for volunteers to respond verbally. One of the initial questions asked of students is "What are some ways in which people use products?" The teacher will lead the class in a discussion concerning the importance of products to everyone.

Brainstorming will also be used later as students identify potential products which could be produced in the classroom. At the end of the unit, students may be asked to brainstorm ways for improving the production activity.

Career Exploration

As part of this strategy, students are given assignments to identify various types of workers who are involved in manufacturing. They are also to identify some of the training received by the workers and some of the tasks carried out by the workers. Parents who work in manufacturing industries may be involved as guest speakers to provide insights into the values and feelings held by workers in manufacturing. Through the use of occupational information literature and systems, students acquire some insights into the training, type of work and responsibilities of the workers.

Likes/Dislikes

In this strategy, all of the types of work responsibilities (simulated jobs) for this classroom activity are placed on a sheet and distributed to each student. Students are asked to identify those tasks which they think they would like doing and those tasks they feel they would dislike. The same information could be obtained by having students complete a "job application" form. Similar results could also be obtained by using the "Rank-Order" strategy or the "Value Continuum" strategy. This information should help each student select the most appropriate occupation to simulate during the activity.

Role-Playing

All students can be involved in at least one role-playing episode. Students may be asked to brainstorm situations about the workers which would have relevance to the tasks they are about to perform in the activity. During the role-playing activity, small groups of students will demonstrate to the rest of the class some of the values workers hold, some of the problems workers face, or some of the ways they are likely to solve certain problems.

Decision-Making

Opportunities for decision-making will be presented to the students throughout the activity. During most of these decision-making opportunities, several additional teaching strategies will be introduced to focus on various elements of the decision-making process. For example, a "Rank Ordering" technique may be used to help students determine feelings and attitudes. Brief questionnaires or interviews may be used by students to survey other students in the school to determine the type of product they might purchase and the price they would be willing to pay. A "Consequence Search" may also be included in regard to some of the alternatives which have been considered. Brainstorming alternatives to some of the manufacturing processes should eventually involve consideration of the consequences. Students should be encouraged to insure that all decisions have included a careful consideration of values and that a proper decision-making procedure was followed.

Record Keeping

Several different types of records will be kept during the production activity. Most of these records will relate to the accounting necessary for operation of the company. However, the teacher will stress the necessity of being precise in certain situations and of keeping records. Students may be asked to brainstorm advantages of keeping accurate records.

Feelings Analysis

After the activity has been completed, students are asked to identify any strong feelings they may have had during the activities in the unit. If certain feelings are expressed which others might have had, the teacher may also wish to use the "voting" technique and ask "How many of you had the same feelings?"

Self/Peer Evaluation

During the teaching strategy students are given an opportunity to evaluate their own performance regarding how successful they were in completing their part of the activity. They may also identify how they might have performed better. This information is usually not shared with the entire class. Students may, however, wish to make statements to the entire class concerning the evaluation of the activity without mentioning individual workers by name.

INFUSING AFFECTIVE EDUCATION INTO MIDDLE SCHOOL INDUSTRIAL ARTS

At the middle school level, students in industrial arts classes are often rotated every ten-twelve weeks to study a different aspect of industry. Typical classes include woodworking, metalworking, drafting, electricity, and power and energy. In some schools several of these areas will be combined into one area and called a "general shop." These courses are usually designed to help students develop skill and understanding with regard to the processes and materials used in industry. In this type of educational setting, affective learning is usually limited to discussions and control of behavior regarding laboratory organization, safety, and maintenance. Additional utilization of affective learning may be promoted by a classroom incident and would be discussed at the discretion of the teacher.

More recent and innovative industrial arts curriculums, such as the Industrial Arts Curriculum Project and the American Industries Project, have shifted the emphasis of study. Rather than focusing almost entirely on projects, materials, and skills relating to the construction of projects, the student learns about many of the careers, processes, and problems associated with industry. Career education and affective learning are already a part of the class content in these programs. For example, at the end of each chapter in the IACP Construction textbook (Lux, 1970), a section is titled "Think About It." This offers students the opportunity to reflect on some of the feelings, values, attitudes, or decisions, associated with topics in that chapter. The teacher has more opportunity to incorporate affective learning into this type of class because more topics are covered which can be related directly to the student's life.

One of the most common content areas of study in middle school industrial arts classes is woodworking. In a typical introductory woodworking class students are involved in learning facts and in developing special woodworking skills. The facts learned often relate to information concerning the identification, use, and maintenance of tools, machines, materials, and processes. The skills developed relate to such actions as measuring, calculating, cutting, shaping, fastening, and finishing. The result is usually some type of project which the student will proudly display.

The nature of these laboratory activities already involves students in some aspects of value clarification and decision-making. However, there is often a lack of awareness on the part of the students that they are formulating and using values, attitudes, and feelings to make decisions. Teachers can help students become more aware of their values and attitudes and the decision-making process by including some additional affective learning teaching strategies in the curriculum.

Common goals for students in a middle school woodworking course are to:

— Develop skills and acquire knowledge regarding the use of woodworking tools and machines and materials;

— Develop and use proper laboratory operating procedures including safety, clean-up, maintenance, and conservation of materials;

— Develop an understanding of industry and how it utilizes raw materials (especially wood) to produce products.

In most industrial arts laboratory situations, the teacher is expected to make a concerted effort to encourage student behavior which will result in a safe, efficient, and organized laboratory. Using various teaching strategies, the teacher will encourage students to think about their values and feelings concerning various issues and to apply these values as they make decisions. Educational films, magazine and newspaper articles, guest speakers, and personal experiences may all have an influence on the student in clarifying values.

Several issues may be introduced to the class to help students understand the role that wood plays in everyone's life. This may include discussions concerning the use of national forests; characteristics of occupations associated with wood products; our daily use of wood products; and the previous and future reliance on wood as a major material for products.

The teaching strategies listed below can be used effectively by the middle school industrial arts teacher in a woodworking class to promote affective learning.

1. Feelings Analysis
2. Attitude Inventory
3. Valuing Skills
4. Brainstorming and Questioning Techniques
5. Career Exploration
6. Reaction sheets
7. Decision making
8. Public Display

Feelings Analysis

The strategy of using "Feeling Analysis" is often effective at the introduction of a discussion or activity and in evaluation after the discussion or activity has taken place. Following are some of the ways in which this teaching strategy can be used in a woodworking class at the middle school level.

On the first day of class, students may be asked to identify their feelings concerning a number of issues which might be of some concern to them. Following are some possible questions which could be asked. Students may respond either verbally or in writing depending upon the teacher's purpose in asking the question and the type of questions posed.

1. Do you feel apprehensive about using any of the machines in the laboratory?
2. Do you feel capable of making this particular project? (An example is shown by the teacher.)
3. Do you feel that safety procedures should be followed in the laboratory?
4. How do you feel about sharing a locker with one of your classmates?
5. How do you feel about the way the class is cleaning up the laboratory at the end of the class period?
6. How do you feel about your finished project? How do others feel about your finished project?

Attitude Inventory

If teachers want to assess feelings and attitudes more accurately, they may wish to use a pre-test and post-test "Attitude Inventory." The pre-test is given to students during one of the first class periods and asks each student to circle either the "Yes" response, "Undecided" response, or the "No" response. Following are sample questions which a teacher may wish to ask students in a woodworking course. Comparing the results of the post-test with the results of the pre-test will indicate a percentage of change of attitudes on the subjects covered.

Attitude Inventory

1. Trees have many beneficial uses.
   YES   UNDECIDED   NO
2. Many of the products we use are made from wood.
   YES   UNDECIDED   NO
3. There is an unlimited supply of wood for people to use.
   YES   UNDECIDED   NO
4. Most of the workers in a company which makes wood products work with handtools and small machines.
   YES   UNDECIDED   NO
5. I enjoy making things using wood.
   YES   UNDECIDED   NO

6. All people should clean up their own work areas after working on a project.
   YES   UNDECIDED   NO

7. All people should put away the things that they get out at home.
   YES   UNDECIDED   NO

8. I don't mind getting my hands dirty.
   YES   UNDECIDED   NO

9. Students should follow safety rules while working in the laboratory.
   YES   UNDECIDED   NO

10. People should follow safety rules while at home and in the community.
    YES   UNDECIDED   NO

11. Mathematics and science are not used by people who make products in a woodworking laboratory.
    YES   UNDECIDED   NO

12. I like working with machines.
    YES   UNDECIDED   NO

13. This course will provide me with information and skills which I can use in the future.
    YES   UNDECIDED   NO

14. I will try to do my very best work on each project I make.
    YES   UNDECIDED   NO

15. I should select a project to make that I like and can use.
    YES   UNDECIDED   NO

16. Someday, I might like to work as a carpenter.
    YES   UNDECIDED   NO

17. With extra effort, a wooden project can be constructed and finished to look very attractive.
    YES   UNDECIDED   NO

18. I could make some of the expensive wood products I see in stores.
    YES   UNDECIDED   NO

19. Pieces of wood can be used to help accomplish many different types of tasks.
    YES   UNDECIDED   NO

20. Before making major decisions, I usually identify the possible alternatives.
    YES   UNDECIDED   NO

Valuing Skills

On the first day of class, the industrial arts teacher asks all students to complete the information requested regarding their assessment of their own skills. Students respond by placing the information on a card. Questions may include the following:

1. What previous experiences have you had using hand tools and machines to construct some type of wooden project?
2. With assistance from the teacher, will you be able to use the woodworking hand tools with confidence?
3. With assistance from the teacher, will you be able to properly use the power woodworking machines located in the laboratory with confidence?
4. With assistance from the teacher, will you be able to construct a project which you will feel proud of?
5. With your skills and abilities, could you design a woodworking project which you and others would appreciate?
6. With your present skills and abilities, could you put a finish on a project which you and others would appreciate?

Information gained from this teaching strategy will help the teacher determine which students need more self-confidence in their laboratory experiences. Also, in completing this survey, students are analyzing their own skills, which is one aspect of affective learning.

Brainstorming and Questioning Techniques

The technique of brainstorming is very useful in helping students identify alternatives for solving a problem. It may also be used to help students formulate thoughts about various issues presented in the class. Following are several issues which might be brainstormed and discussed by students in a beginning woodworking course.

1. What are some uses of trees?
2. What types of products in our society still require the use of large quantities of wood?
3. What skills will be necessary to successfully complete a given project?

4. What are different types of injuries which might occur in the woodworking laboratory?

5. What are some of the desirable characteristics of a good project which you should consider?

6. What clean-up procedures should be used to insure that all tools and materials are replaced at the end of the class period?

7. What are some rules which you would recommend for everyone using the woodworking laboratory?

For added emphasis, each of these questions may be preceded with a problem situation. For example, prior to asking question number six above, the teacher may indicate that many problems exist with the present clean-up system. Tools have not been put away properly and some machines have not been cleaned. Students in following industrial arts classes have had to spend extra time cleaning the machines before they could use them, and several students have been delayed working on their projects because the special tools they needed were not properly returned to the tool rack. This description of the situation will help students become more aware of the existing problems, require some thought and consideration for solutions, and help students feel they have contributed to the solution of the problem.

Career Exploration

Students will be given an assignment to select an occupation which involves working with trees, using substantial amounts of wood, or making some type of wood products. The teacher may have a list of occupations prepared for students to select from. Each student is to seek information about that occupation concerning the type of work done, education, training and skill requirements, and characteristics of the work. Next, students are to identify those characteristics of the work which they feel they would most enjoy and those characteristics which they would not like. They may also identify aspects of the job which they might be qualified to do. Near the end of the course, each student makes a brief verbal report to the class presenting interesting and pertinent information about the occupation they selected.

This teaching strategy brings awareness to the students concerning the number and types of occupations which use wood as a major material for products. This strategy also helps students assess their own likes/dislikes, feelings, and values concerning future occupations which they might consider. A variety of other student activities can be used to help students explore careers.

Reaction Sheets

Several weeks after the industrial arts class has started, the teacher provides each student with a reaction sheet. Each student is asked to react to the questions on this sheet. Some of the questions should be answered each week. Others may be answered whenever the student desires. Each entry is dated. The questions need not relate exclusively to industrial arts. Following is a sampling of questions which might be used:

1. What important decisions did you make this week?
2. What important decisions did you make relating to your industrial arts classwork?
3. Were your values and/or feelings involved in these decisions?
4. Did you rely heavily on the advice of someone else to make these decisions?
5. Do you feel good about the things you attempted and/or accomplished during the past week?
6. What happened this week that you felt very good about?
7. What went wrong during the week?
8. What are some things which you learned that you feel are very important to remember?

The purpose of this technique is to promote student thinking concerning value clarification and decision-making. Periodically, the teacher will review the responses with the student. After several responses have been made, students may wish to make some resolutions concerning their future actions.

Decision-Making

Decision-making skills should be reinforced at all grade levels. Students should be encouraged to carefully identify problems, search for alternative solutions, consider the consequences of each alternative, make the best decision, and initiate action required by the decision. To reinforce these skills, each student is given a problem to solve which will require application of the decision-making process. Problems solved by the student may be real or contrived by the teacher. Following is a statement of an example problem:

"Only one lathe exists in the industrial arts laboratory. Not enough class time exists for each student to have ample time to make a lathe project and develop some skills and understanding of the lathe."

After identifying the problem, students will be asked to identify several possible alternative solutions to the problem and to indicate the probable consequences of each alternative action. The chart shown below may be used as a guideline.

Desired Consequences

ALTERNATIVES	MACHINE SHOULD GET MAXIMUM USE	POLICY SHOULD BE FAIR TO ALL	ALL STUDENTS LEARN A SKILL
Alternative #1 No one uses the lathe		XX	
Alternative #2 First student there uses the lathe	X		
Alternative #3 A few students are selected to use the lathe	X		
Alternative #4 Each student uses the lathe briefly for an introduction	X	XX	

After identifying alternatives and consequences, students may wish to rank the consequences as to their importance. If one consequence is desired more than the others, a second "X" may be placed on the chart indicating the significance of that consequence. Different results from the same problem may be due to some students placing a different value on the desired consequences. The teacher should review the information presented on the charts and the resulting decision to determine if students used a proper decision making procedure.

Public Display

Placing an article of some type on public display may often generate thoughts and feelings by those who view it. In some cases, the article might represent a student's outstanding effort at design or workmanship. Placing a project on display which demonstrates excellent craftsmanship, skill, creativity or design may generate enthusiasm in others to improve their level of performance. Other displays might represent an attempt by the teacher to have students heed certain safety rules. Displaying a broken hammer handle or a broken wood chisel blade may serve as a reminder to students that tools should be used properly and safety rules followed. Other reactions may be felt and could be shared.

INFUSING AFFECTIVE LEARNING INTO INDUSTRIAL ARTS AT THE SENIOR HIGH SCHOOL

At the senior high school level industrial arts courses are often specialized and technical, focusing on just one area of industry or technology. Although affective learning activities are usually not part of the planned course content, they can be infused with some effort by the teacher. To demonstrate how opportunities for affective learning could be created in senior high industrial arts, several teaching strategies are provided in the following pages. These strategies are designed to enhance affective learning in an introductory auto mechanics course.

Students in a typical auto mechanics course are involved primarily in learning about systems of the automobile. Course objectives might include having each student diagnose specific problems using automotive testing equipment and also disassembly and assembly of automotive components which may need repair.

Some of the diagnosis and problem solving procedures used in an auto mechanics class are very similar to aspects of the decision-making process used in affective education. For example, in both areas, the student must first identify the problem. This may include considering several possible alternatives to test. Once the problem has been identified, alternatives and their consequences are considered for solving the problem. Students may be asked to make a decision selecting the solution they feel is best. They may also be asked to provide a recommended solution for a customer and to justify that recommendation. In both situations the decision-making process should be similar and the student will be involved in reinforcing decision-making skills.

Many of the same aspects of affective learning presented at the elementary and/or middle school level will be repeated at the senior high school level. Most industrial arts teachers will make some efforts to encourage students to develop certain attitudes and behavior regarding classroom safety, clean-up, and work skills. However, additional opportunities can be created. Some of the affective learning areas to pursue could include: job values, decision-making, personal skill and goal development, value clarification, and occupational work skills.

Several specific examples of teaching strategies for infusing affective learning in senior high school industrial arts are presented below.

Rating Sheets

Near the beginning of the course, the teacher prepares and distributes to all students a list of qualities which might be important to a successful auto mechanic. Students are asked to indicate their responses by circling those letters which best represent their feelings about each statement.

To be successful, auto mechanics must:

	Strongly Agree	Agree	Undecided	Disagree	Strongly Disagree
1. Have a college degree.					X
2. Be honest.		X			
3. Work long and hard hours.		X			
4. Get along well with people.		X			
5. Know how to repair foreign autos.			X		
6. Be precise in their work.					
7. Own their own tools.					
8. Enjoy getting their hands dirty.				X	
9. Be able to read and write.					
10. Communicate their ideas to others.					
11. Be punctual.					
12. Follow safety rules.					
13. Carefully clean up tools and the work area.					
14. Have a high level of technical information about automobiles.					
15. Be physically strong.					
16. Be a Caucasian male.					
17. Be certified by the State Department.					
18. Not smoke or be overweight.					
19. Be able to operate a microcomputer.					
20. Have good work habits.					

After students have reacted individually to each of these statements, group ratings can be tabulated for discussion by the entire class. Job characteristics identified on this rating sheet can be related to several aspects of the students' lives and especially to any future jobs the students may be interested in pursuing. A few of these statements rated "very important" for an auto mechanic, may become classroom goals for some of the students to achieve.

First Hand Experiences (Field trip)

Providing students with a field trip to a local auto repair shop, a service station, or an automobile manufacturing plant can give them an opportunity to experience some realistic working conditions. This trip may be combined with a "reactions strategy" in which students are to identify their reactions and feelings to the things they observed and felt on the field trip. Reactions may be either positive or negative. Students may also be asked to identify and make a record of specific job characteristics or working conditions which they may observe. These may be discussed later to insure that all students are fully aware of the existing conditions.

Action Project

Near the conclusion of the course, arrangements are made by the teacher for students in the auto mechanics course to apply their knowledge and skills by participating in specific diagnostic tests on personal automobiles. For a minimal charge, students will evaluate the condition of several systems of each automobile. Feelings and attitudes associated with meeting deadlines, dealing with customers, and accuracy and pride in one's work may be discussed after the project is completed. If specific problems develop during the project this will most likely provide opportunity for one or more students to utilize their decision-making and problem-solving skills.

Group activities may later be used to involve other students in determining how they would react in a similar situation.

Contrived Incident

During the action project, the teacher may wish to arrange one or more "contrived incidents" for the purpose of enhancing affective learning. This might include such incidents as "pre-arranging" a customer to become very angry and demand his money back because of poor service or workmanship. Or, a part on one of the automobiles may be arranged to break just as the student attempts to remove it for testing. Values, attitudes, feelings, may all enter into the student's decision in solving the "contrived" problem. The teacher may wish to have several follow-up discussions relating to the incident to determine if alternative actions might have been better. The teacher should be sure to fully explain the purpose and arrangements of the contrived incident to the students after it has been completed.

Resumé

Every student should have some knowledge of how to develop a resumé. A resumé is a record of the student's most significant skills, experiences, and achievements which will indicate probable success in a job. Many students will need to prepare and use a resumé before they graduate from high school. The efforts required to complete a resumé can contribute significantly to the student's affective learning.

The industrial arts teacher may ask the auto mechanics students to develop a personal resumé which would help convince an employer to hire them. This assignment would require each student to select a job related to the field of automotives (mechanic, manager, engineer, designer, product worker, sales person, etc.) for which they are most suited.

To develop the resumé, students must identify themselves. They must analyze their skills, experiences, and achievements, make a record of the most notable things and use this information to convince others of their overall ability to be a successful worker. Students must give careful thought to identifying their strengths and weaknesses.

During the process of preparing a resumé they will become involved in self-evaluation, valuing, organization, and eventually in decision making and expression. Some students who identify a personal deficiency may make a resolution to do something about it. In addition to self-identification, most students will also become more aware of the requirements for getting and holding a job.

Although the teacher may present general guidelines to the class for developing the resumés, the teacher should work with each student to insure that resumés are accurate and effective.

Job Interview

Most people will experience many job interviews during their lives and for some students their first opportunities for interviews will happen while they are still in high school. Students must realize that just being qualified for a job may not result in getting the job. Employers may often rely heavily on impressions gained from an interview as an additional consideration for hiring employees. Being prepared for the interview will help students insure their success at the interview. Teachers can help students realize that they must convince the employer that they are the best person for the job. The efforts required to prepare for a job interview can also provide students with many opportunities for affective learning.

Initially, the industrial arts teacher should provide students with general information and suggestions for successful interviewing. This information could be appropriate for any job. A variety of educational materials about interviewing are available.

In the previous assignment, students were asked to prepare a resumé which could be used in making application for a job at a selected company. For this assignment, students are to assume they have been granted an interview with this same company. The initial part of this assignment requires each student to list all steps necessary to prepare for a job interview. This includes:

— Gathering knowledge about the job;
— Gathering knowledge about the company;
— Identifying items to take for the interview;
— Identifying questions which might be asked by the interviewer;
— Preparing answers which might be given in response to anticipated questions;
— Preparing questions which might be asked of the interviewer;
— Preparations which should be made for a personal appearance;
— Do's and Don'ts to remember during the interview.

Next, each student must use a variety of resources to complete these tasks.

After students have had the opportunity to make all of the preparations for their interview, several students are selected to role-play an interview situation. The teacher or another student may serve as the interviewer. Interview questions are prepared ahead of time.

After the role-playing has been completed, the teacher or other class members should critique the conversations and actions of the interview sessions.

These and many other teaching strategies will be successful for the industrial arts teacher if used in a receptive environment. The atmosphere of the classroom is important for affective learning to take place. Students and teachers must have mutual respect for each other and be willing to communicate. Without some degree of rapport, teaching strategies may not be very effective. With efforts from all teachers, students can become more confident and skillful in developing values and making decisions.

SUMMARY

A major educational goal for all students is to have them become self-actualized. To accomplish this, students must develop an understanding of their feelings, attitudes, and values, and be capable of using their values to make good decisions.

Adult guidance for helping students develop these skills and understandings will range from a domineering environment where students are allowed little or no opportunity for independent decision-making, to complete freedom in an unsupervised environment. A careful blending of both is necessary to insure guidance for the student in times of need, and provide opportunity to experience independent decision-making.

The industrial arts teacher has ample opportunities to provide this required guidance and assistance. However, the teacher must first be self-actualized — aware of his or her own feelings and attitudes; aware of the importance and the process of clarifying values; and aware of the decision-making process. It also requires a conscious effort on the part of the teacher to include affective learning experiences for the students. Some of these experiences are often inherent in industrial arts courses, while others need to be planned and added.

A variety of teaching strategies exist which the industrial arts teacher may use to provide students with affective learning experiences. These strategies will encourage students to think about their feelings, attitudes, or values and to develop a systematic approach to valuing and decision-making. Many of these strategies will require some type of adaptation in the course content or the laboratory situation. Most of them are not designed to result in the student's selection of a particular value or decision, but rather to develop the skills for the process of valuing and decision-making.

REFERENCES

Bell, Julia; Bennett, S.; & J. Fallace. "From Inculcation to Action: A Continuum for Values Education." In Alfred S. Alschuler (editor) *Values Concepts and Techniques.* Revised edition, National Education Association, Washington, D.C., 1982.

Brown, George Isaac. *Human Teaching for Human Learning.* Viking Press, New York, 1971.

Eberle, Bob and Rosie Emery Hall. *Affective Education Guidebook.* D.O.K. Publishers, Inc., Buffalo, New York, 1975.

Fraenkel, Jack R. *Helping Students Think and Value.* Strategies for teaching the social studies, second edition. Englewood Cliffs, N.J.: Prentice-Hall, 1980.

Hawley, Robert C., and Isabel L. Howler. *Human Values in the Classroom.* Hart Publishing Company, Inc., New York, 1975.

Industrial Arts/Technology in West Virginia Schools. (K-4) West Virginia Department of Education, Ed. James F. Snyder, 1979.

Kniker, Charles R. *You and Values Education.* Charles E. Merrill Publishing Company, Columbus, Ohio, 1977.

Lux, Donald and Willis Ray (Co-Directors). *The World of Construction.* Industrial Arts Curriculum Project. McKnight & McKnight Publishing Company, Bloomington, Illinois, 1970.

Moral Education . . . It Comes With the Territory. Edited by David Purpel and Kevin Ryan, McCutchan Publishing Company, Berkeley, California, 1976.

Peter, Richard and Virginia Peter. "Values Clarification Skills: Helping Problem Solvers to Become Decision Makers." *Man/Society/Technology,* November, 1978, pp. 28-31.

Raths, Louis; Harmin, Merrill, and Sidney Simon. *Values and Teaching.* Charles E. Merrill, Columbus, Ohio, 1966.

Rosser, Arthur. *The Development Growth of Elementary School Students and the Role of Industrial Arts in the Process.* ACESIA Monograph 5, 1978.

Simon, Sidney B.; Howe, Leland W. and Howard Kirschenbaum. *Values Clarification.* New York: Hart Publishing Company, 1972.

Thayer, Lou and Kent D. Beeler. *Affective Education: Innovations for Learning.* Handbook Series — N.3, 1977.

Thrower, Robert and Robert Weber (editors). *Industrial Arts for the Elementary School.* 23rd Yearbook, American Council on Industrial Arts Teacher Education, 1974.

Valett, Robert E. *Humanistic Education.* The C.V. Mosby Company, St. Louis, Missouri, 1977.

Valett, Robert E. *Self-Actualization.* Argus Communications, Niles, Illinois, 1974.

Values and Attitudes Handbook. The Wisconsin Guide to Local Curriculum Improvement in Industrial Education, K-12, 1980.

Chapter 4

The Evaluation of Affective Behavior in Industrial Arts Education

H. James Rokusek, Ph.D.
Professor and Head
Department of Business and Industrial Education
Eastern Michigan University
Ypsilanti, Michigan

As indicated in previous sections, industrial arts educators, and educators in general, have tended to place a greater amount of emphasis on teaching and evaluating behaviors associated with the cognitive and psychomotor domains than any forms of behavior associated with the affective domain. This has been evidenced in the formulation of goals and objectives, the design and implementation of learning experiences, and the preparation and administration of specific evaluation activities. Yet, over the years, several essentially affective goals for industrial arts have been given some consideration at the national, state and local levels in curriculum guides, courses of study and various mission statements.

It is also apparent that numerous industrial arts educators cite affective goals when discussing the inherent values of industrial arts to individuals and groups both inside and outside the profession. Unfortunately, most of these goals have not undergone behavioral analysis, and have fallen somewhat short of implementation in the classroom or laboratory.

This chapter will focus on some of the reasons for the neglect of affective goals; the importance of assessing these affective goals;

the necessity for stating affective objectives in behavioral terms; a brief discussion of the affective domain taxonomy, and some of the principles which might be employed to assess affectivity in industrial arts students and programs.

REASONS FOR THE APPARENT NEGLECT OF AFFECTIVE GOALS AND OBJECTIVES IN AMERICAN EDUCATION

Several reasons have been suggested for the neglect and subsequent omission of affective goals and objectives by educators. These may be summarized as: (1) the controversial nature of affective goals, and (2) the reluctance of educators to evaluate affective behavior.

Affective goals have been the subject of considerable controversy for many years in American education. As a result they have not met with the same acceptance as their cognitive and psychomotor counterparts. Not only have affective goals aroused conflict in the minds of educators and lay people, but there has been a definite lack of clarity and a certain amount of disagreement in specifying the types of behavior that students would manifest if they were to accomplish these goals. Problems of differentiation among various types of attitudes and values both at the philosophical and operational levels have also surfaced. In other words, statements of objectives pertaining to values and attitudes such as: respect for the individual, the democratic way of life, and responsible citizenship, appear frequently as curriculum goals, but generally fall short of behavioral analysis (Taba, 1962).

The controversial nature of affective behavior assessment is aptly described by Bloom, Madaus and Hastings (1981) who state:

> One of the reasons for the failure to give instructional emphasis to affective outcomes is related to the Orwellian overtones which attitudinal and value-oriented instruction often conjures up in the minds of teachers and the public. Can we teach attitudes and values without espousing a particular political or sectarian position and without employing the techniques of preachment, indoctrination, and brainwashing which are so foreign to our democratic system? (p. 298)

Scriven (1966), responds to the question by indicating that the teaching of both cognitive and affective goals can be accomplished by meeting the following conditions:

1. We teach as facts only those assertions which can be objectively established . . . ; others we teach as hypotheses. Hence, we do

not violate the rights of others to make their own choices where choice is rationally possible, nor their right to know the truth where truth is known.

2. Good teaching does not consist primarily in requiring the memorization of conclusions the teacher thinks are true, but in developing the skills needed to arrive at and test conclusions . . .

3. That certain conclusions should now be treated as established does not mean they cannot ever turn out to be wrong. (pp. 44-45)

In addition to the concern raised about indoctrination expressed above, there is another area of controversy that has been debated over an extended period of time. Many people believe that the home and church should assume the task of affective education and that the school should assume the primary role in developing the students' cognitive and psychomotor behavior. Although there is much to be said for the significant roles to be played by the family and religion, there are numerous areas within the affective domain where the school can and should play an appropriate role.

The recurring insistence on the part of parents, school boards, and others for the schools to place greater emphasis on basic education and the 3R's has no doubt impeded some of the progress made in the 1960's for affective education.

> . . . There tends to be more concern about the attainment of cognitive outcomes, and less controversy associated with them, than there is for affective goals. Clearly, schools are more frequently criticized over students' shortcomings in such cognitive areas as reading and mathematics than any other shortcomings related to affective objectives. When a school district *does* seek to develop affect concerning a contemporary social issue, it can find itself embroiled in controversy (Bloom, Madaus and Hastings, p. 297).

The preoccupation with cognitive learning in the schools has severely curtailed the emphasis and consideration that our educational systems have given to affective behavior and development. This situation is aptly described by Weinstein and Fantini (1975) who state:

> Today cognitive processes and content are riding the peak of the educational wave. Cognitive development is equated with mastery of institutionally prescribed content, with "understanding of" or "knowledge about" a variety of *academic* subjects rather than understanding or knowledge of how these subjects can serve the needs of the student. The entire machinery of the school, including its reward system, reflects this stance; grades, promotion, recognition, and so on are based on the degree of mastery of the cognitive. In fact, the operational definition of learning used in the

school is a cognitive definition. The classical notion of learning as a "change in behavior" is commonly interpreted by our schools to mean a change in cognitive behavior, measured by paper and pencil tests and verbalization. (p. 108)

B.O. Smith provides a compelling reason for considering both cognitive and affective outcomes in specific subject matter areas. Smith (1966) states:

> ... to teach any concept, principle, or theory is to teach, not only for its comprehension, but also for an attitude toward it — the acceptance or rejection of it as useful, dependable, and so forth. (p. 53)

A broader view of the societal consequences of severely limiting and sacrificing affective outcomes is held by Weinstein and Fantini (1975):

> The pervasive emphasis on cognition and its separation from affect poses a threat to our society in that our educational institutions may produce cold, detached individuals, uncommitted to humanitarian goals. Certainly, a modern society cannot function without ever increasing orders of cognitive knowledge. Yet knowledge per se does not necessarily lead to desirable behavior. Knowledge can generate feeling, but it is feeling that generates action. For example, we may know all about injustice to minorities in our society, but until we feel strongly about it we will take little action. A link to the affective, or emotional, world of the learner is therefore necessary. *Unless knowledge is related to an affective state in the learner, the likelihood that it will influence behavior is limited.* (p. 109)

In industrial arts education, a considerable amount of controversy has ensued regarding the amount of emphasis accorded to the development of psychomotor skills as opposed to both cognitive and affective objectives. But why must educators design learning experiences and evaluation activities so narrowly as to address only one domain and relatively few educational outcomes? Clearly, industrial arts educators must view all of the domains in the design, implementation, and evaluation of their students' learning experiences. Students do not perform a manipulative task or produce a product in the laboratory without thinking and feeling about it in some way. As educators, we need to consider the interaction of these behaviors in the planning, structuring and evaluation of our activities.

Perhaps this is best summarized by Krathwohl, Bloom and Masia (1956):

> ... although there may be varying relations between cognitive and affective objectives, the particular relations in any situation are determined by the learning experiences the students have had. Thus one set of learning experiences may produce a high level of cognitive achievement at the same time that it produces an actual distaste for the subject. Another set of learning experiences may produce a high level of cognitive achievement as well as great interest and liking for the subject. Still a third set of learning experiences may produce relatively low levels of cognitive achievement but a high degree of interest and liking for the subject. (p. 86)

Finally, a considerable amount of controversy has revolved around the notion that affect is considered to be a private rather than a public concern. Many people believe that their attitudes on social, political and religious issues are private matters and that the Constitution protects their privacy. Therefore, many educators have refrained from entering into these areas in planning instructional or evaluation activities. In addition to the controversy over affective goals, there appears to be a general reluctance on the part of educators to assess affective behavior, even after long- or short-range goals have been identified and included in curriculum guides or courses of study. In some instances the assessment dimension has been neglected after affective behavioral objectives have been specified. One reason for this problem is that affective objectives are viewed by educators as long-range, developmental paths to learning; consequently, most classroom teachers feel that they can not be accomplished in the relatively short time that they have with the student. In fact, a number of these teachers believe that most of these values and attitudes will not evidence themselves until well after the student has left the formal school environment.

Although teachers have assumed that attitudes, interests, and personality characteristics develop slowly, Krathwohl, Bloom and Masia (1956) indicate that it is possible that the opposite may be true and that affective behaviors may be developed more suddenly than their cognitive counterparts. But the authors go on to say:

> ... What is even more probable is that certain objectives in the cognitive and affective domain may be quickly learned or developed, whereas other objectives in both domains may be developed only over a long period of time. Implicit in the *Taxonomy* is the assumption that objectives which fall into the first categories (e.g., *Knowledge, Receiving*) are likely to be learned more rapidly and more easily than objectives which fall into the later and "higher" categories (e.g., *Synthesis, Generalized set*). (p. 19)

Recently, Bloom, Madaus, and Hastings (1981), stated that:

> While the time it takes to bring about an affective behavioral change is undoubtedly a function of the complexity of the behavior being sought, this is also true for desired changes in cognitive behavior. There is evidence however that, like certain cognitive objectives, many affective objectives *can* be attained relatively quickly and *are* amenable to evaluation. (p. 299)

Another reason why teachers have hesitated to consider the evaluation of affective behavior is that educators do not consider it appropriate to enter a letter grade to assess such personal characteristics as feelings, attitudes and interests.

Krathwohl, Bloom and Masia (1956) elaborate on this dilemma:

> . . . Cognitive achievement is regarded as fair game for grading purposes. Examinations may include a great range of types of cognitive objectives and teachers and examiners have little hesitation in giving a student a grade of A or F on the basis of his performance on these cognitive achievement examinations. In contrast, teachers and examiners do not regard it as appropriate to grade students with respect to their interests, attitudes, or character development. To be sure, a student who is at one extreme on these affective objectives may be disciplined by the school authorities, while a student at the other extreme may be regarded so favorably by teachers that he receives whatever rewards and honors are available for the purpose. (e.g., the teacher's attention, appointment to prestige classroom positions, etc.). (pp. 16-17)

The authors state further:

> A considerable part of the hesitation in the use of affective measures for grading purposes stems from the inadequacy of the appraisal techniques and the ease with which a student may exploit his ability to detect the responses which will be rewarded and the responses which will be penalized. (p. 17)

As considered previously, many educators do not believe that one's beliefs, attitudes, values, and personality characteristics are public matters, and consequently the use of affective measures for grading purposes is something to be avoided. (Krathwohl, *et. al.* 1981, p. 299)

Bloom, Madaus and Hastings (1981), however, respond in this way to the two concerns presented:

... it is possible to attain affective outcomes and to evaluate them without violating an individual's right to privacy. The point is that when teachers disregard affective outcomes in the evaluation process, they are apt to disregard them unintentionally in the instructional process. (p. 300)

There are at least two other reasons that have been given for the apparent neglect of affective goals in education. First, educators have been quick to point out that a general lack of precision characterizes a large number of the instruments used to assess affectivity. While this criticism was probably valid ten years ago, the argument does not stand up as well as it once did since many new and improved assessment materials are currently available. Secondly, some school administrators have been known to admonish their faculties for providing low grades to otherwise "good" students because they displayed "poor student attitudes." It is not difficult to understand why a teacher might "back off" from considering affective outcomes in subsequent circumstances, particularly in those instances where the administrator has not taken the time to discuss the necessity of appropriately stating affective objectives and the various ways to assess student outcomes in addition to using letter grades.

As with most things in life, people can find reasons for not doing something, and can even advance compelling arguments for defending their behavior and the practices they employ. If affective education is to receive greater emphasis in our schools, the general citizenry and educators at all levels must become convinced that the increased attention given to this domain is warranted.

WHY IS IT IMPORTANT TO ASSESS AFFECTIVE GOALS?

Should the schools take time from their busy schedules to devote attention to the climates they provide for affective learning and to the affective learning of their students? The answer to the question is clearly, "Yes!" (Bills, 1975, p. 4)

Although educators have been able to provide reasons for not assessing affective behavior, many of which have already been discussed, the overwhelming majority of curriculum and evaluation specialists believe that it is essential to evaluate such individual characteristics as interests, attitudes, and values. To put it simply, if the aims of the school, and the individual curriculum areas, i.e., industrial arts, persist in including affective outcomes, there is an obligation to evaluate the effectiveness of the total curriculum in bringing about these behaviors. If this practice is not followed, educational personnel do not have a basis upon which to recommend curriculum change or modifications in teaching strategies.

Over the past several decades, a number of goals have been stated for industrial arts which have clearly had an affective focus. The *1953 AVA Guide to Improving Instruction in Industrial Arts*, in particular, was replete with statements of this type. The following seven goals of industrial arts have been extracted from the nine major goals included in that publication to illustrate the point:

1. To develop in each pupil an active interest in industrial life and in the methods and problems of production and exchange.
2. To develop in each pupil the appreciation of good design, materials, and workmanship and the ability to select, care for, and use industrial products wisely.
3. To develop in each pupil the habits of self-reliance and resourcefulness in meeting practical situations.
4. To develop in each pupil a readiness to assist others and to join happily in group undertakings.
5. To develop in each pupil desirable attitudes and practices with respect to health and safety.
6. To develop in each pupil a feeling of pride in his ability to do useful things and to develop certain worthy free-time interests.
7. To develop in each pupil the habit of an orderly, complete, and efficient performance of any task. (p. 18)

It would appear that the more recently formulated goal statements for industrial arts have tended to reflect fewer affective outcomes. This is probably due, in large measure, to the emphasis given to substantive content or cognitive learning in the preponderance of the curriculum projects undertaken in the 1960's. It was during this period that educators representing a wide variety of subject matter areas were concerned with developing goals that focused on the unique substantive contributions of the discipline, and the industrial arts educators were no exception. As an illustration of the changing stance of that decade, the *1968 AVA Guide to Improving Instruction in Industrial Arts*, included the following five major goals:

1. Develop an insight and understanding of industry and its place in our culture.
2. Discover and develop talents, aptitudes, interests and potentialities of individuals for the technical pursuits and applied sciences.
3. Develop an understanding of industrial processes and the practical application of scientific principles.
4. Develop basic skills in the proper use of common industrial tools, machines and processes.
5. Develop problem-solving and creative abilities involving the materials, processes and products of industry. (pp. 9-11)

It is also evident that a number of curriculum specialists and school administrators viewed affective types of goal statements as having a schoolwide or total school curriculum flavor and that all subject matter areas in their own ways would contribute to these aims. Consequently, the number of objectives included in curriculum guides focusing on the development of student attitudes, values, and interests was greatly reduced or completely eliminated.

The erosion of affective objectives was also noted by Krathwohl, Bloom and Masia (1964) who stated:

> We studied the history of several major courses at the general education level of college. Typically, we found that in the original statement of objectives there was frequently as much emphasis given to affective objectives as cognitive objectives. Sometimes in the early years of the course, some small attempt was made to secure evidence on the extent to which students were developing in the affective behaviors.
>
> However, as we followed some of these courses over a period of ten to twenty years, we found a rather rapid dropping of the affective objectives from the statements about the course and an almost complete disappearance of efforts at appraisal of student growth in this domain. (p. 16)

It appears that the erosion of objectives in the affective domain continues to evidence itself in the literature and in actual practice, and but for a very few exceptions we have not experienced a reversal in this trend in industrial arts education. But beyond the erosion problem concerning affective objectives is the additional problem of locating evaluation techniques and devices of an affective nature. This problem, pointed out by Krathwohl, Bloom and Masia (1964), is not of recent origin.

When we looked for evaluation material in the affective domain we found it usually in relation to some national educational research project or a sponsored local research project (for which a report had to be written). Only rarely did we find an affective evaluation technique used because a group of local teachers wanted to know whether students were developing in a particular way. It was evident that evaluation work for affective objectives was marginal and was done only when a very pressing question was raised by the faculty or when someone wished to do "educational" research.

It is not entirely fair to imply that evaluation of the attainment of affective objectives is completely absent from the regular activities of schools and teachers. Undoubtedly almost every teacher is on the alert for evidence of desirable interests, attitudes and character development. However, most of this is the noting of universal characteristics or dramatic developments when they are almost forced on the teacher's attention. What is missing is a systematic effort to collect evidence of growth in affective objectives which is in any way parallel to the very great and systematic efforts to evaluate cognitive achievement. (pp. 15-16)

However, even though there has been some elimination of these outcomes and a shortage of evaluation materials, there is ample evidence to suggest that affectivity is an essential component in the education process. And since educators persist in giving lip service to the importance of teaching the whole child and promoting affective objectives in our schools, it is time to determine the extent to which the students and programs are successful in these undertakings.

Basically, there are two important reasons for evaluating affective characteristics: (1) to gain a better understanding of students prior to instruction, (2) to determine the extent to which students have met the affective objectives of a course or program.

Anderson and Anderson (1982) elaborate on this issue by indicating that affective characteristics can either be means or ends in themselves. They are a means to an end when affective characteristics are assessed so that instruction can be altered for certain types of students with the hope that such modifications will promote increased learning. Affective characteristics can be ends in themselves when programs are designed and implemented to help students achieve affective outcomes.

The authors continue by saying:

> Whether affective characteristics are important as means or ends has consequences for the type of characteristics assessed. If they are viewed as means, those chosen for assessment must relate

to one or more of the available alternative classroom settings or teaching styles, to the cognitive objectives of the course or curriculum, or both. If they are viewed as ends in themselves, then the characteristics selected for assessment must conform to the goals and objectives of the course or curriculum. (p. 524)

Other things being equal, a student who begins a course with a positive affect should learn more easily and quickly than the student who begins with a negative one. A negative affect for a student enrolling in his/her first course in industrial arts can be illustrated by the following feelings of fear, insecurity, or inadequacy:

"I am not very good with my hands."
"I get nervous around woodworking equipment."
"I'm not mechanically inclined."
"I don't like to work with tools and materials."
"I've heard some things about this teacher, I don't think he'll like me."

Obviously, the above feelings and manifestations can lead to failure, which in turn strengthen and reinforce the negative affect. An industrial arts teacher who knows something about the student's affective entry level should be able to provide some of the needed reinforcement and encouragement to help the student become more positive in his/her outlook.

Another term used for describing the "means" or the kind of evaluation that would take place to determine the student's feelings as indicated in the example above is "formative evaluation." Bloom, Hastings, and Madaus (1971) consider formative evaluation in this way: "Formative evaluation . . . intervenes during the formation of the student, not when the process is thought to be completed." (p. 20)

In another section of the same book, the authors state, ". . . every effort should be made to use it [formative evaluation] to improve the process. This means that . . . one must strive to develop the kinds of evidence that will be most useful in the process . . ." (p. 118)

On the other hand, if a large number of students do not achieve the affective objectives of the course, such as those quoted from the 1953 AVA Guide, this information would be gathered as part of the evidence in the summative evaluation. Summative evaluation, as it is considered in this context, refers to the degree to which the larger outcomes have been realized over the entire course, or some substantial part of it. (Bloom, Hastings, Madaus, p. 61) Obviously then, both formative and summative activities are important and necessary ingredients of an appropriate affective evaluation system.

STATING AFFECTIVE OBJECTIVES IN BEHAVIORISTIC TERMS

... unless there is some clear conception of the sort of behavior implied by the objectives, one has no way of telling what kind of behavior to look for in the students in order to see to what degree these objectives are being realized. (Tyler, 1950, p. 72)

As would be the case in the formulation of cognitive objectives, it is equally appropriate for the teacher to state affective outcomes in behavioristic terms. Objectives such as those reprinted in the previous section from the *1953 AVA Guide to Improving Instruction in Industrial Arts* are really too vague and ambiguous to communicate their educational intent, and consequently must be reduced and restated.

Because teachers have typically spent a larger portion of their time writing cognitive objectives in behavioristic terms, they probably feel more adept and comfortable in doing so than in operationalizing affective objectives. Some, perhaps, feel that it is impossible to define appropriate affective statements of student behavior. If teachers will start with the general construct and then reduce that construct by writing statements of observable student performance, or products of student performance, that will serve as indicators of the construct, they should be able to perform the task.

The following summary of a four-step process suggested by Bloom, Madaus, and Hastings (1981) which is a partial reiteration of the above statement, should be helpful to the teacher in stating affective objectives.

1. Identify the affective objective in terms of a broad general construct such as appreciation, interest, etc.
2. Narrow down the broad construct into component constructs.
3. Describe each component construct in terms of an action verb.
4. Develop specific situations or items to elicit evidence of the presence or absence of construct. (p. 303)

Another suggestion that has been made by several authors for formulating behavioral objectives is to develop a list of action verbs that will provide some clues for describing affective outcomes. Figure 4-1 is illustrative of such a list. (Eiss and Harbeck, 1969)

selects	defends	tests
chooses	obeys	delays (response)
participates	keeps (preserves)	qualifies
challenges	investigates	designs
attempts	attempts	suggests
seeks	tries	supports
persists	specifies	recommends
asks	offers	shares
joins	proposes	disputes
gathers (information)	rejects	subscribes
organizes	accepts	promotes
visits	consults	spends (money)
argues (a position)	questions	annotates
objects (to an idea)	queries	advocates
adopts	weighs (judges)	volunteers
submits	criticizes	sleeps
perseveres	evaluates	yawns
praises		

Figure 4-1. Action Verbs with Particular Value for the Affective Domain

Much has been said and written about the advantages of stating objectives in behavioral terms. Beginning with the work of Ralph Tyler in the 1930's and continuing through the next several decades to the writings of the present, most curriculum and measurement specialists have taken the position that the careful and systematic writing of objectives in behavioral terms is essential to both the improvement of the curriculum and the instructional materials required. Bloom, Madaus and Hastings (1981) have summarized eight benefits associated with explicitly stated behavioral objectives:

1. The process of writing or selecting clear, specific behavioral statements of objectives requires a teacher to think quite seriously about the changes he or she wants to help the student realize.
2. The process helps teachers recognize trivial objectives and identify those that are missing.

3. Clearly stated goals help the teacher in making decisions about the proper placement of students.
4. A list of the ends of instruction is itself an aid in selecting methods, materials, and experiences for their attainment.
5. Clearly stated instructional objectives suggest the most direct methods for evaluating students' achievement.
6. Clearly stated instructional objectives help ensure communication between teachers.
7. Appropriately stated objectives can improve communication between the teacher and the students.
8. Clearly stated objectives can improve communication between the teachers and parents. (pp. 18-21)

Although authors such as Atkin (1968), Raths (1968), and Caffyn (1968) express reservations about utilizing behavioral objectives, the majority of curriculum writers feel that unless behavioral outcomes are appropriately specified, it will be difficult for the teacher to know what to do, how to do it, or when the objectives have been attained.

Probably most industrial arts teachers have written behavioral and performance objectives in the cognitive and psychomotor domains. Consequently, they should be able to draw on this valuable experience to successfully develop affective statements of student behavior.

Mager (1962) who has written extensively on the subject of clearly specifying the type of terminal behavior to be manifested by the student has said: "If you give each learner a copy of your objectives, you may not have to do much else." (p. 53)

THE AFFECTIVE DOMAIN TAXONOMY

The two volumes, *Taxonomy of Educational Objectives: Handbook I, Cognitive Domain* and *Handbook II; Affective Domain*, were developed primarily to facilitate communication among measurement specialists and their colleagues about such considerations as objectives, test items, and test procedures. *Handbook I* categorizes objectives which refer to intellectual tasks of the learners. *Handbook II*, on the other hand, classifies objectives which involve feeling, emotion, or the degree of acceptance, or rejection.

An extremely valuable guide, in that it provides examples for evaluating behavior, the affective domain taxonomy written by Krathwohl, Bloom and Masia first appeared on the educational scene in the mid 1960's, but is still considered to be a key resource for educational personnel.

Commenting on the affective taxonomy, Bloom, Madaus, and Hastings (1981) summarize the classification system in the following manner:

> The *Taxonomy* arranges objectives along a hierarchical continuum. At the lowest point on this continuum, the students are merely aware of a phenomenon, simply able to perceive it. At the next level they are willing to attend to the phenomenon. The next step finds the students responding to the phenomenon with feeling. At the next point they go out of their way to respond to the phenomenon. Next they conceptualize behavior and feelings and organize these into a structure. The highest point in the hierarchy is reached when the structure becomes an outlook on life. (p. 304)

The *Affective Taxonomy* (Krathwohl, Bloom, Masia, 1956) is comprised of five major categories arranged in the following ascending order in the hierarchical structure:

1.0 Receiving (attending)
2.0 Responding
3.0 Valuing
4.0 Organization
5.0 Characterization by a Value or Value Complex

Similar to the cognitive domain, each of the above listed categories has then been subdivided into levels. For example, in the case of 1.0 Receiving (the willingness of the learner to receive or attend to certain phenomena and stimuli), the levels for that category have been identified as: 1.1 Awareness; 1.2 Willingness to receive; and 1.3 Controlled or selected attention. For each of the levels in the five major categories, the authors have supplemented the rather detailed descriptions of the levels with illustrative educational objectives and test items. And although the material as presented is very helpful, Krathwohl, Bloom and Masia (1964) apologize for the general lack of illustrative test items and the almost complete absence of instruments to measure affective outcomes of instruction in the physical and biological sciences, mathematics, and the social studies.

Metfessel, Michael, and Kirsner (1969) have further facilitated the use of the taxonomy by suggesting appropriate infinitives which the teacher may consider to achieve a precise or preferred wording of the desired behavior. Additionally, they have suggested general terms, or direct objects, relative to the subject matter properties. Thus, the direct object may be put together with one or more of the infinitive forms to provide the basic structure of the objective.

Figure 4-2 has been extracted from Bloom, Madaus, and Hastings (1981) as adapted from the table earlier presented by Metfessel, Michael, and Kirsner (1969) in their article on the "Instrumentation of Bloom's and Krathwohl's Taxonomies for the Writing of Educational Objectives." The table provides the categories and levels of the affective domain in the first column, the infinitives or action verbs in the second column, and the direct objects in the third column.

Metfessel, Michael and Kirsner (1969), who have developed a similar table for the cognitive domain, state:

> ... Certainly use of these tables should lead to a substantial gain in the clarity and speed with which teachers and curriculum specialists, as well as those involved in construction of ... tests, may state curricular objectives. The writers have found that these tables have been of considerable help to their students, as well as to personnel in public schools who are concerned with writing objectives prior to curriculum development, constructing test items, or to carrying out evaluation studies. (p. 230)

The *Taxonomy* can be of great assistance to all teachers in defining more clearly the objectives contained in the affective area. It can also help teachers become more aware of the techniques that are available for assessing affective behavior in their students.

ASSESSING AFFECTIVITY

Generally speaking, we think of educational evaluation as having two distinct and useful purposes — the evaluation of student outcomes and the evaluation of the instructional program. Clearly, both purposes have significance when considering affective education. This section will describe some of the principal measures and techniques that may be used for each of these two purposes.

Once the teacher has defined his/her objectives in behavioristic terms, the next step is to consider ways that the student can demonstrate or manifest the anticipated affective behavior. This, of course, should be considered in the design and implementation of both learning experiences and evaluation procedures.

	EXAMPLES OF INFINITIVES	EXAMPLES OF DIRECT OBJECTS
1.0 Receiving (attending) The first category is defined as sensitivity to the existence of certain phenomena and stimuli, that is, the willingness to receive or attend to them. A typical objective at this level would be: ''The student develops a tolerance for a variety of types of music.''		
1.1 Awareness	To differentiate, to separate, to set apart, to share	Sights, sounds, events, designs, arrangements
1.2 Willingness to receive	To accumulate, to select, to combine, to accept	Models, examples, shapes, sizes, meters, cadences
1.3 Controlled or selected attention	To select, to posturally respond to, to listen (for), to control	Alternatives, answers, rhythms, nuances
2.0 Responding ''Responding'' refers to a behavior which goes beyond merely attending to the phenomena; it implies active attending, doing something with or about the phenomena, and not merely perceiving them. Here a typical objective would be: ''The student voluntarily reads magazines and newspapers designed for young children.''		
2.1 Acquiescence in responding	To comply (with), to follow, to command, to approve	Directions, instructions, laws, policies, demonstrations
2.2 Willingness to respond	To volunteer, to discuss to practice, to play	Instruments, games, dramatic works, charades, burlesques

Figure 4-2. Translating the levels of the affective taxonomy into statements of objectives. (Adapted from Metfessel, Michael, & Kirsner, 1969, pp. 227-231.)

Figure 4-2 Continued.

	EXAMPLES OF INFINITIVES	EXAMPLES OF DIRECT OBJECTS
2.3 Satisfaction in response	To applaud, to acclaim, to spend leisure time in, to augment	Speeches, plays, presentations, writings
3.0 Valuing Behavior which belongs to this level of the taxonomy goes beyond merely doing something with or about certain phenomena. It implies perceiving them as having worth and consequently revealing consistency in behavior related to these phenomena. A typical objective at this level would be: "Writes letters to the press on issues he feels strongly about."		
3.1 Acceptance of a value	To increase measured proficiency in, to increase numbers of, to relinquish, to specify	Group membership[s], artistic production[s], musical productions, personal friendships
3.2 Preference for a value	To assist, to subsidize, to help, to support	Artists, projects, viewpoints, arguments
3.3 Commitment	To deny, to protest, to debate, to argue	Deceptions, irrelevancies, abdications, irrationalities
4.0 Organization Organization is defined as the conceptualization of values and the employment of these concepts for determining the interrelationship among values. Here a typical objective might be: "Begins to form judgments as to the major directions in which American society should move."		

Figure 4-2 Continued.

	EXAMPLES OF INFINITIVES	EXAMPLES OF DIRECT OBJECTS
4.1 Conceptualization of a value	To discuss, to theorize (on), to abstract, to compare	Parameters, codes, standards, goals
4.2 Organization of a value system	To balance, to organize, to define, to formulate	Systems, approaches, criteria, limits
5.0 Characterization The organization of values, beliefs, ideas, and attitudes into an internally consistent system is called "characterization." This goes beyond merely determining interrelationships among various values: it implies their organization into a total philosophy or world view. Here a typical objective would include: "Develops a consistent philosophy of life" [Krathwohl et al., 1964, pp. 176-185].		
5.1 Generalized set	To revise, to change, to complete, to require	Plans, behavior, methods, effort(s)
5.2 Characterization	To be rated high by peers in, to be rated high by superiors, in, to be rated high by subordinates in and	Humanitarianism, ethics, integrity, maturity
	To avoid, to manage, to resolve, to resist	Extravagance(s), excesses, conflicts, exorbitancy/ exorbitancies

As indicated by Henerson, Morris and Fitz-Gibbon (1978) the task of measuring attitude is not an easy one, and attempting to demonstrate attitude change is particularly so. According to the authors:

> ... the concept of attitude, like many abstract concepts, is a creation — a construct. As such it is a tool that serves the human need to see order and consistency in what people say, think and do, so that given certain behaviors, predictions can be made about future behaviors. An attitude is not something we can examine and measure in the same way we can examine the cells of a person's skin or measure the rate of her heartbeat. *We can only infer that a person has attitudes by her words and actions.*

> When we attempt to measure a complex attitude, as for example, attitude toward school, we find that it has many *facets* — feelings and beliefs about one's teachers, teachers in general, classmates, school subjects, activities. We find it has many *manifestations* — school work, attention in class, interaction with others, verbal responses. When we attempt to measure an attitude like racial prejudice, we find it blurred by peer group pressure, the desire to please, ambivalence, inconsistency, lack of self-awareness. (pp. 11-12)

Yet, say the authors, it is these types of complex attitudes that educators should be the most interested in influencing and measuring, and they encourage us to proceed with these precautions in mind:

- When we measure attitudes, we must rely on *inference*, since it is impossible to measure attitudes directly.
- Behaviors, beliefs, and feelings will not always match, even when we correctly assume that they reflect a single attitude; so to focus on only one manifestation of an attitude may tend to distort our picture of the situation and mislead us.
- We have no guarantee that the attitude we want to assess will "stand still" long enough for a one-time measurement to be reliable. A volatile or fluctuating attitude cannot be revealed by information gathered on one occasion.
- When we study certain attitudes, we do so without universal agreement on their nature. Is there, for instance, such a thing as a single "self-concept?" Perhaps, but perhaps not. (p. 13)

Erickson and Wentling (1979) in their book, *Measuring Student Growth*, identified and defined five approaches to the measurement of affective behavior:

1. Direct Observation: Viewing and recording a student's behavior with regard to a stimulus object and making inferences about the underlying affective causes for the behavior.
2. Interview: Asking a student open- and closed-ended questions in a face-to-face situation regarding a certain stimulus object.
3. Questionnaires and Inventories: Presenting a student with a printed set of questions similar to interview questions or seeking a student's self-report of affect through a rating scale or checklist.
4. Projective Techniques: Presenting a task or object to a student for reasons unknown to the student. An example would be to require a student to write an essay on some value-laden topic.
5. Unobtrusive Measures: Observing, either directly or indirectly, the behavior of students without their being aware that their behavior is being measured. (pp. 195-196)

The authors indicate that the questionnaire and inventory are "probably the most popular in terms of traditional use," but that "the other four approaches have considerable potential for expanding and improving our affective measurement efforts."

Henerson, Morris and Fitz-Gibbon (1978), identify four approaches for evaluating the attitudes of members of a group or groups:

Approach 1 — Self-Report Measures — consists of interviews, surveys, polls, questionnaires, attitude rating scales, logs, journals and diaries.

Approach 2 — Reports of Others — includes interviews, questionnaires, logs, journal reports, and observation procedures.

Approach 3 — Sociometric Procedures — concerns peer ratings and social choice techniques.

Approach 4 — Records — incorporates counselor files and attendance records.

Figure 4-3, which has been extracted from their book, *How to Measure Attitudes* indicates when each of the four approaches can be most effectively used; the kinds of questions that can be determined by the measures; and the examples of the kinds of conclusions the measures can provide. This figure should be helpful to industrial arts teachers in making decisions about the kinds of instruments and measurement approaches that will best serve their evaluation needs.

	WHEN IS THIS APPROACH MOST APPROPRIATE?
Approach 1: SELF-REPORT MEASURES (Members of Group X report directly about their own attitudes) • interviews, surveys, polls • questionnaires and attitude rating scales • logs, journals, diaries	When the people whose attitudes you are investigating • are able to understand the questions asked of them • have sufficient self-awareness to provide the necessary information • are likely to answer honestly and not deliberately falsify their responses
Approach 2: REPORTS OF OTHERS (Others report about the attitudes of members of Group X) • interviews • questionnaires • logs, journals, reports • observation procedures	When the people whose attitudes you are investigating are unable or unlikely to provide accurate information. When you want information about how people *behave* under certain circumstances. When you can assume that the reporter will be unbiased and will present objective information. When you can assume that the reporter has sufficient opportunity to observe a representative sample of behavior.
Approach 3: SOCIOMETRIC PROCEDURES (Members of Group X report about their attitudes toward one another) • peer ratings • social choice techniques	When you want a picture of the social patterns within a group.
Approach 4: RECORDS • counselor files • attendance records	When you have access to records that provide information relevant to the attitudes in question and when these records are complete.

Figure 4-3. Four approaches for evaluating the attitudes of Members of a Group or Groups

WHAT KINDS OF QUESTIONS CAN BE ANSWERED BY THE MEASURES?	EXAMPLES OF THE KINDS OF CONCLUSIONS THE MEASURES CAN YIELD
[as a member of Group X] How do you feel about it? How strongly do you feel about it? ["It" may be any aspect of a program, focus of interest, or element of concern.] What do you believe about it? What are your reasons for believing as you do? What *should* you do? What have you done in the past? Which do you prefer to do?	Students in Program A have a greater tendency to attribute their school successes to their own efforts than do students in the control group. Teachers in Program A are highly satisfied with the materials. Parents of children in Program A report greater satisfaction with the school and the progress of their children than do parents of children in Program B. Seventy-five percent of the students in Program A have asked to continue in the program next year.
[from your observations of Group X] What do they believe about it? How do they feel about it? How strongly do they feel about it? What do they do when confronted with it?	Parents of children in Program A report significant improvement in their children's work habits since the beginning of school. Teachers in Program A report that classroom friendship patterns indicate successful integration and acceptance of the bussed students. Observers report a significant difference in the number of helping behaviors exhibited in Program A classrooms as compared with control group classrooms.
[as a member of Group X] Who in your group fits this description? Whom would you choose in this situation? Who associates with whom?	The sociometric choices of students in Program A indicate that handicapped students are establishing friendships with students in the larger group.
What do past records indicate they [Group X] know about it? What inferences can be made from past records concerning their feelings about it? What do past records indicate they do when confronted with it?	Students in Program A tend to be absent less than students in Program B. There have been significantly fewer disciplinary referrals in Group X.

In the same chapter, Henerson, Morris, and Fitz-Gibbon provide specific advantages and disadvantages of the four major approaches. They conclude the chapter with the following figure (Figure 4-4) which suggests a process to help answer the question, "What kinds of instruments will best serve my measurement needs?"

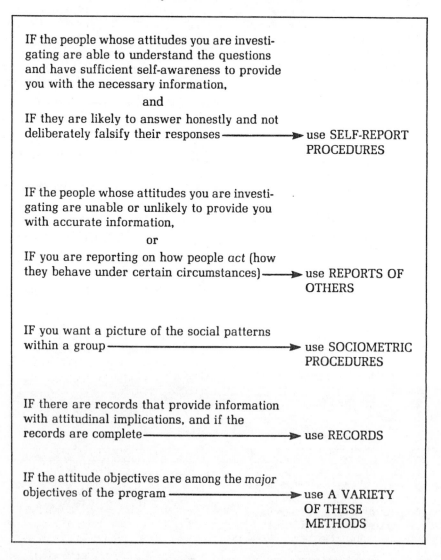

IF the people whose attitudes you are investigating are able to understand the questions and have sufficient self-awareness to provide you with the necessary information,

and

IF they are likely to answer honestly and not deliberately falsify their responses ⟶ use SELF-REPORT PROCEDURES

IF the people whose attitudes you are investigating are unable or unlikely to provide you with accurate information,

or

IF you are reporting on how people *act* (how they behave under certain circumstances) ⟶ use REPORTS OF OTHERS

IF you want a picture of the social patterns within a group ⟶ use SOCIOMETRIC PROCEDURES

IF there are records that provide information with attitudinal implications, and if the records are complete ⟶ use RECORDS

IF the attitude objectives are among the *major* objectives of the program ⟶ use A VARIETY OF THESE METHODS

Figure 4-4. Summary of Selected Approaches

After the teacher has determined what types of instruments will best suit his/her needs, there are two alternatives that may be considered: (1) to find an appropriate existing measure, or (2) to develop a new measure.

The great advantage in using an already existing instrument is that one may save a great deal of time. However, there are at least two other reasons why it would be well to conduct a search of existing measures. First of all, much can be gained from other people's experience in creating and trying out the instrument and secondly, it should be possible to locate some validity and reliability data. At any rate, the following three-step process recommended by Henerson, Morris and Fitz-Gibbon (1978) appears sound:

1. Determine what the attitude you want to measure is likely to be called in the literature or in catalogs of available tests.

2. Find reference books that list, describe, and/or evaluate existing measures.

3. Obtain and examine the measures that seem appropriate for your evaluation needs. (p. 41)

After the teacher has obtained a copy of the instrument that seems appropriate, Henerson, Morris, and Fitz-Gibbon (1978) suggest that before it is used, the following six questions should be raised about it:

1. *Does the measure seem to be doing what it says it does?* To help you answer this, think about how a skeptic would criticize the instrument by reinterpreting a score at either extreme. For example, suppose that an instrument purporting to determine a young child's comfort in the school environment presents the child with sets of pictures depicting these activities, one of which is school related. The non-school related activities include such things as staying at home, going to the zoo, watching television, and so forth. The child is asked to circle the one he likes best. Now suppose the child scores low, that is, consistently chooses non-school activities. The skeptic might say that the child's consistent preference for non-school-related activities does not necessarily indicate discomfort or unhappiness in school. That child might just happen to like other activities better.

   Turn yourself into a skeptic through this brief exercise: Imagine that you are committed to a particular program which you feel is having positive effects. The evaluation instrument under consideration has been given and has shown that the program is producing no effect — or even negative effects. How would you explain away this unwanted result? In other words, how would you attack the instrument's credibility? If such an

attack could be mounted with plenty of ammunition — for example, if you could make a case that many of the items are silly
and misleading — then the instrument is not very credible and
might not be valid.

2. *How close a fit is there between the objectives of the measure
and your program objectives?* Let us say, for example, that you
are examining a self-esteem instrument. In your examination you
discover only one item that relates to pride of accomplishment.
Yet this dimension of self-esteem is heavily emphasized in your
program goals. If you decide to purchase the instrument, you
will have to tap this dimension through the use of some other
measure. You should look for the measure that reflects your program objectives most accurately; in this case, one that you want
to measure. Otherwise, you might find yourself attempting to
evaluate the program using either irrelevant or insufficient data.

3. *Is there information on the reliability of the measure, and is this
information persuasive?* Reliability information . . . can tell you
how stable a measurement you are making. As you read about
a particular instrument, you will notice that the degree to which
it yields consistent results is expressed as a "reliability coeffi-
cient" which is a decimal. It is helpful to think of this decimal
as representing the correlation between two administrations of
the measure without intervening influences (i.e., instruction,
acquisition of new information, change of attitudes, etc.). Thus
a reliability of 1.00 would indicate perfect correlation: two
administrations of the measure without intervention yield exactly
the same results. A reliability of zero would mean that the
measure is totally useless. In general, a measure used to make
decisions about an individual should have a reliability of at least
.90. One for making decisions about different groups or programs
may be useful even if its reliability is as low as .50. Quite often
an attitude instrument will not be accompanied by reliability
estimates. In this case you will have to make an assessment of
the instrument's credibility based on your own critical judgment.

4. *Does the measure seem appropriate for the age and ability level
of the group whose attitudes you are measuring?* The instrument
may be wrong for the group you have in mind for any one of
several reasons: vocabulary, formatting, tone, etc. People have
developed, for example, group measures for first graders with
answer sheets requiring the children to record their responses
on a complex matrix. Knowing the young children's perceptual
skills are not up to this task, one can be sure that there will be
many errors on such a measure simply because children will lose
their places on the answer sheets. Older students, on the other

hand, given an attitude measure that is "below them" in language and format, will find it silly. Your data will be distorted accordingly.

5. *Can you anticipate any problems that might arise from the use of this measure?* Before you decide upon an instrument, try to see it through the eyes of those who will be involved — teachers, parents, administrators, or students. If the measure is likely to offend one group or another, then you must balance the potential discomfort against the usefulness of the measure. Information that is not required for appropriate program decisions is not worth collecting — especially if its collection causes resentment.

6. *Do you have the wherewithal to do what has to be done to use this instrument?* This is the issue of practicality. For example, an observation schedule using an elaborate coding system will provide data that have to be decoded before they can be analyzed. Decoding is an extra step which will require extensive clerical assistance.

Before you decide on a measure, think of the step-by-step procedures involved in its use so that you can determine if the available time, money, and staff are adequate for the task. (pp. 55-56)

In those instances where it is not possible to find an existing measure, the industrial arts teacher may have to develop his/her own measure. Contrary to what many teachers believe, it is not that difficult to develop appropriate measures of affective behavior. This view is also held by Erickson and Wentling (1976) who state:

For some reason occupational educators have assumed that affective instruments require developmental techniques that are beyond the competency of individual teachers. It is unfortunate, however, that this assumption has been made, since attitude and interest measures for some purposes are not more difficult to construct than the average cognitive-achievement test. Many teacher-made or locally developed instruments can be prepared with simple and less formal techniques than are typically used by developers of standardized instruments. (p. 194)

A number of authors, Eiss and Harbeck (1960); Krathwohl, Bloom and Masia (1964); Baldwin (1971); Girod (1973); Erickson and Wentling

(1976); Henerson, Morris, and Fitz-Gibbon (1978); and Bloom, Madaus, and Hastings (1981), have provided some excellent suggestions and examples for developing affective instruments and individual items. The reader is advised to consult these sources to become better informed about the process of constructing appropriate evaluation devices.

In addition to evaluating student behavior to determine the extent to which certain affective objectives have been realized, it is also desirable to evaluate the effectiveness of the instructional program in facilitating affective outcomes.

Maley (1978) makes particular reference to the environmental setting and indicates that the emotional environment is one of great importance to the student. He states:

> The emotional environment pertains to the non-physical atmosphere in the classroom or laboratory that tends to have a psychological impact on the learner. This impact may take the form of acceptance or rejection, stimulation or discouragement, trust or lack of trust, as well as a number of other student attitudes that may contribute to or hinder affective learning and/or development. This emotional environment is, in some cases, a result of the interpersonal relations that the teacher establishes with the student(s). The administration of the school may play a strong part in establishing the tone of the emotional environment. Other contributors to the quality of the emotional environment would include the students, parents, and community. (p. 338)

There are many standards and evaluative criteria that have been written to assess various categories of the instructional program; however, the guidelines suggested by Maley (1978) for evaluating the effectiveness of the emotional environment are particularly appropriate at this time:

1. The students feel that the teachers and the administrative staff are there to help the individual.
2. There are appropriate degrees of freedom allowed each student in his or her pursuit of the educational experience.
3. The teachers are positive in their efforts to assist the students.
4. There is an overt effort made to establish a positive self-attitude on the part of all students.
5. The requirements of the program are challenging to every student, and at the same time, within the capability of each.

6. There is an atmosphere of mutual trust between the students and the teachers in the classroom or laboratory.

7. The students feel that the school and the individual's program is for them.

8. The teachers and all other support personnel demonstrate a genuine interest in the work and needs of the student.

9. The students play an important part in decisions regarding programs, evaluation, activities, and involvement.

10. There are many forms of recognition given to students in return for their learning accomplishments. (p. 339)

The recently completed *Standards for Industrial Arts Programs* (Dugger 1982), contains several statements within the standard topics that reflect a concern for the affective domain. Although some statements speak more directly to affective development than others, the following eight clearly address the need for affective education in industrial arts programming:

Standard Topic 1 Philosophy
    1.1 Development
        c) The philosophy addresses the value of industrial arts including industrial and technological literacy; career orientation, exploration, and preparation; avocational activities, economic concepts; consumer skills; creative talents; personal and social growth; and problem solving skills.

Standard Topic 2 Instructional Program
    2.1 Goals
        b) Emphasis is placed upon improving student ability to make informed and meaningful occupational choices.
        d) Emphasis is placed upon developing student talents, creative abilities, positive self-concepts, and individual potentials related to industrial-technical areas.
        f) Emphasis is placed upon developing student problem-solving and decision-making abilities involving industrial materials, processes, and products.

> h) Emphasis is placed upon developing leader-
> ship ability, encouraging and promoting
> responsibility, and developing positive social
> interaction through AIASA.

2.3 Content
> 4) Course content includes the development of personal
> and leadership skills through AIASA.

Standard Topic 4 Instructional Staff
4.3 Personal Qualities
> 5) The industrial arts teacher exhibits good work habits
> such as safe practices, punctuality, neatness, and
> attendance that have a positive effect upon the edu-
> cational environment.
> 6) The industrial arts teacher is sensitive to student
> needs, recognizes individual student abilities, and
> practices appropriate teaching methods that moti-
> vate students to maximum performance.

Inherent in the statements is the concern for providing an environment which is conducive to developing positive attitudes, values, and
feelings in industrial arts students. This, as indicated in the statement
pertaining to the instructional staff, can probably best be accomplished
by teachers who are appropriate role models and genuine professionals in every sense of that word. By employing the *Standards* it
should be possible to assess the extent to which the program has provided for affective outcomes.

SUMMARY

A considerable amount of controversy regarding the inclusion and
subsequent evaluation of affective learning has surfaced over the
years. Nevertheless, most authorities agree that affective objectives
should become integral goals of American education.

Because of the nature of industrial arts and the many significant
contributions that can be made to affective learning, evaluations
should be conducted of both the students and program. In order to
be successful in these undertakings, industrial arts teachers must be
able to: (1) clarify their affective objectives prior to making decisions
about specific measurement techniques and (2) determine whether the
intended measures should focus on processes or outcomes.

Once these concerns have been addressed, teachers will have to determine whether an appropriate assessment measure already exists or whether they will have to develop a new one. In either instance, teachers can do much to help themselves by carefully reviewing the various types of instruments available, studying the suggestions and examples given by affective measurement specialists, and sharing the products of their labor with their colleagues.

With the proper resolve, study and reflection, industrial arts educators can assess the affective objectives so frequently neglected in the development of our students and programs. Affective assessment must rest on the appropriate clarification of objectives and the development and implementation of learning experiences. All of these ingredients are essential if affective education is to be successfully accomplished.

REFERENCES

Anderson, Lorin W., and Anderson, J. Craig. "Affective Assessment Is Necessary and Possible." *Educational Leadership*, April 1982, pp. 524-522.

American Vocational Association. *A Guide to Improving Instruction in Industrial Arts.* AVA, Washington, D.C., 1953.

American Vocational Association. *A Guide to Improving Instruction in Industrial Arts.* AVA, Washington, D.C., 1968.

Atkin, H. Myron. "Behavioral Objectives in Curriculum Design. A Cautionary Note." Presented in February, 1968 at the annual meeting of the American Educational Research Association in Chicago, 1968.

Baldwin, T.S. "Evaluation of Learning in Industrial Education." In B.S. Bloom, J.T. Hastings and G.F. Madaus. *Handbook on Formative and Summative Evaluation of Student Learning.* New York: McGraw-Hill Book Company, 1971.

Bills, Robert E. *A System for Assessing Affectivity.* University, Alabama: University of Alabama Press, 1975.

Bloom, Benjamin S.; Hastings, J. Thomas and Madaus, George F. *Handbook on Formative and Summative Evaluation of Student Learning.* New York: McGraw-Hill Book Company, 1971.

Bloom, Benjamin S.; Madaus, George F. and J. Thomas Hastings. *Evaluation to Improve Learning.* New York: McGraw-Hill Book Company, 1981.

Caffyn, Lois. "Behavioral Objectives: English-Style," *Elementary English*, XLV, No. 8, December 1968, pp. 1073-1074.

Dugger, William E., Project Director. *Standards for Industrial Arts Programs.* Blacksburg, Virginia: Virginia Polytechnic Institute and State University, 1982.

Eiss, Albert F. and Harbeck, Mary Blatt. *Behavioral Objectives in the Affective Domain.* Washington, D.C.: National Science Supervision Association, 1969.

Erickson, Richard C. and Wentling, Tim L. *Measuring Student Growth.* Boston: Allyn and Bacon, Inc., 1976.

Girod, Gerald R. *Writing and Assessing Attitudinal Objectives.* Columbus, Ohio: Charles E. Merrill Publishing Company, 1973.

Henerson, Marlene E.; Morris, Lynn Lyons and Fitz-Gibbon, Carol Taylor. *How to Measure Attitudes.* Beverly Hills, California: Sage Publications, 1978.

Krathwohl, David R.; Bloom, Benjamin S. and Masia, Bertram B. *Taxonomy of Educational Objectives. The Classification of Educational Goals. Handbook II: Affective Domain.* New York: David McKay, 1964.

Mager, Robert F. *Preparing Instructional Objectives.* Belmont, California: Fearon Publishers, 1962.

Maley, Donald A. *The Industrial Arts Teacher's Handbook.* Boston: Allyn and Bacon, Inc., 1978.

Metfessel, N.I.; Michael, W.O. and Kirsner, D.A. "Instrumentation of Bloom's and Krathwohl's Taxonomies for the Writing of Educational Objectives." *Psychology in the Schools,* 1969, 6 (3), 227-331.

Raths, James D. "Specificity as a Threat to Curriculum Reform." Presented in February, 1968 at the Annual Meeting of the American Educational Research Association in Chicago, 1968.

Scriven, M. "Student Values as Educational Objectives." *Proceedings of the 1965 Invitational Conference on Testing Problems.* Princeton, N.J.: Educational Testing Service, 1966.

Smith, B.O. "Teaching and Testing Values." *Proceedings of the 1965 Invitational Conference on Testing Problems.* Princeton, N.J.: Educational Testing Service, 1966.

Taba, Hilda. *Curriculum Development: Theory and Practice.* New York: Harcourt, Brace and World, Inc., 1962.

Tyler, Ralph W. *Basic Principles of Curriculum and Instruction.* Chicago: The University of Chicago Press, 1950.

Chapter 5

The Role of Industrial Arts Teacher Education in Affective Learning

Harold E. PaDelford, Ph.D.
Professor
Department of Business and Industrial Education
Eastern Michigan University

> *Your children are not your children.*
> *They are the sons and daughters of Life's longing for self.*
> *They come through you but not from you,*
> *And though they are with you yet they belong not to you.*
>
> *You may give them your love but not your thoughts,*
> *For they have their own thoughts.*
> *You may house the bodies but not their souls,*
> *For their souls dwell in the house of tomorrow, which you cannot*
> *   visit, not even in your dreams.*
> *You may strive to be like them, but seek not to make them like you.*
> —Gibran, 1923/1963, p. 17

This quotation from Gibran expresses the gravity and caution with which affective learning must be approached. If we, as teacher educators, are to seek to inculcate feelings and values in our students so they, in turn, are able to transmit to their students similar feelings and values we must search for ways to encourage the student to examine thoughts and outcomes and then make choices.

THE TASK ASSUMED

Values, value clarification, and value acquisition have received varying amounts of emphasis in education over the past three decades.

179

It seems that the emphasis has shifted so much and so often that many teachers are confused as to the proper role of education in addressing the issue. Just what is the responsibility of education in response to a "new" demand for inculcating societal values?

Responsibility of Teacher Education

The issue of feelings and values in education cannot be avoided. It is part of both the explicit and implicit curriculums. There exists a continuum of thought and action regarding feelings and values which transverses the hardline to the softline. Some communities expect, even demand, that values be taught and that students react in approved ways (*Policies and Procedures*, 1981-82). Schools are looked upon as being agents for change in our society. Schools, i.e., teachers and administrators, must accept the grave responsibility of bringing about an adjustment in the personal desires of the individual in favor of the group (*Discipline Handbook for Faculty*, 1981).

At the other end of the continuum from this strong commitment to values and their imposition one finds a humanistic tradition. Learning models must be created in which students learn how to learn, not just to learn, and to value a commitment, not be committed (Morris and Krajewski, 1980).

The fact is, feelings and values cannot be escaped. If they are not publicly expressed, they are concealed in the curriculum. Shaver and Strong (1982) indicate this hidden curriculum "Includes the unintended implications of content and of teaching behavior, as well as the many 'noninstructional' encounters that students have with teachers and other school people. Much of the hidden curriculum has to do with values" (p. 1). There should be no pretense that teachers and teacher educators can avoid feelings and values in the curriculum. The question is what to do about feelings and values and to be aware of the responsibility of our influence.

Accepting the task. Teacher educators must realize that how they teach and how they act are more important than what they teach. Whether one cares to admit it or not, we possess a certain philosophy of life, personal values, and beliefs. These form a foundation for interaction with our students. Our teaching effectiveness is the result of using our unique self.

If values are conveyed through teaching methods, knowledge, and procedures, then teacher educators must be aware of these powerful affects. The unique self should be evaluated and emphasis should be placed on factors which increase teaching effectiveness. The organization of the course, student evaluation, interaction with students, and one's role in the teaching-learning process are all affected by the unique self. We canot remain neutral, we must be aware of the values we espouse or portray (Dobson, et al., 1982; Shaver and Strong, 1982).

Making the difference. Now is the time to question the goals and processes of teaching-learning. As Podeschi (1982) so powerfully states:

> We need emigrants into the global village, who will learn and teach about the rest of the world, reducing our fatty ethnocentrism. We need pioneers who have the independence and courage to live ethnically in a new world of cassettes, commercials, and computers with something more than the guidance of "looking out for number one." And in this America of changing lifestyles, we need explorers into strange social and psychological regions — persons who are not seduced by new rhetoric covering old, but powerful, values. (p. 162)

As society (and we and our students) changes, values become conflicting. Because the potential of value conflict is so pervasive, teacher educators and students ought to learn to recognize and deal with value dilemmas openly and with rational thought. We can help students understand values and value acquisition by helping them be aware that value conflict is inevitable and by helping them to evalute and judge values in terms of consequences (Shaver and Strong, 1982).

Feelings and values can be dichotomous. Children are encouraged to be autonomous and this self-centeredness is seldom questioned. The child is encouraged to make his own decisions, to develop his own opinions, to have his own possessions, to solve his own problems, and to see the world through his own eyes. Yet, young people need to have friends, exhibit team spirit and cooperation, work in a group, and conform to the group. This dichotomy can, and usually does, result in conflict and anxiety. Teacher educators and their students must explore the problems and search for solutions to this dilemma. They can make a difference. The Quality of School Life scale (Epstein and McPartland, 1976) searches for, among other items, anxiety about school, classroom integrative environment, control of environment, self-esteem, self-reliance, social involvement, class participation, and participation in family decision making. As reported by Epstein and McPartland, the trend for Quality of School Life scores to decrease as the child grows older may be due primarily to real differences in the quality of school experiences. The quality of school experiences may be an indicator of the conflicting feelings and values the student encounters as he/she confronts the needs of the self and of the group. If the self-concept, to self and to the group, is a guide and mediator of feelings, thoughts, and actions, then the image of self (be it teacher educator, teaching student, or student) is of utmost importance. If good teacher educators and good students have a positive view of self, then more opportunities should be provided for both preservice and inservice teachers to acquire positive self-perceptions. A potent area for research is the extent to which the school climate affects self-perceptions.

Teacher Educators as Role Models

How often do teacher educators impress upon their students the idea that when the students become the teachers they will serve as models for their own students? How often do teacher educators feel rejection when their students repudiate that role as model? How often do teacher educators examine *their roles* as models?

Teacher educators must examine the role they play as models for students. Affective teaching is done explicitly and implicitly. What the teacher educator does and says is "read" by the student. Also, the development of a definite rationale for teaching about the affective domain is essential. Among the areas needing clarification are assumptions about society and the schools' relationships to society, the nature of young people and how they learn, and the nature and worth of feelings and values. An important reason for developing a rationale is to avoid the unintended imposition of one's own feelings and values upon the students. To explore values, yes; to impose them, no.

If teacher educators transmit values, and transmit means a sense or knowledge about values, it must be done in a non-propagandized manner. It is the individual learner's task to uncover the emotions and beliefs which will affect his life and to be able to integrate them into his own unique value system. But there is a shared responsibility between teacher and learner which Buber (1958) described as the *I-Thou relationship*. In the I-Thou relationship there is implicit trust, shared experiences, decision making, and acquisition of values to live by. The trust and sharing which are the foundation of the I-Thou relationship comprise the basis for student dependency upon the teacher as a realistic model for values acquisition without leaning upon indoctrination or propaganda.

In viewing the great teachers of morals and values — those like Buddha, Christ, Mohammed, and Moses — whose influence has been felt over the centuries, we discover that they used more than words to transmit meanings. The teachings of the prophets and teachers have been made more real by symbolism and action; in lives lived, in responsibility, in dedication, and in concern for others.

The Effect on College Curriculums

New emphasis is being placed upon the inclusion of values education in liberal arts curriculums, especially in liberal arts colleges (Brown, 1982; Langerak, 1982; Merrill, 1982; Perry, 1982). Consciousness raising, moral training, moral action, value identification, valuing, and decision making are topics that receive considerable attention. Learning about values rather than value inculcation seems to be a common theme.

Is there room in a teacher education curriculum for a course on values? Probably not. There is room, however, within courses to discuss feelings and values, and more importantly, to focus on teaching models which enhance the process. Teaching methods make a difference in what is learned, as well as how it is learned. Some methods of teaching emphasize values — they highlight the value implications of the content. Examples of personal models of teaching include Carl Rogers' nondirectional teaching, William Schultz' awareness training, David Hunt's conceptual systems, and William Glasser's social problem-solving (Joyce, 1978). These or similar models can be taught to teacher education students in order to prepare them to teach about values.

VALUES IN INDUSTRIAL ARTS TEACHER EDUCATION

There are values which have traditionally been considered a partial function of industrial arts teacher education such as craftsmanship, safety, dedication to task, organization, etc. Considering that industry and technology have changed and that social values have apparently changed, it is appropriate to consider the feelings and values of students in industrial arts teacher education.

Values Related to Industrial Arts

Value, as a term, has many definitions and undoubtedly no one definition is entirely correct. Shaver and Strong (1982) have derived the following definition which may suffice for this discussion, "*Values* are our standards and principles for judging worth. They are the criteria by which we judge things (people, objects, ideas, actions, and situations) to be good, worthwhile, desirable; or, on the other hand, bad, worthless, despicable; or, of course, somewhere in between these extremes" (p. 17). Values may be applied consciously or unconsciously; that is, the standards that we apply are either definitively stated or implied through actions or words.

The identification of value constructs can be made through philosophical means, that is, man-object, man-man, or man-group (Gephart, 1981). If we revere objects (money, things, knowledge), then objects become the basis for judgment. Likewise, if man or the group become the locus of valuing then their well-being becomes the standard for values. Conflicts arise when a dichotomy exists between value judgments made toward two or more loci, such as when students receive an individual grade for work in a group rather than the group being graded as a whole.

Types of values can be identified as moral, esthetic, performance, intrinsic, or instrumental (Shaver & Strong, 1982). Another viewpoint (Joyce, 1978) is that values can be viewed as personal capacity, that is, self-organization, productive thinking, personal meaning, self-teaching and problem solving, aesthetic capacity, and motivation.

In direct relationship to industrial arts, Kazanas & Beach (1978) have defined work habits, work values, or work attitudes that are considered desirable and important by industry and teachers. These affective work competencies include: ambition; cooperation, helpfulness; adaptability, resourcefulness; consideration, courtesy; initiative; accuracy; carefulness, alertness, perceptiveness; pleasantness, friendliness, cheerfulness; responsiveness, willingness to follow; perseverance, endurance; neatness, orderliness; dependability, punctuality, reliability, responsibility; efficiency, speed; and dedication, honesty, loyalty, and conscientiousness. We set the standards for whatever it is we judge to be worthwhile. These standards can be identified and placed in context; whether it be cottage industry, industrial technology, or high technology/communications technology that we emphasize in industrial arts.

Value of Values

As distinct from attitudes which are feelings or opinions converging toward an object or thing such as a person, car, food, or situation; values are standards or established measures of worth or significance. We possess literally thousands of attitudes and relatively few real values. Values are the essential components used in defining society and its functions. Attitudes are judged against values; values are the verification factors for our attitudes.

As such, a teacher educator cannot give a rationale for teaching, built on values, to teaching students. The students must develop a rationale which accommodates their own values. The task is to stimulate the students' thought processes concerning commitment to teaching and to all that it entails. Values must have worth to the individual in order to be acceptable. When values are identified and accepted it is then possible to assist the learner in adjusting attitudes. Adjusting attitudes is crucial to making decisions regarding quality of work, career decisions, relationships with others, relationships to the environment, and worth of objects.

Does teaching about values have an effect on attitudes? Greenstein's study, as reported by Engle and Seyfarth (1982) seems to indicate affirmation. The study utilized a Values Reeducation Model and the findings give evidence that student teachers exposed to self-confrontation feedback changed their attitudes and behaviors. Engle and Seyfarth (1982) state, "It was noted that when student teachers had a ten-minute exposure to the values of good teachers and to the values of mediocre teachers, the student teachers incorporated the values of the good teachers into their own value system. Furthermore, student teachers exposed to this technique received higher student teacher evaluations" (p. 477).

VALUE ACQUISITION IN INDUSTRIAL ARTS TEACHER EDUCATION

"If he is indeed wise he does not bid you enter the house of his wisdom, but rather leads you to the threshold of your own mind" (Gibran, 1923/1963, p. 56).

A Worthy Effort

Our attitudes toward others, either students or teachers, come from our interactions with them. The kind, quality, and amount of inter-action between student and teacher shows considerable divergence. Feelings of attachment, indifference, concern, or rejection can dominate relationships with students (Gaite, 1975). If we are able to alter the quality of these interactions we may be able to alter the attitudes, for the purpose of instruction is to assist students in developing their own potential for learning and satisfaction. As Howard (1978) notes, *"The secret to learning is in the students' attitudes towards themselves and their feelings of power over their own destiny"* (p. 164, italics in original). A feeling of knowing what values we possess can have a powerful effect on learning. Dorfman and Stephan (1981) state, "that people whose high expectancies are accompanied by positive affect are the most likely to work hard in order to achieve favorable outcomes. Individuals who feel good because they perform well, and who perceive that they have some responsibility for their performances are likely to work hard in the future" (p. 18).

Teacher educators, and teachers, should not seek to impose personally held values upon students. But they should encourage some sort of commitment to the basic values of society such as honesty, punctuality, and dependability. Students should also be assisted in identifying values and their meaning to society, and to understand and be able to resolve conflicts of values. An individualized system of value recognition and appraisal is an evolutionary process rising from the individuality of the learning process and of the relationship between learner and teacher (Haladyna & Thomas, 1979).

We live in a dichotomous society; one in which "individualism, self-determination, and self-centeredness are in conflict with the needs of the group, group conformity, and the need for friends" (Podeschi, 1982). Anxiety appears to be a direct result of these conflicting needs. Understanding one's attitudes toward these needs can assure the individual that action, that is, behavior, need not be either-or, but relativistic. A dualistic view requires that answers or actions be either wrong or right. A relativistic view only asks what is best (Perry, 1982).

To ignore an emphasis on attitudes and values is to deny they exist, to deny their importance, or to deny their place in teacher education. Teacher education students need assistance in recognizing values and their effect in order that they, in turn, are able to help their students.

Implementing Change in the Individual

Change seems inevitable; society changes, weather changes, and technology changes. Yet, from observation, individuals all too often shield themselves from change. As teachers we must plan for change in ourselves and in students. In view of this, Castillo (1974) states, "The teacher (must) be actively involved in *his own* development and learning. He must know how he responds to change" (p. 35, italics in original). The teacher must understand the effect of anger, love, happiness, frustration, and content upon his/her actions and attitudes. The teacher must know the effects of saying "I cannot" versus "I will not." It is necessary that the teacher engage in introspection to discover the anxieties and abilities associated with change. Security is an important factor for without it little change occurs.

Varying instructional techniques can assist with teaching the student to analyze his/her capabilities and also his/her capacity for change. Rokeach (1979) found that a self-confrontation technique, in which students compared their values with those of a desired norm group, resulted in significant self-dissatisfaction with personally held values. The results of the study indicated that the subjects (students) changed their personal values more towards the direction of those from the normative group of values. Further, the adjusted values, as eveluted by attitudes and behavior persisted for at least seventeen months.

Working in groups seems to assist learners to focus on inner change. Slavin and Karweit (1981) used cooperative learning in which students worked in small cooperative groups (teams) to master academic materials. The group, as a whole, was rewarded for achievement. They report that students gained in liking of school, felt less anxious, and gained in academic and general self-esteem.

Some suggestions for college class instruction include open group work on values and beliefs, discussion of anxieties and behavior, simulation of experiences with ethical and moral intent, and survey-ing of opinions concerning feelings and emotions. It's worth a try.

Self-Actualization: Awareness, Readiness, Commitment

It is never too early or too late to self-actualize commitment. Young people are quite aware of feelings and attitudes of commitment. Nelson (1974) developed an affective assessment questionnaire for children in grades 1-3. The tenor of the questionnaire is shown by the follow-ing items to which children are asked to respond: not finishing a job you start, making your own choices, not getting work done on time, wasting time after school, doing good work, people should go to work every day if they are not sick, and being the best person you can be. If children can respond to such thoughts, college students can also respond.

In a study which related vocational maturity to self-concept, Put-nam, Hosie, and Hansen (1978) found a positive relationship between the individual's view of his/her moral-ethical self and vocational atti-tude maturity. The subjects were eleventh grade boys and girls. The feelings of adequacy, worth, value as a family member, and percep-tion of self were significant.

One goal of teacher education is to produce thinking, feeling, com-municating, decision making, and committed teachers who are not afraid to act upon their beliefs while out in the real world of teaching. Self-evaluation is the key to developing a personal methodology for improving one's abilities. Some helpful hints include scheduling one's own weekly "think back time," practicing a new procedure, obtain-ing evaluations of one's teaching, and setting new goals. It is difficult, but imperative, to schedule a definite time for reflection on the previous week's activities. It is a time to identify results of specific teaching behaviors such as efficiency of time on task and student learning.

Practicing a new procedure might include a new grading pro-cedure, a new teaching style, or restructuring time on teaching tasks. Evaluation of one's teaching can be done through audio-visual feed-back, student evaluations, peer evaluations, and peer evaluations of student actions. Set a new goal for each course each semester. The goal need not be great enough to drastically change the course but it should be noticeable. Communicate the change to the students. The time spent with students should be "lived" and efficient.

Value Palatability and Rejection

Values and attitudes are not universally held, nor should they be. In a practical manner, however, setting the tone or atmosphere of the laboratory or classroom requires standards of study and behavior. End-of-class clean-up and placement of tools and equipment is done on the assumption that orderliness and cleanliness have a positive effect on learning. Regular and punctual attendance, completion of assignments, and craftsmanship are usually viewed as attributes of a good student. Individual students, however, may not view as acceptable these teacher-held values; they may, in fact, reject them.

Interpersonal value conflict, as between teacher and student, is a reality. While we can expect the dilemma because of the teacher's attempt to broaden the learner's interests and attitudes the dilemma also provides a learning situation as the dilemma is resolved. The students will hopefully become more aware of their priorities. As Shaver and Strong (1982) explain, "Helping your students to become aware of their values, to define and apply value terms, to be aware of conflicting commitments and their implications for action, and to develop conceptual frames that will enable them to do all this for themselves out of the classroom — these goals are consistent with our societies' commitment to individual worth and dignity" (p. 89).

TEACHING/LEARNING STRATEGIES

Industrial arts education holds a logical place in the curriculum for assisting young people to be aware of values and attitudes. The activities and responsibilities usually conducted offer numerous opportunities for working with attitudes, feelings, emotions, and values. Industrial arts teacher education also holds a great potential for assisting teacher education students, both preservice and inservice, to appreciate the opportunities for helping their students in the affective domain.

Developing an Attitude Toward Teaching

Attitudes of teachers toward teaching are reflected in the variety of teaching methods utilized, the breadth of materials employed, the classroom organization, and relationships between the teacher and the learner.

It is noted, however, that the normal teaching styles of most teachers are extremely restricted (Joyce, 1978). Expanding the teacher's repertoire of models of teaching should be an immediate goal of industrial arts teacher education. Teachers are able to learn a variety of models that they could use at will. The greater the repertoire of models or styles gained the greater the possibility that teaching will become more effective. Improved effectiveness of teaching will boost teachers' attitudes toward the task.

Four assists to teachers allow for the acquisition of an expanded repertoire of teaching models or styles. These are: providing practice, with feedback, with small groups of students in the particular skills required for each model to be learned; acquaintance with the theory of the models; observation of demonstrations so that features can be seen and comprehended; and knowledge of when and with what material the model can be used (Joyce, 1978). Can teachers acquire an expanded repertoire of teaching models? Most can, and with ease. An expanded repertoire gives confidence in one's ability to perform. The teacher's comfort with new models will influence his or her effectiveness.

A more positive attitude toward teaching can be developed by focusing on teacher variables such as clarity of presentation, variability of teaching models, enthusiasm for learning, behavior that is task oriented, ability to accept critical review, and being able to adapt to new situations and tasks. Victor and Otis (1980) found that teachers who emphasize subject matter, per se, and maintain a social distance between themselves and the students tended to be closed to new ideas. Teachers who considered the student's views, were concerned with the student's adjustment, and believe that learning should relate to broad perspectives tended toward willingness to accept new ideas and to reveal their inner self. Teachers and prospective teachers need to focus on teaching styles or models and their own ability to explore and accept new ideas.

An interesting side issue regarding attitudes is how a person expresses or reveals them. Expressive behavior, though often masked or altered, eventually reveals one's true attitudes. Masking or altering is done because our culture determines the appropriateness of expression, our coping behaviors function to relieve discomfort, and/or we wish to deceive others. Teachers often feel that the job requires a stern countenance so that no student would dare take advantage. We mask our discomfort such as appearing angry when we wish to laugh, or cover anger with a thin smile. Lastly, due to some failure, we might actually intend to deceive the student (Saarni, 1981). Attitudes usually can be detected, for expressions communicate. Learning is an intensely interpersonal experience and honesty of expression will enhance the exchange.

One's attitude toward teaching affects performance. Attitudes can be changed with assistance. An enlarged repertoire of teaching models or styles enhances one's attitudes toward teaching. Honesty of expression appreciably enlivens students' acceptance of values and beliefs.

Acquiring or Changing Values

Values are the primary determinants of attitudes. We possess many attitudes but few values. Although values are intricate and involved, it is generally acknowledged that by having students reflect on their known values, their attitudes and resulting behavior can be influenced, even changed (Shaver and Strong, 1982). Values are standards toward which we judge our attitudes and actions. New values are acquired when we do not have a standard to judge by. Values can be modified when judgments cause actions which are not acceptable to the individual, especially when the actions run contrary to significant others, i.e., friends, family, and society. By focusing on attitudes and actions in light of desired results such as conformity, equilibrium, self-worth, etc., the individual can adjust his/her values.

Several ways and means can be utilized to assist the teacher and student to make meaningful changes in the values they possess or to acquire new values.

Modeling is the process of exhibiting attitudes, behavior, feelings, beliefs, and self-esteem which the learner may observe and emulate. Verbal and nonverbal communication play important roles in modeling. Everything that is said and done, appearance, and expression affect the learners' responses to their own set of values. Everyone, teacher and student alike, serves as a role model of some kind. Teacher educators can determine the role they play which students may emulate.

Learner attitude and behavior can also be influenced (modified) by changing the conditions or events of learning. Remember the gold stars rewarded for good work in elementary school days? The events may be either negative or positive. Some of us may also remember the green stars we received. Learners respond to external prizes or inducements and in responding modify their attitudes.

Contingency contracting is a method of bringing about desired changes in the learner's attitude and behavior (Homme, 1973). A contract is made between the teacher and the student, with conditions of reward, specifying the desired changes or behavior. An advantage of contingency contracting is that the learner becomes very much aware of the modified value. There are, however, several cautions: the contract must be fair, attainable, clear, honest, and positive.

Snyder (1977) identified several formal structured teaching activities to implement the process of attitude adjustment. Included were group processes which focused on goals and roles, leadership and teaming, and cooperation and trust. Other teaching activities for attitudinal change included using problem solving (analyzing causes, considering alternatives), human relations (discovering relationships, resolving conflicts), and personal growth processes (strategies for achievement, self tabulation).

Establishing or modifying values and subsequent behavior and attitudes requires a planned effort. The instructor must be accepting and non-judgmental to be effective. Learner responses to value activities must be respected. Teacher educators must respond to the challenge of raising the awareness of teacher education students regarding acquiring or changing values.

The Teacher's Effect on the Affect

Much has been written in the popular press concerning the need for some sort of "values education" which can be interpreted to mean fewer discipline problems and vandalism. Kiwanis, a service club organization, is being approached to financially support a "character education curriculum" in the public schools, K-12. A quote from John Ruskin on the cover of a brochure gives evidence of their intent, "Education does not mean teaching people to know what they do not know; it means teaching them to behave as they do not behave" (Character Education Curriculum, 1980).

Public pressure, at this time, seems aimed at changing some of the negative behavioral actions of students. The promoters of the Character Education Curriculum claim an 80 percent reduction in window breakage and less writing on lavatory walls; a message that the public can understand.

Hopefully, this yearbook discusses more than reversal of discipline problems, but there is an indicator that the schools and teachers will be put in a position of teaching some sort of "moral education." This may overshadow the total task of affective education. Teachers must have a larger goal than alleviating discipline problems.

Industrial arts teachers and teacher educators can have a particular effect on affective education. Activities, organization, meaningful content, and ensuing results are all trademarks of industrial arts which can have an important effect on learning. When expectancies are high and accompanied by positive effects the learner is more likely to work hard to achieve favorable results. Also, learners who feel good because they perform well (have good results) and who perceive that they have some responsibility for their performance are likely to work hard in the future. Studying, participating, completing, producing, responding, etc., are all interchangeable with "working hard." Industrial arts teachers do determine the type and extent of organization in classroom management. Class activities and the resulting products or outcomes greatly influence the participation of the learner. Content which reflects state of the art technology gives meaning to the learning task.

These hallmarks of industrial arts which can so profoundly affect the learner are all determined and managed by the teacher. There are few subject matter areas as fortunate and productive as industrial arts. Teacher educators share the responsibility for affective education because they determine the content and method of industrial arts teacher education.

Determining and Evaluating Outcomes

Industrial arts teachers are very much aware of their teaching responsibilities. Two major responsibilities are maintaining an appropriate atmosphere in the classroom and laboratory, and providing learning experiences that enhance student achievement (Medley and Crook, 1980). Teachers rate their effectiveness by evaluating student performances in cognitive, psychomotor, and affective learning. This information is corroborated by colleagues and administrators (and sometimes students) who share formal and informal observations of students. Being aware of and using information feedback is a teaching skill that needs to be emphasized in teacher education. Heilman and Cole (1980) present a tangible guideline for discussions on responsibility, behaviors and responses, teacher stance, and communication.

In the affective domain it is quite possible to evaluate student level and growth in attitudes, interests, values, preferences, self-esteem, responsibility, and anxiety (Anderson, 1981). A number of evaluative scales; Guttman, Likert, Thurstone, and Semantic Differential; are available in many forms (Anderson, 1981; Henerson, et al., 1978) or can be teacher made. Skill in using scales for assessing affective learning must be part of industrial arts teacher education.

Approaches to Teaching

The purpose of affective education is not to make the students feel and think the way the teacher does, but to assist the learners to develop their own potential for perceiving, valuing, feeling, believing, and behaving. It is the teacher's task to select and create opportunities for learning.

But teachers also perform other tasks, often simultaneously, such as instructor, counselor, manager, and evaluator. Competence in teaching is the ability to fulfill all these roles expertly. Mastering the repertoire of approaches to teaching is part of this competence. Teaching capability can be expanded by increasing the number of teaching strategies and by increasing the skill in the use of strategies.

The affective domain may be focused upon by employing relevant strategies or models. The strategies must emphasize the relationships between the learner and society (friends, family); between the learner and the plethora of information (technical and otherwise); and between what the individual is and what he/she wishes to be (selfhood).

Among social interaction strategies or models, *Group Investigation* developed by Thelan (1960) cultivates skills for participation in democratic social processes through emphasis on interpersonal/group skills and academic inquiry skills. An additional goal is growth in personal development. Another model, *Role Playing*, is designed to have students inquire into personal and societal values. One's own values, attitudes, and behavior are the basis for analysis (Shaftel and Shaftel, 1967). A third model worth utilizing is Boocock's (1968) *Social Stimulation*, in which students experience various social processes and realities and then examine their own reactions to the processes and realities.

Information processing models assist the learner to process stimuli from the environment, sense problems, organize information, form concepts, find solutions, and use symbols. The *Concept Attainment* model by Bruner, Goodnow, and Austin (1967) was designed to develop reasoning and concept development and analysis. Ausubel's (1963) *Advance Organizer* model is useful to the learner for increasing the efficiency of information processing capabilities. The *Inductive Thinking* model (Taba, 1967) assists the learner in developing the inductive thinking processes.

Personal models or strategies share an orientation toward the individual and the growth of one's inner self or character. Personal models emphasize the processes by which the learner can construct and organize his/her own unique reality; to see themselves as persons who are capable and have potential for further growth.

Rogers' (1951) *Nondirective Teaching* model places emphasis on strengthening the learner's capacity for personal growth in terms of self-awareness, understanding, independence, and self-esteem. *Awareness training* is a strategy for increasing the learner's ability for self-awareness and self-exploration. Body and sensory awareness can also be focused upon. Awareness training also places importance on the development of interpersonal awareness and comprehension (Perls, Hefferline, and Goodman, 1977; Schutz, 1967). Glasser's (1969) *Classroom Meeting* model is useful in assisting the learner in understanding one's self and the responsibilities the individual has to self and community.

A repertoire of strategies is essential for the teacher if industrial arts education has the goal to assist the learner in increasing potential for perceiving, valuing, feeling, believing, and behaving. Teacher education has the responsibility of incorporating models into the curriculum and assisting the teacher to acquire the necessary skills to utilize them.

Student Club Activity in Teacher Education

A student industrial arts club is a natural and efficient vehicle for providing experiences in the affective domain that are not otherwise attainable in the classroom or laboratory. Teacher educators see far too little of teacher education students. A student club can help students develop attitudes, perceptions, and behaviors which they in turn can impart to their students. Also, students can gain self-esteem through practicing social and leadership skills.

A student industrial arts club should be an integral part of the total curriculum in teacher education. Students need the club experience so they have the capability and desire to organize and/or operate an American Industrial Arts Student Club when teaching. Organizing and managing a student club requires extra effort and time, but it is well worth it to give students experiences which draw so heavily on the affective domain.

Many teaching/learning strategies can be used in industrial arts education to assist the teacher education student in gaining a larger repertoire of skills. Developing a positive attitude toward teaching should be part of the affective curriculum. Teacher education students need assistance in exploring attitudes and acquiring or changing values. We industrial arts teacher educators can help.

REFERENCES

Anderson, L.W. *Assessing Affective Characteristics in the Schools*. Boston: Allyn and Bacon, Inc., 1981.

Ausubel, D.P. *The Psychology of Meaningful Verbal Learning*. New York: Green and Stratton, 1963.

Boocock, S.S. *Simulating Games in Learning*. Beverly Hills, CA: Sage Publications, 1968.

Brown, P. Liberal arts clusters. In P. Brown (Ed.) Teaching about values and ethics. *The Forum for Liberal Education*, 1982, 4, 5-7. (ERIC Document Reproduction Service No. ED 212 248)

Bruner, J.S.; Goodnow, J.J.; & Austin, G.A. *A Study of Thinking*. New York: Science Editions, Inc., 1967.

Buber, M.M. *(I and Thou)* R.G. Smith (trans.). New York: Charles Scribner's Sons, 1958.

Castillo, G.A. *Left-Handed Teaching*. New York: Praeger Publishers, 1974.

Character Education Curriculum (and) Achievement Skills: Guidelines for Personal Success, Level I Junior High, Ages 11-14, Course Description (and) Level II, High School, Ages 15-18, Course Description. Pasadena, CA: Thomas Jefferson Research Center, 1980. (ERIC Document Reproduction Service No. ED 200 463)

Discipline Handbook for Faculty. Springfield, IL: Springfield Public Schools, 1981.

Dobson, R.L.; Dobson, J.E.; & Koetting, J.R. The language of teaching effectiveness and teacher-competency research. *Viewpoints in Teaching and Learning*, 1982, 58, 23-33.

Dorfman, P.W. & Stephan, W.G. *Cognitive, Affective, and Behavioral Determinants of Performance: A Process Model*. Paper presented at the annual convention of the American Psychological Association, Los Angeles, 1981. (ERIC Document Reproduction Service No. ED 212 970)

Engel, J.B. & Seyfarth, L. Teaching values: does it make a difference? *The Educational Forum,* 1982, *46,* 475-482.

Epstein, J.L. & McPartland, J.M. The concept and measurement of the quality of school life. *American Educational Research Journal,* 1976, *13,* 15-30.

Gaite, A.J.H. Teachers' attitudes. *Instructor,* 1975, *84,* 30.

Gephart, W.J. *Values, Valuing, and Evaluation.* Research Report Series (interim draft). Portland, OR: Northwest Regional Education Laboratory, 1981. (ERIC Document Reproduction Service No. Ed 216 047)

Gibran, K. *The Prophet.* New York: Alfred A. Knopf, 1963 (originally published, 1923).

Glasser, W. *Schools Without Failure.* New York: Harper and Row, 1969.

Haladyna, T. & Thomas, G. The attitudes of elementary school children toward school and subject matters. *Journal of Experimental Education,* 1979, *48,* 18-23.

Heilman, J. & Cole, B. *Behavioral Management: An Affective Approach.* (Affective Education Trainers Manual.) Sacramento: California State Department of Education, 1980. (ERIC Document Reproduction Service No. ED 202 854)

Henerson, M.E.; Morris, L.L.; & Fitz-Gibbon, C.T. *How to Measure Attitudes.* Beverly Hills, CA: Sage Publications, 1978.

Homme, L.E. *How to Use Contingency Contracting in the Classroom.* Champaign, IL: Research Press, 1973.

Howard, E. *School Discipline Desk Book.* West Nyack, NY: Parker Publishing Company, 1978.

Joyce, B.R. *Selecting Learning Experiences: Linking Theory and Practice.* Washington: Association for Supervision and Curriculum Development, 1978. (ERIC Document Reproduction Service No. ED 156 673)

Kazanas, H.C. & Beach, D.P. *Affective Work Competencies Inventory,* 1978, as cited in Beach, D.P. *Development of an Instructional Model for Helping Youth Acquire Necessary Work Habits, Attitudes, or Values.* Paper presented at the Eastern Educational Research Association Annual Conference, Philadelphia, 1981. (ERIC Document Reproduction Service, No. ED 199 569)

Langerak, E.A. Values in the curriculum. In P. Brown (Ed.), Teaching about values and ethics. *The Forum for Liberal Education,* 1982, *4,* 2-4. (ERIC Document Reproduction Service No. ED 212 248)

Medley, D.M. & Crook, P.R. Research in teacher competency and teaching tasks. *Theory Into Practice,* 1980, *19,* 294-301.

Merrill, K. Values throughout the curriculum. In P. Brown (Ed.), Teaching about values and ethics. *The Forum for Liberal Education,* 1982, *4,* 7-8. (ERIC Document Reproduction Service No. ED 212 248)

Morris, R.C. & Krajewski, R. Humanism and the futuristic perspective. *Theory Into Practice,* 1980, *19,* 129-133.

Nelson,, K. *Affective Assessment Questionnaire for Career Education Grade 1-3.* Minneapolis: Minnesota Research Coordinating Unit for Vocational Education, University of Minnesota, 1974.

Perls, F.S.; Hefferline, R.F.; & Goodman, P. *Gestalt Therapy: Excitement and Growth in the Human Personality.* New York: Crown Publishers, 1977.

Perry, W.G., Jr. Students developing views of pluralism in knowledge and value. In P. Brown (Ed.), Teaching about values and ethics. *The Forum for Liberal Education,* 1982, *4,* 4-5. (ERIC Document Reproduction Service No. ED 212 248)

Podeschi, R. Education and American values. *The Educational Forum,* 1982, *46,* 159-165.

Policies and Procedures. Saginaw, MI: School District of the City of Saginaw, Michigan, 1981-82.

Putnam, B.A.; Hosie, T.W.; & Hansen, J.C. Sex differences in self-concept variables and vocational attitude maturity of adolescents. *Journal of Experimental Education,* 1978, *47,* 23-27.

Rogers, C.R. *On Becoming a Person.* Boston: Houghton-Mifflin Company, 1951.

Rokeach, M. Introduction. In M. Rokeach (Ed.), *Understanding Human Values: Individual and Societal.* New York: Free Press, 1979.

Saarni, C. *Emotional Experiences and Regulation of Expressive Behavior.* Paper presented at the Biennial Meeting of the Society for Research in Child Development. Boston, 1981. (ERIC Document Reproduction Service, No. ED 207 700)

Schutz, W.C. *Joy: Expanding Human Awareness.* New York: Grove Press, 1967.

Shaftel, F.R. & Shaftel, G.A. *Role-Playing for Social Values: Decision Making in the Social Studies.* Englewood Cliffs, NJ: Prentice-Hall Inc., 1967.

Shaver,, J.P. & Strong, W. *Facing Value Decisions: Rationale-Building for Teachers.* New York: Teachers College Press, 1982.

Slavin, R.E. & Karweit, N.L. Cognitive and affective outcomes of an intensive student team learning experience. *Journal of Experimental Education,* 1981, *50,* 29-35.

Snyder, T.R. *Affective Education: a Comprehensive Program to Promote Student Self-Actualization and Human Relations Skills.* Columbus, OH: Development Institute, 1977. (ERIC Document Reproduction Service, No. ED 175 755)

Taba, H. *Teacher's Handbook for Elementary Social Studies.* Reading, MA: Addison-Wesley Publishing Co., 1967.

Thelen, H.A. *Education and the Human Quest.* New York: Harper and Row, 1960.

Victor, J.B. & Otis, J.P. Teacher strength and sensitivity behavior: attitude personality correlates. *Journal of Experimental Education,* 1980, *49,* 9-15.

Chapter 6

An Annotated Bibliography of Sources in Affective Learning

Gerald L. Jennings, Ph.D.
Professor
Department of Business and Industrial Education
Eastern Michigan University
Ypsilanti, Michigan

This chapter offers annotations of over fifty books, periodicals, research reports and instructional programs that may be useful to the student, teacher or researcher in industrial arts education who is interested in reviewing in greater depth the topics in this yearbook. It is by no means an exhaustive collection, for there are many more items available which are related to aspects of affective learning. Those included here were either recommended by the authors of this yearbook, or appeared to have particular relevance to industrial arts education.

In the process of conducting research necessary for the yearbook project, it became evident that there are very few items (virtually none) reported in the literature directly relating industrial arts education to affective learning. Many items are available which discuss affective education in a general context — primarily under humanistic education. A very significant number of items exist on the topics of values and value clarification, especially with reference to studies in the humanities. It has been necessary, therefore, to look at sources in a number of areas — psychology, philosophy, learning theory, guidance and counseling, as well as the humanities — to identify the theories, concepts, principles and generalizations pertaining to affective learning that might have implications for industrial arts education. Nearly all of the items cited by the yearbook authors have been used in that manner.

It is hoped that with these sources the reader will be encouraged to take a closer look at the meaning of affective learning, and select some approaches for teaching affectively in an industrial arts classroom. Considering the paucity of material that currently exists on affective learning in industrial arts, and in view of the proposal for a major study of industrial arts to reflect technology education, the need for a more adequate study of affective learning by professionals in the discipline seems to be quite urgent.

Alloway, T.; Lester, K. & Pliner, P. (Eds.) *Communication and Affect: A Comparative Approach.* New York: Academic Press, 1972.

> This collection of research papers deals with the importance of communication to the development of affective or emotional feelings. The view expressed is that at the present time in our history, it appears that we may be approaching a crisis in affective communication produced by the growing difficulties which individuals face in establishing meaningful interpersonal relationships in an increasingly impersonal society. The rhetoric, alienation and frequent criticism of traditional institutions seen today, as well as the decline in the family as an institution, reflect the crisis that is growing. New techniques for building interpersonal relations are needed and being studied. The papers in this book focus on some of the problems in affective communication between man and man, man and machine, man and animals, and among animals. The basic research findings and theoretical recitations provided should be useful to psychologists, linguists and educators interested in the evolution and development of communication and affect in mammals.

Aspy, D.N. *Toward a Technology for Humanizing Education.* Champaign, IL: Research Press, 1972.

> The work of Aspy over a period of a decade is summarized by him in an effort to show educators the concepts, procedures and techniques which he used to maximize learning in the classroom. He offers the results of the empirical research and the research tools which he used to search his theses as well as train his teachers and students. Both the rationale for humane classrooms and specific processes for developing them are presented. Each chapter describes a specific dimension of humane interpersonal relationships followed by a specific instrument for assessing the dimension, and a study which both validates the dimension and illustrates how it can be used in schools.

Aspy, D.N. and Roebuck, F.N. *Kids Don't Learn from People They Don't Like.* Amherst, MA: Human Resource Developing Press, 1977.

These authors explore the questions of how to transform the school classroom into the kind of humane environment which would promote real student growth. This book represents a ten-year effort by Aspy and Roebuck to find ways in which teachers and educators could achieve this goal. Research conducted during the latter part of those years, with the assistance of the National Consortium for Humanizing Education, as documented in this text, dispels any doubts about the critical need for interpersonal skills in the public school classroom. The ongoing battles in education between "values" and "skills," "learning" and "training" must be reconciled, "for in the end there can be no values without the skills needed to live them, no learning without the effective teaching that makes such learning possible." The first section provides a narrative account of the background and development of the NCHE, a summary of literature and preliminary pilot studies used for the research. Section two offers a research summary of the National Consortium work. Section three describes the tools used in the research, and section four contains references and a bibliography.

Association for Supervision and Curriculum Development, *Measuring and Attaining the Goals of Education.* Washington, D.C.: The Association, 1980.

An ASCD committee on research and theory worked for three years to complete this text. Ten major goals of education are used in an effort to give readers a perception of educational goals and their relationship to cognitive, affective and psychomotor learning. Operating from the premise that humanistic education is concerned with all aspects of learning and developing the "whole" child, the committee accepted the ASCD charge to examine: (1) how the valued goals were interrelated; (2) the types of school programs and/or experiences that are likely to maximize achievement in all goals, and (3) how educators might design research and evaluation programs to acquire comprehensive measures of student achievement. A virtual catalog of instruments currently available for measuring each of the goals resulted from the committee's efforts. A research model was also developed and is included to illustrate how educators can determine the relationships among goals of schooling, specific outcomes representing those goals, processes of teaching and learning employed by schools, and environmental factors influencing those processes.

Association for Supervision and Curriculum Development. *Improving Education Assessment and An Inventory of Measures of Affective Behavior.* Washington, D.C.: The Association, 1969.

> Speeches by Ralph Tyler, Robert Stake, Daniel Stufflebeam and Walcott Beatty provided the basis for development of this text by the ASCD Council on Assessment of Educational Outcomes. Major efforts of the Council were directed at: (1) developing a theory of educational assessment; (2) defining problems in carrying out effective assessment and developing a means for coping with the problems, and (3) reviewing existing instruments in the area of self-concept. Motivation for their work came from a concern that measurement theory which currently exists appears to be much too restrictive to serve the purposes of evaluating the effectiveness of educational procedures. In addition to the four papers, a large section is devoted to an inventory of measures of affective behavior, including attitude scales, and instruments on interaction, motivation, personality readiness and self-concept.

Berman, L.M. & Roderick, J.A. (Eds.) *Feeling, Valuing, and the Art of Growing: Insights into the Affective.* (Yearbook of the Association for Supervision and Curriculum Development.) Washington, D.C.: The Association, 1977.

> This collection of writings offers significant insights into the character of affective processes. Twelve contributors present a broad picture of the conditions and opportunities for affective learning in the schools. A key concern of the editors was that affective learning discussion tends to focus too often on the lower level affective process, such as those involving feeling behavior. Their attempt in this yearbook was to describe the higher level processes and to deal more directly than does much of the literature with the problems of maturing, growing, and becoming more complete persons. A wide variety of views are offered concerning the affective by artists, writers, psychologists and educators, with the result that the principles underlying humanistic education are given greater meaning. Includes a very extensive bibliography organized to guide the student toward the several components of affective development.

Bloom, B.S.; Hastings, J.T. & Madaus, G.F. *Handbook on Formative and Summative Evaluation in Student Learning.* New York: McGraw-Hill Book Co., 1971.

> A book about the "state of the art" of evaluating student learning for use by both present and future teachers, it is intended to help teachers as they encounter various evaluation problems at the

beginning of the school year, at each stage of the academic cycle (formative evaluation) and in the final (summative) stage. Related to Bloom's earlier text on the *Taxonomy of Educational Objectives*, it offers a framework and techniques for test construction. Part one addresses the evaluation problems all teachers are likely to encounter. It concludes with a discussion of some major new developments taking place in evaluation. Part two considers evaluation in each of the major subject fields and levels of education. It offers teachers ways of using evaluation to improve learning in their own interest area and level of teaching.

Bloom, B.S.; Hastings, J.T. & Madaus, G.F. *Evaluation to Improve Learning.* New York: McGraw-Hill Co., 1981.

A guide for teachers and students in teacher education who are concerned for the improvement of student learning, it speaks to the proper use of teacher-made quizzes, progress tests, and other examinations. Mastery learning is viewed as a significant new development in instruction, and is used by these authors as a goal in developing evaluation processes. Chapters 1 to 3 deal with how evaluation may be used to help bring students up to mastery levels of learning. Chapters 4 to 6 discuss the purposes of evaluation and the ways to use evaluation instruments in the classroom. Diagnostic, formative and summative evaluation techniques are described. Writing and selecting test items is reviewed in Chapter 7. Chapters 8 to 11 are organized around taxonomies of educational objectives and present models and techniques for constructing valid evaluation instruments for different types of objectives.

Brown, G.E. *Affectivity, Classroom Climate and Teaching.* American Federation of Teachers, Washington, D.C., 1971.

"Confluent education" is defined as the integration of the affective and cognitive elements. Overemphasis on either element can be a detriment to the other, and will lead to serious complications. Techniques in affective learning are described briefly and suggestions are offered on how to integrate those techniques into conventional classroom practices and content.

Combs, A.W. (Ed.) *Perceiving, Behaving, Becoming: A New Focus for Education.* (Yearbook of the Association for Supervision and Curriculum Development.) Washington, D.C.: The Association, 1962.

Four authors, Earl C. Kelley, Carl R. Rogers, Abraham H. Maslow, and Arthur W. Combs present position papers describing what they view as the fully-functioning or self-actualized person. From those papers a number of implications for education are developed in the areas of: motivation and growth of self; positive view of self; creativity and openness to experience; the feeling of identification; the adequate person; convictions, beliefs, and values; dignity, integrity and autonomy; and the process of becoming. This new focus on education espouses "third force" psychology, which is considered neither behavioristic nor Freudian, but accounts for the larger concerns for developing a self-actualized person. This is one of the most highly regarded sources and yearbooks offered by ASCD.

Curwin, R.L. & Curwin, G. with the editors of *Learning* magazine. *Developing Values in the Classroom.* Palo Alto, CA: Education Today, Ind., 1974.

Teachers who are looking for activities to use in developing values in the classroom will find this a valuable handbook. A brief introduction to values clarification is followed by a list and explanation of strategies to be used. They deal with: (1) building trust; (2) helping children discover their true selves; (3) integrating values and curriculum areas. It concludes with a description of ways to create activities for the classroom, methods of evaluating, record keeping and processing, and a bibliography of resources.

Curwin, R.L. & Fuhrmann, B.S. *Discovering Your Teaching Self: Humanistic Approaches to Effective Teaching.* Englewood Cliffs, NJ: Prentice-Hall, Inc., 1975.

This book presents a program of self-improvement for teachers and prospective teachers based upon humanistic criteria. A collection of activities designed to help teachers be more effective through an examination of their own "self." The activities are internally focused and utilize fictional logs and discussions of the teacher's role and teaching behavior. Their intent is to make the teacher's classroom behavior congruent with his or her ideas. Teachers are directed to carry out assignments in their own classroom teaching.

Darling, D.W. Why a taxonomy of affective learning? *Educational Leadership.* (April 1965) Vol. 24, pp. 473-522.

A rationale is presented for the use of a taxonomy of learning in planning curriculum. A taxonomy in the affective domain can help the teacher focus on developing the students' interests, attitudes and values. A systematic approach can be developed and implemented to help students make commitments to appropriate values. The school's responsibility for promoting affective learning can be clarified through the use of a taxonomy.

Dinkmeyer, D. & Dinkmeyer, D, Jr. *DUSO: Developing Understanding of Self and Others.* (Revised) Circle Pines, MN: American Guidance Service, 1982.

A two-level instructional program to be used for the affective development of children, DUSO-1 is prepared for grades K-2 and DUSO-2 for grades 3-4. Working under the premise that positive self-concept and social skills are necessary conditions for learning, the Dinkmeyers prepared these instructional units to help teachers help children feel good about themselves and others. Activities in the programs are organized into three units: (1) Developing Understanding of Self; (2) Developing Understanding of Others; (3) Developing Understanding of Choices. The units are made up of a number of specific goals with activities which can be used sequentially, presenting a goal each week, or according to specific needs. The first activity for each goal is a story, which may be followed by such things as a guided fantasy, dramatic play, a problem situation, discussion activities, career activities, role playing, music, or worksheets.

DUSO-1 focuses on developing awareness of feelings, priorities, and choices, with related activities directed at building the child's positive self-image, appreciation of individual strengths, and acceptance of personal limitations. The activities also deal with beginning social skills and demonstrate the value of careful decision making to achieve goals. DUSO-2 moves the student from the awareness of feelings, goals and values to an understanding of the purposive nature of behavior. Students are also shown how to apply behavioral goals to self, relationships with others, and personal accomplishments. A teacher's guide, story books, audiocassettes, activity cards, and puppets are some of the materials in the program packages.

Dinkmeyer, D.; McKay, G.D. & Dinkmeyer, D., Jr. *Systematic Training for Effective Teaching.* Circle Pines, MN: American Guidance Service, 1980.

An inservice program for teachers, grades K-12, who are seeking practical ways of communicating with, disciplining, and motivating students, the STET program is based on a theory of behavior that says authoritarianism doesn't work in correcting student discipline problems. A series of fourteen topics is introduced to a participating group of teachers over a period of several weeks by a leader. Each weekly session will last 1-2 ½ hours depending upon whether the complete or abbreviated program is used. Discussion topics deal with such areas as understanding behavior and misbehavior, using encouragement to motivate, improving communication skills, group dynamics, understanding special needs students and working with parents. Several formats for delivery are suggested to accommodate different teacher inservice schedules, including consecutive sessions, dual semester format, a five-part component plan and an inservice workshop plan. The program package includes a teacher's resource book, a teacher's handbook, and a leader's manual, as well as audiocassettes and items for directing discussions.

Drews, E.M. Beyond curriculum. *Journal of Humanistic Psychology.* (Fall 1968) Vol. 8, pp. 97-112.

A number of assumptions are used as a basis for this discussion of the psychology of self. They deal with unconditional trust and valuation of the student, individualization, group discussions, self-affirmation and commitment, and world as setting and curriculum. Consideration is given to the nature of the teacher's role, ways to change instructional methodology and content, learning to achieve self-actualization, and how to involve students in the world outside the classroom. The point is emphasized that schools can best prepare students to assume appropriate roles in society by helping them become self-actualized persons.

Dupont, H. *Transition.* Circle Pines, MN: American Guidance Service, 1979.

Five instructional kits are designed for use with students aged 12 to 15. Prepared for teachers in any subject area — as well as counselors, social workers and school psychologists — as a tool in helping the early adolescent cope with their difficult age period. The ninety-one activities in the five units present a variety of situations to promote discussion of experiences common to adolescents. Scenarios of conflicts and dilemmas for reading, writing and acting out; discussions, dialogues, debates, games, exercises and questionnaires are all a part of the activities. Transition-1 deals with communication and problem-solving; Transition-2 deals with encouraging openness and trust; Transition-3 with verbal and nonverbal communication of feelngs; Transition-4 with needs, goals and expectations; and Transition-5 with increasing awareness of values. The author believes that when you support adolescents' efforts to cope with emotional and social issues you help them academically as well.

Dupont, H.; Gardner, O.S. & Brody, D.S. *Toward Affective Development.* Circle Pines, MN: American Guidance Service, Inc., 1982.

An activity-centered program is designed to stimulate psychological and affective development of 8- to 12-year-old children. A four-year development and field test period was used in preparing the five sections in this set of instructional aids. Its purpose is to help children examine their thoughts, feelings, and reactions while learning in the classroom. A large variety of techniques is utilized in the process of helping children to: (1) become more open to sensory experience and to use their imagination; (2) increase their awareness of feelings and the ways feelings are communicated; (3) learn and practice skills and attitudes basic to working together successfully; (4) consider their individual characteristics, interests and aspirations while learning about career fields, and (5) put their developing skills to work in resolving interpersonal conflicts — choosing the course of action that is best for them. Among the activities used are games and simulations, role playing, acting out, modeling, imitating, brainstorming, and group discussion.

Eberle, B. and Hall, R.E. *Affective Education Guidebook: Classroom Activities in the Realm of Feelings.* Buffalo, NY: D.O.K. Publishers, Inc., 1975.

> The primary concern of these authors is for the improvement of interpersonal relationships. Since learning and living with others requires social skills, skill building for positive relations should become a part of instruction for all learning groups. In this book they offer an instructional plan and learning activities intended to improve interpersonal relationships. It is intended primarily for elementary and junior high teachers, but has application and adaptive value for other groups which deal with interpersonal problems. Chapter One provides an introduction to the issues and describes the model for achieving effective affective learning in the realm of feelings. Chapter Two presents three steps toward improved relationships, while Chapter Three provides a description of five levels of activities which can be used in helping learners improve interpersonal skills.

Erickson, R.C. & Wentling, T.L. *Measuring Student Growth: Techniques and Procedures for Occupational Education.* Boston: Allyn and Bacon, Inc., 1979.

> This book is designed as a tool for classroom teachers in secondary and post-secondary schools, as well as for advanced graduate students in vocational education. Basic techniques in general measurement, the use of teacher-made instruments, standardized instruments, and how to obtain and use measurement information are discussed with reference to applications in occupational education. The focus is on measurement of student growth and not on measurement of the many other facets of occupational programs. Chapter 7 discusses the process of constructing measures of affect.

The concern for appropriate attitudes, interests, values and appreciations related to job entry provided the basis for this discussion on the use of affective measures. A number of techniques and instruments for this purpose are described and illustrated.

Ferkiss, Victor C. *Technological Man: The Myth and the Reality.* New York: George Braziller, 1969.

The effects of current technological change on society are explored through an examination of "the direction in which mankind must move if it is going to be able to deal with the new challenges put to the social order by technological change." Technological man requires a philosophy that encompasses a new naturalism, holism, and immanentism. Social planning and awareness of the ecological consequences of policies are needed. Offers a basis for considering value formulation in a society experiencing rapid technological change.

Forsyth, A.S., Jr. & Gammel, J.D. *Toward Affective Education: A Guide to Developing Affective Learning Objectives.* Batelle Memorial Institute, Columbus, OH: Center for Improved Education, 1973.

This guide is designed to assist the educator in preparing and implementing a program of affective education. It introduces the affective domain, discusses its importance, and presents a brief history of approaches to affective education. The Batelle Project/Alpha approach is described. A model of the "effective human being" and a hierarchy of objectives in the affective domain are illustrated. A concluding discussion on the educator or facilitator includes a general presentation on how to proceed in the structuring of a complete program in affective education. Emphasis throughout the guide is on helping the educator understand affective education, feel comfortable with it, and improve his skills in the affective domain.

Girod, G.R. *Writing and Assessing Attitudinal Objectives.* Columbus, OH: Charles E. Merrill Publishing Co., 1973.

A programmed text for persons interested in writing behavioral objectives for attitude development and change, materials are designed to aid users in selecting and writing attitudinal objectives and measures in order to be better prepared to change attitudes. Each chapter begins with a brief statement defining terms and introducing concepts which follow in the programmed materials. Pre- and post-tests are also used to help readers determine their own positions relative to the process of writing attitudinal objectives and measures.

Hargrove, W.R. Learning in the affective domain. *Peobody Journal of Education.* (November 1969) Vol. 47, pp. 144-146.

>   According to this author there are five affective goals which must be considered in the schools today. They involve: (1) quiet contemplation; (2) relationship to nature; (3) valuing the good and beautiful; (4) respect for the self and others, and (5) development of values and behaviors necessary for sustaining a democracy. Hargrove describes a number of specific ways to begin implementing these goals in schools to establish affective education.

Harmin, M.; Kirschenbaum, H. & Simon, S.B. *Clarifying Values Through Subject Matter: Applications for the Classroom.* Minneapolis: Winston Press, Inc., 1973.

>   These authors discuss three levels of teaching: facts, concepts, and values. The goals of values-clarification are explained. Examples of values-level teaching in all of the different subject areas of the curriculum are presented, as well as values strategies that might be used with subject matter. A book that would be useful to teachers who are looking for ways to incorporate values education into the curriculum.

Henerson, M.E.; Morris, L.L. & Fitz-Gibbon, C.T. *How to Measure Attitudes.* Beverly Hills: Sage Publications, 1978.

>   Intended for use in evaluation activities, this is one of eight books in a kit. Extensive field testing of kit materials was carried out in Canada and the United States by these authors. Recommended measurement procedures, rules of thumb and practical strategies for performing evaluation tasks related to the assessment of peoples' attitudes are offered. Deals with the major issues and procedures surrounding the design and use of attitude instruments. Materials include both formative and summative evaluation tasks. Attitude is defined as having to do with affect, feelings, values and beliefs. For use primarily by people who have been assigned to the role of program evaluator.

Hillman, A. Concepts and elements of confluent education (life is possibilities, not probabilities). *DRICE Monograph 3 Development and Research in Confluent Education.* Santa Barbara, CA. Ford Foundation, New York, February, 1973.

>   This is a report of a project that attempted to find ways in which emotional learning could be brought to a level commensurate with intellectual learning. Confluent education considers the process of teaching a person through both cognitive and affective approaches. The project defines nine critical elements that should be present in

a teaching situation for confluent education to exist: (1) responsibility — the ability to respond creatively and positively to any situation; (2) convergency — relating and experiencing what is done or what is happening to the self; (3) connectedness — a sense of positive affiliation with others; (4) divergency — relating and experiencing what is happening or will happen; (6) gestalt — gaining closure or satisfaction through positive frustration and explication; (7) identify — a feeling of self-worth, self-esteem, and ego identity; (8) context — learning to understand communications through general semantics and environment; and (9) evaluation — eliciting individuals' opinions concerning values.

Humanizing education through technology: symposium. *Educational Technology.* June 1971. Vol. 11, pp. 9-33.

An entire issue of this journal discusses the impact of technology in education. Articles include:

Landers, R.R. "An approach to humanizing education through technology," pp. 9-11. Three primary elements are described: humanizing, education and technology. Humanizing may be "soft" or "hard." Education can be humanized through technology as long as the failure modes, defects and hazards in the revised educational system are identified, analyzed and eliminated or controlled.

Goshen, C.E. "The humanizing process," pp. 12-14. Technology in education should not be viewed as either humanizing or dehumanizing. Technology can serve a humanizing effect on the classroom by freeing teachers from monotonous routines, and permit them to develop more interpersonal relationships with students.

Martin, J.H. "Self-growth and self-enhancement through technology," pp. 15-18. A technology is needed that can respond positively to such criteria as: (1) does it involve many senses?; (2) does it permit the learner to get into the curriculum?; (3) does it make possible the braided trilogy of sound, text and picture?; (4) does it bring freedom to the act of learning in the unique random style of each and every learner?

Persselin, L.E. "Humanizing education through technology: the view from an ivory fox hole," pp. 18-20. Educational technology can be defined in terms of three component elements: (1) Programmed Learning; (2) Mediated Instruction; (3) Educational Accountability in Effective Technology, Product and Process are Inseparable.

Barnes, D.E. "Humane benefits for education: some direction in technology," pp. 21-23. Technology will exert increasing influence on instruction and may do so with humane results. Rising costs and limited resources, as well as the problem of achieving greater cost-effectiveness, will be significant forces in this process.

Canfield, J.T. "Dear machine, don't call us, we'll call you," pp. 23-26. Offers programs designed to teach in the affective domain. A key factor is the teacher's attitude toward his pupils. There is a need to train teachers to develop nurturing capability.

Williamson, M. "Some reservations about humanizing education through technology," pp. 26-27. Undesirable elements should be taken out when developing the humanizing process. Teachers may be either positive or negative models in teaching. They need to recognize actions and attitudes that dehumanize people.

Sharp, B.B. "Contract learning and humanistic education," pp. 28-30. The goal must be to educate human differences, if education is to be humanized through technology. Both human and technological resources must be reallocated to enable machines to produce sameness and humans to produce differences.

Kranzberg, M. "The new role of the humanities and social sciences," pp. 31-33. The 21st century will be characterized by accelerating social changes and a larger technological base. Discusses the interface of science and technology with humanistic and social concerns. Education should prepare future citizens to understand the social forces accompanying technological change.

Junell, J.S. *Matters of Feeling: Values Education Reconsidered.* Bloomington, IN: Phi Delta Kappa, 1979.

This book examines the philosophy, confusion and ignorance that pervade the teaching of values as conducted in schools today. The author argues that values, to the degree that schools can teach them at all, can be taught only through emotionally related processes of identification and through the arts of persuasion and drama. He is, therefore, taking issue with the popular concept that values can be taught through the methods of logical analysis and science. The qualities of a teacher are critical to the process of shaping values. Junell believes that all the hard evidence concerning attitudes formulation indicates that teachers must espouse the arguments that favor the attitudes and beliefs we wish to instill. What exerts the greatest impact on children's attitudes is not that their intelligence is exposed to reason, but that they are exposed to dynamic teachers. He also argues against the use of moral dilemmas approaches and values clarification activities. Children learn values by becoming emotionally involved in the lives of individuals and groups locked in struggles of significant moral consequence.

Kolesnik, W.B. *Learning: Educational Applications.* Boston: Allyn and Bacon, Inc., 1976.

> For beginning or prospective teachers, this book describes in a nontechnical nature how learning takes place and how it can be facilitated. Kolesnik discusses the concepts of teaching and learning as strongly interdependent functions. Numerous examples of learning principles are offered in a rather casual, conversational style in an effort to make the study of the teaching-learning process interesting to a wide range of readers. Each chapter is supplemented with an annotated list of recommended readings, in an effort to encourage a more detailed study of basic learning principles.

Kolesnik, W.B. *Humanism and/or Behaviorism in Education.* Boston: Allyn and Bacon, Inc., 1975.

> A discussion of the two dominant psychological theories in contemporary education, Kolesnik presents in a nontechnical manner a comparison of humanism and behaviorism through a review of educational issues and psychological principles surrounding each of these seemingly conflicting approaches. In the end discussion is directed at synthesizing and integrating the features of each in an effort to help readers determine their own position relative to the meaning of behaviorism and humanism. Kolesnik suggests that the two are not diametrically opposed on either a theoretical or practical level. He concludes: "Schools can help develop the free and happy, self-actualizing people envisioned by the humanists while at the same time contribute to the development of the good citizens envisioned by the behaviorists."

Krathwohl, D.R.; Bloom, B. & Masia, B. *Taxonomy of Educational Objectives. Handbook II: Affective Domain.* New York: David McKay, 1964.

> Terminology in the affective domain is organized and defined in this book so that research and thinking on the subject can follow a more logical and consistent path. It begins with a description of the nature of the affective domain and the classification structure prepared for it. The classification structure is then detailed and the evaluation of affective objectives discussed. A great deal of effort is given to providing examples of affective objectives and evaluation approaches which could be used for those objectives. The

appendices contain condensed versions of both the cognitive and affective domains. A book which has been used extensively as a basic guide in writings and research on the affective domain.

Leeper, R.R. (Ed.) *Humanizing Education: The Person in the Process.* (22nd ASCD Annual Conference, Dallas, 1967.) Washington, D.C.: The Association, 1967.

Presents ten major addresses at the ASCD annual conference, including those by the well known humanists Carl Rogers and Arthur Combs. The message in this collection is summarized by Combs: "We have produced a world capable of freeing humanity as never before, but capable also of producing a terrible loneliness and alienation. What we sought to help us be free has the potential to make us slaves." The issue is "that education is a people business in which the goals we seek and the things we try must eventually be judged in terms of the persons in the process." This book sounds a clarion call for a re-emphasis on the affective domain in education.

Macpherson, C.B. Democratic theory: ontology and technology. In Spitz, D. (Ed.) *Political Theory and Social Change.* New York: Atherton Press, 1967, pp. 203-220.

Western democratic theory has been based on two internally inconsistent assumptions. The first — associated with capitalism and the market — sees man as an infinite desirer and consumer of utilities. The second — which provided the justification for liberal democracy — views man as a exerter of his uniquely human capacities and asserts the equal right of every individual to make the most of himself. The two conflict because, if each man is allowed to consume in accordance with his infinite desires, some men will accumulate more than others and thereby gain power over others, so that the right of every man to make the most of himself will not be realized. The conflict can be resolved because the technological revolution allows us to abandon the market conception of man, since we are no longer faced with the problem of using men's energies in the material productive process. To retain the values of liberal democracy, the market view of man must be abandoned.

Mager, R.F. *Developing Attitude Toward Learning.* Belmont, CA: Fearon Publishers, 1968.

In straightforward language Mager describes some basic principles for developing in students a positive attitude toward what they learn. The conditions that influence the attitude, how to recognize it, and how to evaluate it are considered in the three major sections of this book. Mager expresses the concern that "when we accept the responsibility for professionally influencing the lives and actions of other people, we must do all we can to make that influence positive rather than negative." The responsibility is not only one for helping students acquire more knowledge and skills, but also for sending them away with the ability and the inclination to use those skills to help themselves and others.

Maslow, A.H. *Motivation and Personality.* (2nd Ed.) New York: Harper and Row, 1970.

One of the best known and most influential humanists offers a unified theory of motivation and psychological growth in this book. He expresses concern for total personality development, rather than classroom motivation, and discusses the self-actualizing individual and presents his views on human nature and potentialities.

Mesthene, E.G. *Technological Change: Its Impact on Man and Society.* Cambridge, MA: Harvard University Press, 1970.

Mesthene discusses the nature of strains placed on our values and beliefs by technological innovation. New goals must be defined by society and people must organize themselves differently from before in order to take advantage of opportunities offered by the new tools of technology. As new goals are defined, old value systems tend to become displaced. The result is often reflected in economic, political and ideological conflict. The effects of technology on society are much more complex, and demanding of much more knowledge than many have considered. An annotated bibliography is offered with numerous references on the nature of technology and its impact on society. Mesthene developed these materials while being involved at the Harvard University Program on Technology and Society.

National Special Media Institute. *The Affective Domain.* (A Resource Book for Media Specialists.) Washington, D.C.: Gryphon House, 1972.

A collection of papers on research and studies, this book describes the meaning of affect for educational technology. As the field of education technology moved from its traditional audiovisual product orientation to consider the impact of new systems on learning, a more critical look has been given to the cognitive and affective domains. Seven facets of human feelings, or affect, are discussed in terms of approaches which might help the instructional technologist who is involved in designing, developing, or revising instructional systems. The behavioral sciences provide the basis for theories developed in the approaches which are described.

Patterson, C.H. *Humanistic Education.* New Jersey: Prentice-Hall, Inc., 1973.

> For the teacher, this text emphasizes the humanistic approach for teacher education as well as the primary and secondary classroom. The author considers the issues of teaching subject matter in a more human way and educating the affective aspect of the student. It begins with a historical introduction to affective education, outlines goals for this type of education, and then describes the process of developing human teachers, promoting affective teaching and affective learning.

Peter, R. & Peter, V. Values clarification skills: helping problem solvers to become decision makers. *Man/Society/Technology.* Nov. 1978. Vol. 38, 2, pp. 28-31.

> These authors offer a problem-solving model for teaching industrial technology values and value judgments in industrial arts classes. An example of a curriculum plan format to include the values level in teaching graphic arts is presented. The value clarification techniques included are intended to help students in solving life problems.

Piaget, J. *Intelligence and Affectivity: Their Relationship During Child Development.* (Translated and edited by Brown, T.A. & Kaegi, C.E.) Palo Alto, CA: Annual Reviews, Inc., 1981.

> Lectures delivered by Piaget at the Sorbonne during the 1953-54 academic year represent his fullest statement not only on the nature of affectivity but also on the relation of affectivity to intelligence throughout development. Developed from lecture notes, the sections of this book have been extensively edited to provide a complete text to represent as accurately as possible the full intent of Piaget's presentations. The first two sections deal with affect as related to the function of intelligence — acting as an energizing force. The last section describes the developmental stages from birth through adolescence, illustrating parallels between characteristics of cognition and emotion-motivation at each level.

Raths, L.E. et al. *Values and Teaching: Working with Values in the Classroom.* Merrill, 1966.

> Raths presents a values theory and describes in detail a value clarifying process. Specific instructional strategies are offered to illustrate how to implement the values theory. The authors' interests

are for how students actually behave rather than how they say they behave. The process a student uses to acquire a value rather than any particular value a student uses in a given situation is also a primary concern discussed in this book. Research on the value-clarifying process is summarized.

Read, D.A. & Simon, S.B. (Eds.) *Humanistic Education Sourcebook.* New Jersey: Prentice-Hall, 1975.

This collection of articles from such authors as Carl Rogers, Arthur Combs, Alfred Alschuler and Arthur Jersild on various aspects of humanistic education provides a very readable description of the humanistic emphasis in student-teacher relationships. Topics such as the meaning of interpersonal relationships, the importance of ideas and feelings in learning and the role of the teacher as psychologist conclude with a discussion of the problems and promises of sensitivity education. A description of current techniques of humanistic education is the final section of this book.

Ringness, T.A. *The Affective Domain in Education.* Boston: Little, Brown and Co., 1975.

The author states a concern for both the attitudes we purposely foster in the schools and those which we unwittingly foster. Since attitudes and values are learned behaviors, schools should help children learn and explore, and find ways to behave that satisfy them as individuals, as well as satisfy and improve society. A description of the affective domain is offered with an analysis of different theories which tend to support the concept of affective learning. The need for the teacher to become "affective" is also discussed, along with suggestions and implications for teaching activities to achieve affective learning. A very practical book which presents the many aspects of affective education in a very logical form.

Rogers, C.R. *Freedom to Learn.* Columbus, OH: Charles E. Merrill Publishing Co., 1969.

Major challenges must be met by education today, according to Rogers, if mankind is to move ahead. Accelerating change, social tensions, international conflicts, a tradition-bound educational system and increasing emphasis upon the depersonalizing of education represent the major challenges to be faced. Changes in the classrooms can help children learn to deal with these problems, if that change is in the direction of experiential learning. The first two sections of this book provide teachers specific ways to experiment with their classes while making the changes. The third section provides a conceptual basis for the experimentation, while the fourth section develops the personal and philosophical basis for this approach. The last section considers the character of self-directed change in an educational system, and the beginnings of the implementation of such a program.

Sahakian, W.S. *Introduction to the Psychology of Learning.* Chicago: Rand McNally College Publishing Co., 1976.

Sahakian offers a very comprehensive analysis and review of the psychology of learning. A systems-oriented approach is used to present an interpretation of numerous experiments, hypotheses, postulates and theories found in the psychology of learning. The point is illustrated that S-R theory dominated the psychology of learning during the first half of the twentieth century. However, during recent years a number of new theories, emphasizing humanistic, cognitive, physiological, and information-processing viewpoints have taken shape. Virtually all recognized theories and theorists are discussed, and the influence they have had upon each other is described.

Simpson, E.L. *Humanistic Education: An Interpretation.* Cambridge, MA: Ballinger Publishing Co., 1976.

This book has two major parts: the first describes the state of the art of humanistic education; the second is a very extensive annotated bibliography of humanistic education. A historical perspective of humanistic education is offered, followed by some examples of humanistic education in practice. Humanistic teachers and classrooms are described and the requirements for humanistic teacher training and curriculum development defined. The annotated bibliography by Mary Anne Gray is comprehensive and well organized.

Thal, H.M. & Holcombe, M. Value clarification. *American Vocational Journal,* (December 1973) Vol. 48, pp. 25-29.

These authors advocate the use of values clarification in vocational education programs. Students in those programs must deal with many conflicts, both personal and social, in the process of developing occupational skills and knowledge. Values clarification can be used to help students recognize and define their own values and to see values in relation to others. Greater motivation for learning in vocational education can result from involvement in values clarification activities. The vocational classroom with its more relaxed atmosphere provides a natural setting for this approach in instruction. A number of examples of classroom strategies are also provided.

Thayer, L. & Beeler, K.D. (Eds.) *Handbook of Affective Tools and Techniques for the Educator.* Ypsilanti, MI: The Special Interest Group: Affective Aspects of Education (American Educational Research Association), 1974.

These 35 different activities could be carried out in the classroom to promote affective development. Each of the 21 contributors begins the activity description with a goal statement. That is followed by an indication of group size, required time, physical setting, necessary materials, specific objectives of the activity, step-by-step procedures and recommendations for conducting the activity. This handbook is intended as a tool to help educators work with from one to one-hundred persons or more in the regular school setting, where up to one hour of time would be available for completion of the activity.

Thayer, L. & Beeler, K.D. (Eds.) *Activities and Exercises for Affective Education.* Ypsilanti, MI: The Special Interest Group: Affective Aspects of Education (American Educational Research Association), 1975.

The second handbook arranged by Thayer and Beeler also offers examples of activities and exercises used to guide the development of affective education experiences in the classroom. In this text, 49 entries have been prepared by 44 educators who have tried and tested their own particular approaches in schools. The focus of this collection is upon the person in the learning process. The learner's values, feelings, attitudes, and perceptions are of primary concern in the experiential approaches to learning that are described. Activities and exercises focus on several topical areas in the affective components of learning, including assessment, self-disclosure, learning climates, communication skills, perceptions of self and others, building trust, and group processes.

Thiagarajan, Sivasailam. Experiential learning packages. *NSPI Journal.* (September 1979) Vol. 18:7, pp. 11-15.

This article makes the point that experiential learning packages help learners effectively attain affective empathetic, interactive, and complex cognitive objectives, and unlearn undesirable cognitive prejudices and affective anxieties. They are recommended for vocational education, in the helping professions and in instructional situations that involve internships. The beginning designer is advised to avoid controversial content and strategies.

Thornburg, Herschel D. *School Learning and Instruction.* Monterey, CA: Brooks/Cole Publishing Co., 1973.

> Reviewing learning theories in a form intended to offer the teacher a more interpretable description of psychological principles useful in teaching, Thornburg establishes a foundation and framework from which teachers can build their own repertoire of problem-solving principles and techniques. The first part of this book deals with learning theory and focuses on the hierarchical learning model advanced by Robert Gagne, which indicates that each person learns at different levels of complexity and in a successive, segmented manner. The second part deals with the teaching-learning situation and the factor of individual differences in teaching. Classroom applications of theories are emphasized throughout to "illustrate how learning principles and instructional theory work in harmony."

Timmerman, T. & Ballard, J. (Eds.) *Yearbook in Humanistic Education 1976.* Amherst, MA: Mandala, 1976.

> This collection of articles was selected and arranged by Timmerman and Ballard in an effort to answer questions on the philosophy of humanistic education and how it works. The articles describe the philosophy, theory, and practices in humanistic education as viewed by 23 authors. It is pointed out that no attempt has been made to provide a final definition of humanistic education since it is a relatively new field for study. It is best represented as a movement, which requires an openness to a variety of forms and theories which may eventually give it more adequate description.

Timmerman, T. & Ballard J. (Vol. 3) *Strategies in Humanistic Education.* Amherst, MA: Mandala Press, 1978.

> The third in three volumes by these authors offers a large selection of strategies for implementing humanistic learning activities in the classroom. The first volume covers their S-I-S-F model, brainstorming, circletime, discussion methods, journals, 6-point continuum, role-play, small-group methods, fantasy and processing; the second offers S-I-P-A Self-Growth Plan, forced choice, rank-order, inventories, spectrum, support groups, and energizers; while this volume presents Phoney Words, Affirming Strategies, Kid-A-Teacher and Whips These are all detailed teaching strategies which can be readily implemented in both the elementary and secondary grades.

Valett, R.E. *Humanistic Education: Developing the Total Person.* St. Louis: The C.V. Mosley Co., 1977.

>   The underlying assumption for this book is "that affective education should be an intrinsic part of a child's education along with the more traditional cognitive and psychomotor education." It is intended to help educators develop humanistic education programs which may assist children in understanding themselves, to develop a more positive self-concept, to be able to express their feelings, hopes and aspirations more adequately, to become more self-determining and actualized persons, and to achieve greater personal and social maturity. A large number of examples and techniques are offered to illustrate how to implement humanistic principles in the classroom.

Values and Attitudes Handbook. The Wisconsin Guide to Local Curriculum Improvement in Industrial Education, K-12. Wisconsin State Department of Public Instruction, Madison, 1980.

>   Designed as a resource for implementing *The Wisconsin Guide to Local Curriculum Improvement in Industrial Education, K-12,* this handbook is intended to aid industrial educators in developing and incorporating values and attitudes in their programs. The first section presents a values rationale to provide a set of ideas to use in developing a statement for local use. The next section contains a variety of activities and strategies for examining and clarifying values, attitudes, and feelings in industrial education. First, some commonly used strategies for values and attitudes activities are summarized. Then a list of value and conflict problems is suggested for several traditional industrial arts concentrations to which the strategies may be adapted. Finally, some activities are provided which represent the strategies described, including value sheets, values continuum, rank ordering, values voting, role playing, questionnaire making and taking (attitude inventories), goal sheets, alternatives search, unfinished sentences, self/peer-evaluation, and simulation. Activities may be used as is, adapted by the teacher, or used as models. The final section of the handbook includes listings of resources such as articles, resources, films, duplicating master, kits, and tape programs.

Vocational Development in Grades Seven, Eight and Nine: A Resource Guide Integrating Selected Vocational Development Concepts with Eight Areas of the Curriculum in Grades Seven, Eight and Nine. Mid-Hudson Career Development and Information Center, Beacon, NY, 1972.

>   Developed by representatives from state guidance, education, and employment agencies, this resource guide was designed to

facilitate the integration of career education concepts into the curriculum of junior high schools. Recognizing that career development is a life-long process, learning experiences to develop work concepts and attitudes are outlined for eight subject areas, including industrial arts. Most of the activities are concerned with development of attitudes and skills associated with vocational awareness, and are designed for teachers who are concerned about, but not necessarily trained in, vocational learning-maturation. Activities emphasize work function and worker trait components and exposure to relevant concepts, and should be adapted by the teacher and used with other related tools. In addition to identifying concepts to be taught, the Guide also outlines content, teaching techniques, and resources. Included in the appendices are data on classifying occupations.

Weinstein, G. & Fantini, M.D. *Toward Humanistic Education: A Curriculum of Affect.* New York: Praeger Publishers, 1970.

A program funded by the Ford Foundation entitled Elementary School Teaching Program is reported by these authors, who served as directors for the project. They present an account of their work, which was designed to develop a fundamental approach to education and relevant curriculum materials to meet the needs of the disadvantaged student. The affective domain of learning is given special emphasis, with a model being offered for development of a curriculum of affect. Specific ways to implement the model in the classroom are presented. Appropriate for persons who are just becoming acquainted with this area of education.

Weller, Richard H. (Ed.) *Humanistic Education: Visions and Realities.* (Symposium on humanistic education.) Berkeley, CA: McCutcheon Publishing Co., 1977.

This is a record and analysis of a symposium on humanistic education conducted by Phi Delta Kappa and the Center for Educational Reform, University of North Carolina, in January, 1976. Contributors were Michael Apple, David Aspy, Walter Feinberg, Nancy King, James MacDonald, Ralph Mosher, Fred Newmann, Robert O'Kane, David Purpel, Flora Roebuck, Thomas Sergiovanni and Richard Weller. The symposium began with a paper on "the hidden curriculum" by Apple and King, which addresses the fact the curriculum extends beyond the stated curriculum. Several approaches are suggested for moving the schools toward more humanized education. Emphases on the individual in the environment, on developmental psychology, and on the improvement of interpersonal skills are suggested by different contributors. Feinberg concludes with a view of the larger issues of implementing humanistic education when the prominent theories of education still serve the critical relationship of schooling and society. A significant change in society must occur if education is to become more humane, according to Feinberg.

Index

Bonser's child-centered approach to education, 30-31
Brain hemispheres and learning, 57
Brainstorming, 123, 129-130, 136-137

Career development, self-assessment of, 92-94
Career education, 130, 137, 143-144
  Vocational Development in Grades Seven, Eight and Nine, 218-219
Challenge versus threat, and promotion of learning, 26
Change —
  of behaviors and attitudes, 189-191
  in teachers and students, 186-187
Climate for optimum learning, 53
Clubs, student, 193-194
Cognition —
  preoccupation with, 149-150
  relation to other domains, 19-20, 34, 61, 69
Combs's studies of teacher effectiveness and perceptual organization, 95-96
Communication, 64-65, 160
  Communication and Affect, 198
Communicativeness of teacher, 73-74
Concept learning, in Gagné's learning theory, 43
Conditioning, and humanistic approach, 62. *See also* Learning theory
Conflict —
  "Democratic Theory," 211
  between teachers' and students' values, 188
Congruence, 70
  defined, 60
  research on, 96-97
Connectionism and S-R theories, 40
Consciousness, *defined*, 59
Consequences. *See* Anticipating decision consequences

Consequence search (strategy for teaching problem-solving skills), 123
Consistency and pattern, strategies for teaching, 126-127
Constructs, attitudes as, 166
Content structures and human needs, 34-37
Contiguity theories of learning, 41
Contingency contracting, 190
Continuum of values, 112
Contrived incident (teaching method), 142
Creativity in person-centered learning, 65
Criticisms of affective education, 26
Cultural differences between teacher and student, 106
Curriculum —
  The Affective Domain, 212
  college, 182-183
  feelings and values in, 180
  and human needs, 34-37
  materials for affective learning, 57-58
  middle school, 131-133
  Toward Humanistic Education, 219

Decision consequences, *See* Anticipating decision consequences
Decision making, 130-131, 138-139, 140
Development. *See also* Affective development; Career development; Change; Values; Whole person
  Intelligence and Affectivity, 213
Discipline problems, 191
Displays, public, 139-140
Domains of behavior. *See also* under Affective; Cognitive; Psychomotor
  and developing the whole person, 19-23

Economic conditions, effect on education, 15
Education, recent influences on, 14-18

Tendency toward self-actualization, *defined,* 59
Threat in learning, 26, 63, 69-70
Tradition —
and person-centered learning, 80
and process of valuing, 110-113
in value development, 109-110

Unconditional positive regard, 71
defined, 60
Unobtrusive measures, 167

Validity of instruments for evaluating attitudes, 171-173
Values. *See also under* Affective
assertion of, 112, 125
assessment of, 120-122
*Clarifying Values Through
Subject Matter,* 207
and curriculum, 180, 182-183
defined, 183
*Developing Values in the
Classroom,* 202
development of, 21, 109-113,
189-191
in industrial arts, 183-188
and learning, 26
Matters of Feeling, 209-210
in taxonomy of affective
domain, 161, 165

teachers' and students'
compared, 106-107, 188
and technology, 27-29
types of, 184
Values and Teaching, 213-214
"Value Clarification," 215
"Values Clarification Skills,"
213
Values continuum (teaching
method), 121-122
Values voting (teaching
method), 120-121
Valuing, in taxonomy of affective
domain, 161, 164
Vandalism, and rationale for
affective education, 25
Verbal associations, in Gagné's
learning theory, 43

Whole person —
*Affectivity, Classroom Climate
and Teaching,* 201
development of, 18-23
education of, 35-37, 150-151
*Humanistic Education: Develop-
ing the Total Person,* 218
Motivation and Personality, 212
and psychology, 44-45
Woodworking, as middle school
teaching unit, 132-140
Wording of behavioral objectives,
158-159, 161-162, 163-165